PRODUCT LIABILITY LAW

Product Liability Law
A guide for managers

Michael Whincup

Gower

© Michael Whincup 1985

All rights reserved. No part of this publication may be reproduced, stored in a retrieval system, or transmitted in any form or by any means, electronic, mechanical, photocopying, recording, or otherwise without the prior permission of Gower Publishing Company Limited.

Published by
Gower Publishing Company Limited,
Gower House,
Croft Road,
Aldershot,
Hants GU11 3HR,
England

Gower Publishing Company,
Old Post Road,
Brookfield,
Vermont 05036,
U.S.A.

British Library Cataloguing in Publication Data

Whincup, Michael
   Product liability law.
   1. Products liability — Great Britain
   I. Title
   344.1063'82   KD1987

ISBN 0-566-02494-2

Library of Congress Cataloging in Publication Data

Whincup, Michael H.
   Product liability law.
   Includes index.
   1. Products liability — Great Britain
   I. Title
   KD1987.W54 1984   346.4103'82   84-13713

ISBN 0-566-02494-2 (U.S.)   344.106382

Typeset by Graham Burn Studios, Leighton Buzzard, Bedfordshire, England.

Printed in Great Britain at the University Press, Cambridge

Contents

Acknowledgements	ix
Statutes	xi
Table of Cases	xiii
Introduction	xxi

1	**On buying and selling**	1
	Intention and certainty	2
	Offer and acceptance	8
	Obligations and remedies	14
	Frustration	21
	Summary	22
2	**Express terms and guarantees**	24
	Consideration	25
	Consumer complaints	34
	Statutory provisions	36
	Summary	37
3	**Terms implied by law**	39
	The Sale of Goods Act	40

	Title	41
	Description	41
	Quality and fitness	43
	Merchantable quality	45
	Reasonable fitness	48
	Used goods	55
	Sale by sample	56
	Acceptance	56
	Strict liability	58
	Hire purchase	60
	Service and hire contracts	62
	Reform	64
	Ownership and risk	65
	Summary	70
4	**Exclusion clauses**	71
	Common law rules	71
	The Unfair Contract Terms Act	78
	Other statutory provisions	87
	Common law and statute	88
	Summary	88
5	**Negligence (1) The general principles**	90
	Burden of proof	91
	Reasonable care	93
	Elements of liability	95
	Defences	99
	Damages	100
	Time limits	101
	Summary	102
6	**Negligence (2) Manufacturers' and distributors' duties**	103
	Materials	103
	Design	108
	Advice and warning	123
	Workmanship	125
	Vicarious liability	126
	Distributors' liabilities	127
	Summary	130

CONTENTS vii

7	Product liability law in America and the Common Market	131
	America	131
	Ireland	140
	France, Belgium, Luxembourg	141
	Holland	144
	Italy	145
	Germany	146
	Greece	149
	Denmark	149
	Summary	151
8	Law reform	152
	The Strasbourg Convention and EEC draft Directive	153
	The Pearson Report	155
	The New Zealand alternative	160
	Insurance	161
	Summary	163
9	Suppliers' criminal liabilities	165
	The Health and Safety at Work Act	166
	Dangerous substances	171
	The Consumer Safety Act	171
	The Food and Drugs Act	176
	Drugs	179
	Motor vehicles	179
	Miscellaneous provisions	180
	The Trade Descriptions Act	180
	Summary	186

Appendix 1 Sales of Goods Act 1979   187

Appendix 2 Supply of Goods and Services Act 1982   214

Appendix 3 Unfair Contract Terms Act 1977   227

Appendix 4 Council of Europe: Convention on Products Liability in regard to Personal Injury and Death, 27 January 1977   250

Appendix 5 EEC Draft Directive on product liability   259

Appendix 6 Health and Safety at Work etc Act 1974	
Sections 1-9	264
Further reading	271
Index	273

Acknowledgements

The author gratefully acknowledges the kind permission of the editors of the *Common Market Law Review* to draw for the purposes of chapter 7 on materials first published in the Review. The permission of Her Majesty's Stationery Office to reproduce the various Acts in the Appendices is also acknowledged with thanks.

Statutes

Accident Compensation Act 1982 (N.Z.)	160–1
Carriage Acts 1924–72	87
Consumer Credit Act 1974	61, 87
Consumer Protection Act 1961	172
Consumer Safety Act 1978	93, 97, 111, 171–6
Defective Premises Act 1972	87
Employers' Liability (Defective Equipment) Act 1969	93
Explosives (Age of Purchase) Act 1976	180
Fabrics (Misdescription) Act 1913	180
Factories Act 1961	104, 112, 165
Fair Trading Act 1974	35
Food & Drugs Acts 1955–82	165, 176–8
Health and Safety at Work Act 1974	94, 103, 107, 111 113, 126, 166–71
Law Reform (Contributory Negligence) Act 1945	99
Law Reform (Frustrated Contracts) Act 1943	22
Limitations Acts 1939–80	101
Medicines Act 1968	178–9

Misrepresentation Act 1967	5, 82
Plant Varieties & Seeds Act 1964	180
Rag, Flock etc., Act 1954	180
Road Traffic Act 1972	87, 179
Sale of Goods Act 1979	14–16, 30, 37 40–70, 80, 90–1, 98 115, 121
Sale of Goods and Supply of Services Act 1979 (Ireland)	35, 140–1
Seeds Act 1920	180
Supply of Goods and Services Act 1982	40, 62, 81
Supply of Goods (Implied Terms) Act 1973	40, 60, 62, 81, 85
Trade Descriptions Act 1968	180–5
Unfair Contract Terms Act 1977	5, 13, 17, 20, 33, 36 40, 72, 77–89, 125
Uniform Product Liability Act 1983 (US)	131, 136, 139
Vaccine Damage Payments Act 1979	93, 157

Statutory Instruments

Agriculture (Tractor Cabs) Regulations 1974	119
Business Advertisements (Disclosure) Order 1977	44
Consumer Safety Act Regulations	93, 172-5
Consumer Transactions (Restrictions on Statements) Order 1978	36–7, 81
European Communities Act Regulations	175, 178
Foods and Drugs Act Regulations	178
Medicines Act Regulations	178
Packaging and Labelling of Dangerous Substances Regulations 1978	171
Price Marking (Bargain Offers) Order 1979	185

Table of Cases

Adams v Richardson (1969) 2 All ER 1221	30
Adler v Dickson (1955) 1 QB 158	75
Allard v Manahan (1974) 46 DLR (3d) 614	99, 125
Aluminium Industrie v Romalpa Aluminium (1976) 2 All ER 552	69
Amherst v Walker ('1983) 3 WLR 334	16
Andrews v Hopkinson (1975) 3 All ER 422	4, 27–8, 60–1
Appleby v Sleep (1968) 2 All ER 265	40
Arcos v Ronnaassen (1933) AC 470	43
Ashby v Tolhurst (1937) 2 All ER 837	79
Ashington Piggeries v Hill (1971) 1 All ER 847	74
Bacceleri v Hipter 597 P.2d 351 (1979)	133
Baker v Jones (1954) 2 All ER 553	3
Banbury v Hounslow LBC (1971) RTR 1	183
Barber v C.W.S. (1983) 81 LGR 762	177
Bartlett v Marcus (1965) 2 All ER 753	54–5
Beale v Taylor (1967) 3 All ER 253	43
Beckett v Cohen (1973) 1 All ER 120	184
Bernard v Kee Manufacturing 409 So 2d 1047 (1982)	137
Beshada v Johns 440 A.2d 1372 (1982)	135

Birnie v Ford (1960) *Times*, Nov. 22	116
Bishops & Baxter v Anglo Eastern Trading (1943) 2 All ER 598	7
Blackmore v Bellamy (1983) RTR 303	45
Board v Hedley (1951) 2 All ER 431	59
British Road Services v Crutchley (1968) 1 All ER 598	10
Brown v Craiks (1970) 1 All ER 823	46
Buchanan-Jardine v Hamilink (1983) S.L.T. 149	46
Buckley v La Reserve (1959) Crim LR 451	165
Bunge v Tradax (1981) 2 All ER 524	15
Burfitt v Kille (1939) 2 All ER 372	129
Burnett v Westminster Bank (1965) 3 All ER 81	73
Burns v Terry (1950) 2 All ER 987	112
Butler v Ex-Cell-O (1970) 1 All ER 965	9–11, 13
Cadbury v Halliday (1975) 2 All ER 226	181
Cammell Laird v Manganese Bronze (1934) AC 402	408
Carlill v Carbolic Smoke Ball (1893) 1QB 256	4, 27–30 32, 33
Cavendish Woodhouse v Manley (1984) *Times*, Feb.4	43, 81
Cehave v Bremer (1975) 3 All ER 739	43
Chapelton v Barry UDC (1940) 1 All ER 356	73
Charnock v Liverpool Corporation (1968) 3 All ER 473	63
Charterhouse Credit v Tolly (1963) 2 All ER 432	58
Clea v Bulk Oil (1984) 1 All ER 129	21
Cremdean v Nash (1977) 244 EG 547	82
Crocker v Winthrop Laboratories 514 SW 2d 429 (1974)	134
Croshaw v Pritchard (1889) 16 TLR 45	6
Crow v Barford (1963) CA 102	120–1 135
Crowther v Shannon (1975) 1 All ER 139	55–6
Curtis v Chemical Cleaning (1951) 1 All ER 631	13, 74
Czarnikov v Koufos (1969) 1 AC 350	19
Daniels v White (1938) 4 All ER 258	92

TABLE OF CASES

Davies v Fareham UDC (1956) AC 696	21
Davies v Sumner (1983) *Times*, Aug. 11	45
Davis v Afa Minerva (1974) 2 L1R 27	63
Demby Hamilton v Barden (1949) 1 All ER 435	70
Devillez v Boots (1962) 106 SJ 552	130
Dixon Kerby v Robinson (1965) 2 L1R 404	48
Donoghue v Stevenson (1932) AC 562	93
Dove v Banham (1983) 2 All ER 833	101
Drummond v Van Ingen (1887) 12 AC 284	56
Drury v Buckland (1941) 1 All ER 269	60–1
Dunlop v New Garage (1915) AC 79	18
Elmore v American Motors 451 P2d 84 (1969)	133
Errington v Errington (1952) 1 All ER 149	26
Evans v Merzario (1976) 1 WLR 1078	12, 74
Evans v Triplex (1936) 1 All ER 283	122, 136
Farnworth Finance v Attryde (1970) 2 All ER 774	49, 54, 58
Farr v Butters (1932) 2 K.B.606	99, 112
Feast v Vincent (1974) 1 NZLR 212	55
Federspiel v Twigg (1957) 1 L1R 240	68
Finlay v Metro Toyota (1978) 82 DLR (3d) 440	54
Fisher v Harrods (1966) 1 L1R 500	128, 130
Foley v Classique Coaches (1934) 2 KB 1	6
Ford Motors v Mathis 322 F2d 267 (1963)	137
French v Olau Lines (1983) Times, May 5	123
Friskin v Holiday (1977) 72 DLR (3d) 289	50
Frost v Aylesbury Dairy (1905) 1 KB 608	59
Gallant v Beitz (1983) 148 DLR (3d) 522	109
Garrett v Nissen 498 P.2d 1359 (1972)	120
Gibbons v Trapp Motors (1970) 9 DLR (3d) 742	54
Goldsworthy v Catalina Agencies (1983) 142 DLR (3d) 281	128
Goodchild v Vaclight (1965) *Times*, May 22	99, 123, 129
Goodrich v Hammond 269 F 2d 501 (1959)	133
Graham v CWS (1957) 1 All ER 654	114
Grant v Australian Knitting Mills (1936) AC 85	48, 92, 126

Green v Cade (1978) 1 L 1 R 602	83, 86
Grenfell v Meyrowitz (1936) 2 All ER 1313	42
Griffiths v Conway (1939) 1 All ER 685	59
Guarantee Trust of Jersey v Gardner (1973) 117 SJ 564	57
Hadley v Baxendale (1854) 1854 9 EX 341	18
Hallmark Pool Corn v Storey (1983) 144 DLR (3d) 56	29
Harman v Mitcham Works (1955) *Times*, June 22	114
Harris v Northwest Natural Gas 588 P2d 791 (1979)	105, 134
Hawes v Railway Executive (1952) 96 SJ 852	104
Head v Showfronts (1970) 1 L1R 140	67
Heaton v Ford Motors 435 P2d 806 (1967)	135
Hedley Byrne v Heller (1964) AC 465	5, 31 100
Heil v Hedges (1951) 1 TLR 512	60, 134
Henningsen v Bloomfield Motors 161 A2d 69 (1960)	122, 133
Hill v Crowe (1978) 1 All ER 812	92, 123 126
Hindustan S S Co. v Siemens (1955) 1 L1R 167	111
Holmes v Ashford (1980) 2 All ER 76	124
Hong Kong Shipping v Kawasaki (1961) 2 All ER 257	15
Hounslow LBC v Twickenham Garden Developments (1970) 3 All ER 326	21
House of Holland v Brent LBC (1971) 2 All ER 296	182
Howard Marine v Ogden (1978) QB 574	5
Hughes v Hall (1981) 125 SJ 255	81
IBA v EMI (1980) 14 Build LR	4, 25
IBM v Shcherban (1925) 1 DLR 964	47
Jackson v Chrysler Acceptances (1978) RTR 474	58
Jackson v West Coast Paint 499 F2d 809 (1974)	133
Jamieson v Woodward & Lothrop 247 F2d 23 (1957)	120
Junior Books v Veitchi (1982) 3 All ER 201	100, 138

TABLE OF CASES

Kendall v Lillico (1969) 2 AC 31	60
Klages v General Ordnance Equipment 367 A2d 304 (1976)	134
Kuschy v Norris 206 A2d 275 (1964)	139
La Rossa v Scientific Design 402 F2d 937 (1968)	138
Lambert v Lastoplex (1971) 25 DLR (3d) 121	124
Lambert v Lewis (1981) 1 All ER 1185	30–2, 60, 100, 110, 134, 139
Lartigue v Reynolds Tobacco 307 F2d 19 (1963)	135
Laurelgates v Lombard (1983) 133 NLJ 720	58
Leaves v Wadham Stringer (1980) RTR 308	51
Lee v York Coach (1977) RTR 35	58
L'Estrange v Graucob (1934) 2 KB 394	13, 75, 79
Licences Insurance v Lawson (1896) 12 TLR 501	3
Lightburn v Belmont (1969) 6 DLR (3d) 692	53, 57
Long v Lloyd (1958) 2 All ER 402	6
Lowe v Lombank (1960) 1 All ER 611	74
MFI v Nattrass	182
McCants v Salameh 608 SW 2d 304 (1980)	135
McDonald v Empire Garage (1975) *Times*, Oct. 8	48
Magrine v Spector 241 A2d 637 (1970)	138
Malat v Bjornson (1981) 114 DLR (3d) 612	117
Maple Flock v Universal Furniture (1934) 1 KB 148	16
Mardorf v Attica (1977) 1 All ER 545	16
Martin v Bengue 136 A2d 626 (1957)	124
Melia v Ford Motors 534 F2d 795 (1976)	135
Mendelssohn v Normand (1969) 2 All ER 1215	72, 79
Microbeads v Vinhurst (1975) 1 All ER 529	41
Millar v Turpie (1976) SLT 66	49–50
Mitchell v Finney Lock (1983) 3 WLR 163	76–7, 85
Moxley v Laramie Builders 600 P2d 733 (1980)	137
Myers v Brent Cross Service (1934) 1 KB 46	62–3
Naish v Gore (1971) 3 All ER 737	184
New Zealand Shipping v Satterthwaite (1975) AC 154	75

Newell v Hicks (1938) *Times*, Dec.7	183
Nicolene v Simmonds (1953) 1 All ER 882	7
Northland Airlines v Ferranti (1970) 114 SJ 845	8
Norton v Streets (1968) 120 CLR 635	124
O'Connor v BTC (1958) 1 All ER 558	117
Olley v Marlborough Court (1949) 1 All ER 127	73
Parker v SE Railway (1877) 2 CPD 416	73
Parsons v Uttley Ingham (1978) QB 791	19
Pearson v NW Gas Board (1968) 2 All ER 669	104, 134
Penelope, The (1928) P 180	22
Philco v Spurling (1949) 2 All ER 882	96
Phillips v Cycle Corp. (1977) CLY 364	42
Phillips v Hamstead (1983) CLY	80
Pirelli v Faber (1983) 2 WLR 6	101
Photo Productions v Securicor (1980) 1 All ER 556	76
Pryor v Lee Moore 262 F2d 673 (1958)	135
Qualcast v Haynes (1959) AC 743	107
R v Ford Motor (1974) 3 All ER 489	181
R v Hammertons Cars (1976) 3 All ER 758	181
R v Sunair (1973) 2 All ER 1233	183
Ray v Alad, 560 P2d 3 (1977)	137
Reardon Smith v Hansen Tangen (1976) 3 All ER 570	43
Richards v Westminster Motors (1975) 119 SJ 626	182
Richardson v Rowntree (1894) AC 217	72
Rimmer v Liverpool CC (1983) *Times*, Dec.15	99, 117
Robertson v Diciccio (1972) RTR 431	181
Robotics v First Cooperative Finance (1983) 80 LSG 3006	28, 58, 61
Rogers v Night Riders (1983) RTR 324	127
Roscorla v Thomas (1842) 3 QB 234	32
Rose & Frank v Crompton (1925) AC 445	3
Routledge v McKay (1954) 1 All ER 855	24–5
Ryan v Camden LBC (1982) *Times*, Dec.16	111
Samways v Westgate (1962) 106 SJ 937	123

TABLE OF CASES	xix

Sandbanks Hotel v Wallman (1962) *Times*, Nov.3	6
Santor v Karagheusian 207 A2d 305 (1965)	138
Scanlon v General Motors 326 A2d 673 (1974)	134
Schawel v Reade (1913) 2 IR 64	25
Schemel v General Motors 384 F2d 802 (1967)	135
Schipper v Levitt, 207 A2d 314 (1965)	137
Scholler v Wilson Certified Foods 559 P2d 1074 (1977)	134
Schuler v Wickman (1974) AC 235	16
Shanklin Pier v Detel Products (1951) 2 All ER 471	28
Sheffield v Ely Lilley 52 LW 2005 (1983)	137
Sheridan v Boots & Kensington AHA (1981) *NLJ* April 30	113–14
Sherratt v Gerald (1970) 114 SJ 147	184
Sigurdson v Hillcrest Service (1976) 73 DLR (3d) 132	63
Simmons v Ravenhill (1983) Crim.LR 749	181
Sindell v Abbott Laboratories 607 P2d 924 (1980)	137
Smedleys v Breed (1974) AC 839	177
Smith v Leech Brain (1961) 3 All ER 1159	95
Spencer v Rye (1972) *Guardian*, Dec.19	51, 54, 58, 59
Spruill v Boyle Midway 308 F2d 79 (1962)	124
Spurling v Bradshaw (1956) 2 All ER 121	73
Stanners v High Wycombe Borough Council (1968) 67 LGR 115	63
Steer v Durable Rubber Co. (1958) *Times*, Nov.20	92
Stennett v Hancock (1939) 2 All ER 578	110
Stevenson v McLean (1880) 5QBD 346	8
Stokes v GKN (1968) 5 KIR 401	106
Suisse Atlantique v NV Rotterdamsche Kolen Centrale (1967) 1 AC 361	76
Sumner v Henderson (1963) 2 All ER 712	133
Sumner Permain v Webb (1922) 1 KB 55	46
Symmons v Cook (1981) High Court, March, unreported	83
Tarling v Baxter (1827) 6 B & C 360	66
Taylor v Fraser (1977) 121 SJ 757	172
Taylor v Kiddey (1968) *Times*, Feb.1	63

Taylor v Rover (1966) 1 WLR 1491	127, 137
Tearle v Cheverton & Laidler (1970) 7 KIR 364	99, 111
Teheran Europe v Belton (1968) 2 QB 545	48
Tesco v Nattrass (1972) AC 153	172, 184
Thompson v LMS Railway (1930) 1 KB 41	72
Tradax v European Grain (1983) 2 L1R 100	42–3
Tradax v Goldschmidt (1977) 2 L1R 604	43
Turriff v Regalia Mills (1971) 222 EG 169	6
Turner v General Motors 514 SW 2d 497 (1974)	110
Tywood v St Anne Co. (1979) 100 DLR (3d) 374	12
UDT v Taylor (1980) SLT 28	62
Vacwell v BDH Chemicals (1970) 3 All ER 553	113
Vandermark v Ford Motors 61 Cal 2d 256 (1964)	136–7
Victoria Laundry v Newman (1949) 1 All ER 997	19
Walton v British Leyland (1978) *Times*, July 13	118
Ward v Bignell (1967) 1QB 534	66
Webster v Blue Ship 198 NE 2d 309 (1964)	134
Wells v Buckland Sand (1964) 1 All ER 41	28–9
Westminster CC v Alan (1981) *Times*, Dec.3	183
White v Blackmore (1972) 3 All ER 158	74, 79
White & Carter v McGregor (1962) AC 413	20
White Cross Equipment v Farrell (1983) TrL 21	86
Williams v Trimm Rock Quarries (1965) 109 SJ 454	111
Willis v FMC (1976) 68 DLR (3d) 127	115
Wings v Ellis (1983) *Times*, Dec.7	183
Woodar v Wimpey (1980) 1 All ER 571	16
Woodman v Photo Trade (1981) Exeter County Court, unreported	86
Woods v Durable Suites (1953) 2 All ER 391	105–6
Wright v Dunlop (1973) 13 KIR 255	107
Wright v Massey Harris 215 NE 2d 465 (1969)	121, 135
Young v McManus Childs (1968) 2 All ER 1169	63

Introduction

Common law and statute law

This book explains concisely and so far as possible without legal technicality the basic principles of liability of retailers, distributors, manufacturers, designers and installers for the unfitness or danger of the goods they supply. Many practical examples of the problems are given, together with the answers provided by the courts. Most of the cases are English but a number of instructive Commonwealth and American cases are also referred to.

Unfitness and danger are two distinct but overlapping issues. The suitability of goods depends very largely on the needs of the parties, as expressly agreed in their contracts of sale, hire purchase or lease. Their freedom of choice and the sort of problems they may encounter in making or breaking their contracts are the subject of chapters 1 and 2. In case of doubt the law will intervene and lay down minimum standards of fitness of goods, as described in chapter 3. Chapter 4 explains the limits on the parties' rights to exclude liability for breach of contract.

Safety standards, on the other hand, are more clearly matters of general concern. Suppliers must therefore comply with the standards laid down by our judges in the rules of common law or with those set by Parliament. The common law provisions are described at length in chapters 5 and 6. Their purpose is to provide compensation for injured parties where fault can be proved and so they are classed as civil matters. The most serious wrongs will involve also prosecution under the criminal law, as laid down by Act of Parliament or regulations made under Acts, or, since 1972, in accordance with Common Market requirements. These various more rigorous provisions are summarised in chapter 9.

In recent years, under the pressure of more advanced American law and worldwide concern over tragedies arising from the side effects of drugs, there has been talk in Britain as elsewhere of making manufacturers' liabilities much more stringent. The Common Market Commission was responsible for one such proposal, the draft Directive on product liability which appeared in 1976, and the Council of Europe produced another, the Strasbourg Convention, also of 1976, which Britain has signed. These agreements are set out in appendices 4 and 5 at the end of this book and discussed in chapter 8. They differ on points of detail but agree on the fundamental principles of reform.

We shall see in the ensuing chapters exactly what changes these principles will involve. We note in chapter 7 that they have long since been adopted in America and that several continental European legal systems have already gone a long way towards putting the proposals into practice. Chapter 8 reminds us that in Britain the Pearson Commission on personal injury litigation reported in 1978 in favour of such reform, as did later reports of the English and Scottish Law Commissions. So far there has been no result, apart from many determined statements of opposition to any change at all. It seems safe to say nonetheless that the movement of events is inexorable and that within the next decade or so Britain must come into line and accept rules of manufacturers' liabilities well established in American law and effectively the norm in many European countries.

Product

Before we begin our review of present and probable future liabilities we should define the word 'product', which for the most part we shall use interchangeably with 'goods' (as we shall also use 'producer' interchangeably with 'manufacturer'). For this purpose we may conveniently adopt the definition given by Article 2 of the Strasbourg Convention: 'The term "product" indicates all movables, natural or industrial, whether raw or manufactured, even though incorporated into another movable or into an immovable.' The EEC draft Directive refers simply to 'movables which have been industrially produced', a definition applying also to movables used in the construction of buildings or which are installed in buildings. This latter definition has the merit of brevity but may be thought more limited or doubtful in its application to raw materials, including foodstuffs, than the Convention. Neither of the agreements expressly resolves the question as to whether intangibles such as gas and electricity are to be regarded as products, but we shall take it that they are.

Law reports

Another matter of definition is the case reference system. Most English cases are in the All England Reports, cited as All ER, or Weekly Law Reports – WLR. Other reports include AC – Appeal Cases – and QB – Queen's Bench. Scottish cases are signified by SLT and Canadian by D (Dominion) LR. American cases are usually reported by region, eg P for Pacific.

1 On Buying and Selling

Until English law responds to international pressures for law reform, the nature and extent of a producer's liability in this country depends essentially on whether or not he has a contract with the injured party. If there is a contract of sale between the two parties the plaintiff's burden of proof is relatively simple and the defendant is usually accessible and responsive to pressure. A buyer's claim is more likely to succeed than one in which the injured person is, say, the buyer's wife or child or employee or some other ultimate user who has no contract with the producer and thus becomes involved in the more complex questions of law discussed in chapters 5 and 6. Since it is entirely a matter of chance who is injured by any given product this requirement of 'privity of contract' may seem an extraordinary anomaly in the law, and its practical consequences are indeed absurd, as will be illustrated. It is this distinction between contractual and non-contractual rights which is the basic issue in the proposed reforms.

Our first enquiry then will be as to the liabilities arising under a contract of sale; but that begs the question as to what exactly a contract is and when exactly it comes into being. The general rule of English law is that *a contract is made when clear reciprocal obligations are undertaken*, typically when one party pays or promises to pay for goods or services delivered or promised by the other. Our law is usually concerned therefore with the enforcement of *bargains*, not merely with promises by one side only which do not then or in the future require any action or promise (which the law calls 'consideration') by the other. It follows that the presence or absence of writing is not the crucial factor. As a rule writing is important only because it helps to prove what has been agreed, which is otherwise a matter of 'your word against mine'.

A seller's duties to his buyer are essentially those he undertakes by the express terms of the contract, though other very important duties may be added in by the law (see chapters 2 and 3). We note in chapter 4 the limits on the seller's rights to evade his responsibilities, but otherwise the law leaves contracting parties to make whatever bargains they please. Contracts thus very largely reflect the economic strength of the parties. The stronger the seller's bargaining position the fewer the burdens he will accept. But, conversely, whatever obligations he *does* accept, he must fulfil. If he fails to supply the number or quality of goods he has promised to supply he must, as a general rule, be liable for breach of contract, and the reasons why he fails are accordingly unimportant. The problem then becomes one of assessing his liability in damages or deciding whether the buyer is entitled also to repudiate the contract, as discussed below. The seller may sometimes seek to avoid liability by reference to the doctrine of frustration of contract, dealt with at the end of this chapter, but it will be seen that this is rarely a successful defence.

INTENTION AND CERTAINTY

Generally speaking, the object of contract law is to give effect to the parties' wishes, as expressed in their words and deeds. There are nonetheless many reasons why this objective might not be fulfilled. It is not enough simply to ask 'What did the parties intend?' In the first place, if the agreement is of a social, domestic or friendly nature, it will almost certainly be presumed on their behalf that they did not intend it to be enforceable by law. If made in a commercial context, then the chances are that each party had different and conflicting intentions, otherwise the case would not have gone to court. And even if they are notionally agreed, the weaker party contracting on disadvantageous terms with a monopoly supplier hardly 'intends' to do so to his own detriment. But the courts cannot take account of what contracting parties privately hope or fear, only of what they openly say or do. In the result the courts try to give effect to what contracting parties *appear to intend*, though there is always the possibility this is not what they actually intended.

Everything depends therefore upon the clarity of the contract. If its terms are disputed and the matter goes to court, the judge will hold the agreement unenforceable unless he can say what the parties wanted and whether they have got it and what should be done if they have not. Commercial men usually express their agreements in detailed standard forms designed to cover every eventuality, but even these often give rise to litigation, as illustrated below, because the terms are still unclear or the forms contradictory.

Doubts may arise over the meaning and effect of a contract for many different reasons, and the law's response varies accordingly. Here we shall consider briefly just a few typical problem areas. First the judge may refuse to enforce an agreement because the parties have expressly said that their bargain was 'binding in honour only' or was a 'gentlemen's agreement', or used other such optimistic phraseology to show they do not intend their agreement to be subject to the scrutiny of the courts. They are free to make agreements of that kind, and to avoid liability accordingly – *Rose & Frank v Crompton*, 1923 – though they would not thereby be allowed to defraud each other, eg by accepting payment but refusing to deliver goods. Nor are they free to say at one and the same time that while their agreement is not to be enforced by the law it can be enforced by one side only, eg 'our decision is final', or by some specified third party such as trade associations: *Baker v Jones*, 1954. Even where there is no 'honour clause' an otherwise clear agreement may still possibly be invalidated because of its informality. So the absence of written evidence in circumstances where writing would normally be expected, for example at a board meeting, might suggest that the parties did not regard their agreement as final or binding, as illustrated in *Licences Insurance Corp v Lawson*, 1896.

ADVERTISEMENTS

Another interesting and important question in sales law is whether advertisements or other pre-contract statements are intended to be binding, or should be so in any event. It would not be right to give legal effect to everything said before agreement was reached. If a dealer says in the course of negotiations that he can meet his customer's requirements, for example, that is not necessarily put forward as a binding promise: *IBA v EMI*, 1980. Advertisements in particular cannot usually be enforced if only because they are expressions of opinion, as when goods are said to be 'bigger' or 'better' or 'whiter' or 'faster', without any standards by which such opinion or 'puff' could be tested. But, conversely, if advertisements state *facts* which can be tested, they may in appropriate circumstances be regarded as contractual promises. So in the famous case of *Carlill v Carbolic Smoke Ball Co*, 1893, manufacturers were held bound by an express promise in their advertisement to pay £100 to anyone who used their concoction but nevertheless caught 'flu, both of which were provable facts. Strangely enough, however, a statement may be factual in one context, but not in another. A dealer's glowing description of a new car, for instance, might be mere puff because he clearly could not say whether this model was more reliable or effective than any other, but if he said the same thing about a used car he could be liable for breach of contract because he has examined that car himself and should know about its quality or condition: *Andrews v Hopkinson*, 1957. The separate question of the enforceability of manufacturers' guarantees, raised here by *Carlill* in particular, is discussed fully in chapter 2.

Sales literature, price lists and the like often disclaim contractual effect, not necessarily because what they say is untrue but perhaps because the seller or manufacturer wants to reserve the right to change his materials or specifications over a period of time. Alternatively, the conditions of sale themselves may make it clear that the parties are contracting only on the basis of what is agreed there and then, and provide that nothing said previously in advertisements or the like is of any significance at all. This may seem like sharp practice, since it is probably in reliance on the advertisement that the customer buys the goods, but the law permits exclusion of liability for precontractual statements if it is reasonable in the circumstances. We shall see what that involves when we look at the Unfair Contract Terms Act in chapter 4.

REPRESENTATIONS

Another possibility is that advertisements or other sales talk may be classed as 'representations', a kind of half-way house between puffs which have no legal effect and the binding terms of the contract itself. The law defines a representation as a statement of *fact* which encourages or induces a person to make a contract but which does not necessarily form part of that contract. It follows that unless there is a duty to disclose information, as eg in insurance contracts, mere silent acquiescence in another person's mistaken belief is not a representation. It would probably be a representation to say, for example, that a car has had only one previous owner or has done such and such a mileage, or that a boat has a certain capacity: *Howard Marine v Ogden*, 1978. Such statements would not usually be made terms of the contract but are still quite important from the buyer's point of view. If the statement is subsequently proved wrong, the buyer's remedy depends on whether the misrepresentation was made fraudulently, negligently, or innocently. He is entitled to repudiate the contract and/or claim damages for fraudulent misrepresentation. The Misrepresentation Act, 1967, allows a claim for damages for both negligent and innocent misrepresentation and independently of any contractual relationship a claim for damages for negligent statements may also be made at common law under the rule in *Hedley Byrne v Heller*, 1964, chapter 5, but in claims brought under the Act the onus of *disproving* negligence is upon the person making the statement. If the representation is negligent or innocent the Act might enable the buyer to rescind the contract, ie give back the goods and recover his money. But if he has used the goods to any extent or resold them, or otherwise seems to have accepted them, that cannot be done. *Long v Lloyd*, 1958, was a particularly hard case of a buyer of a vehicle advertised as 'in exceptional condition', which in a way it was, who lost his money simply because he drove the defective vehicle for a few days and let the seller do some repairs. Further examples of representations are given in chapter 2.

APPROXIMATIONS

Phrases such as 'at a price to be agreed' or 'on the usual hp terms' invite disaster, unless the contract has actually been carried out by one or both parties. If goods have been delivered as requested they have to be paid for, and if no price has yet been agreed the judge must decide what is a 'reasonable' price on all the available evidence of market price and the like: *Foley v Classique Coaches*, 1934. A 'quotation' is usually enforceable, and even an 'estimate' may be, but it is more a matter of the sense of the contract than the precise wording: *Croshaw v Pritchard*, 1889. Promises to 'use one's best endeavours' and similar expressions are probably too vague to be enforceable. Agreements expressed in 'letters of intent' or as 'subject to contract' are similarly inconclusive, unless perhaps acted on by one party to the knowledge and benefit of the other – *Turiff v Regalia Mills*, 1971 – in which case again benefits must be paid for. The phrase 'subject to contract' may also be used to mean only that the parties intend to put into writing commitments already agreed by word of mouth, and if so the mere change in form does not affect the validity of the existing agreement. While written contracts are always preferable, as we have said, they are only *essential* in land, hire purchase and a few other exceptional transactions.

There are of course many kinds of commitments which with the best will in the world cannot be precisely defined. If in such cases the buyer is dissatisfied with what he gets that of itself does not mean he is entitled to reject it or claim compensation. A not very serious but illuminating little example of the problem is *Sandbanks Hotel v Wallman*, 1962. Mr Wallman booked 'a double room' at the hotel. It turned out to be rather a small room

– 5ft long by 8ft 6in wide, with only a 4ft wide bed. Mr Wallman left and refused to pay the bill because in his view this was not a double room. 'The real objection,' said the judge, 'was that the only way the bed could be put in the room for the door to be openable was right up against the wall, so that if anyone wanted to get out of it for any purpose during the night he or she would have to climb either over the other occupant or over the end of the bed.' But he concluded: 'I am not prepared to decide as a matter of law that a double bed is not a double bed unless one can walk all round it', and so Mr Wallman had to pay the bill.

If there is by chance an omission in the contract, or an obscure or meaningless term is put in, one can never be quite sure what the effect will be. It depends how far the uncertainty 'strikes at the root of the contract'. On the one hand it is quite common to reach an 'agreement in principle' which does not require detail to be enforceable, otherwise forward contracts would be impossible, while on the other such agreements are clearly inadequate if the transaction is a very complex one requiring definite agreement on various different aspects. Certain terms may be added in by law, however, as we see in chapter 3.

Again, a contract which is otherwise clear and self-sufficient will not be invalidated just because some incidental part has no apparent meaning. This was the conclusion in *Nicolene v Simmonds*, 1953, where a contract in all other respects complete and clear stated that it was subject to 'the usual conditions of acceptance'. Neither side could explain what these were and so the phrase was struck out. 'It would be strange indeed,' said the judge, 'if a party could escape from every one of his obligations by inserting a meaningless exception from some of them ... The parties treated the contract as subsisting ... It would be most unfortunate if the law should say otherwise. You would find defaulters scanning their contracts to find some meaningless clause on which to ride free.' We should note nonetheless that the mere fact that contracting parties believe themselves bound does not of itself make them so, if subsequently some basic omission or mistake appears which nullifies their agreement: *Bishops & Baxter Ltd v Anglo Eastern Trading Co.*, 1943.

OFFER AND ACCEPTANCE

The next question with regard to this problem of uncertainty in a contract is whether the legal and common sense requisites of offer and acceptance can be established. Do the expressed intentions of buyer and seller coincide? The basic rule of law is that an offer, for example to buy or sell, can only be validly accepted as it stands. However, the seller's statement of the price of his goods is not usually an offer in law. In legal theory it is for the buyer to offer to buy at the stated price and the seller then has the right to accept or reject that offer.

If buyer and seller seem agreed on all terms and then the buyer says: 'I'll take the goods but only if you can deliver them within a week', that may well be a new term, in effect a counter-offer, which effectively nullifies the original offer. If the seller rejects the counter-offer, in legal theory at any rate the whole agreement must then be re-negotiated: *Northland Airlines v Ferranti*, 1980. Or of course the buyer might say: 'I'll take the goods. Can you deliver them within a week?' If that is merely a request for information or for a service the buyer would like but does not insist on, the original contract is not affected: *Stevenson v McLean*, 1880.

THE BATTLE OF THE FORMS

When businessmen contract with each other on their own standard conditions of sale and purchase it is quite likely that some of the terms will be contradictory and irreconcilable. If so, whose terms prevail? Doubt and confusion often arise because neither side reads the other's terms, nor even, it sometimes seems, its own. Each side's form is designed to secure significant bargaining advantages. Sellers seek to escape liability for defects in their goods while buyers draft clauses designed to hold sellers tightly to agreed specifications. A seller might include a price escalation clause while the buyer's form contemplates a fixed price. Or again the forms might make entirely different provision as to risk of accidental loss or damage – the seller seeking to relieve himself of liability at the earliest possible moment and the buyer accepting it only at the latest. In all these cases the two sets of provisions are fundamentally irreconcilable.

While no businessman in his senses wishes to go to law over difficulties of this kind, not only because of the time and expense involved but because litigation is the surest possible way of losing the customer he would probably still prefer to keep, the fact remains that in commercial conflicts settlements are usually reached on the basis of what the parties believe to be their legal rights, and of course the value of the subject matter or the principle at stake may be such as preclude settlement and compel litigation. Some knowledge of the law is therefore bound to be helpful.

Unfortunately, English law's solutions to these particular conflicts of interest are not as clear as they might be. The possibilities were explored by Lord Denning in *Butler v Ex-Cell-O*, 1979:

> In most cases where there is a battle of the forms there is a contract as soon as the last of the forms is sent and received without objection being taken to it... The difficulty is to decide which form, or which part of which form, is a term or condition of the contract. In some cases the battle is won by the man who fires the last shot. He is the man who puts forward the latest terms and conditions and, if they are not objected to by the other party, he may be taken to have agreed to them . . . In some cases however the battle is won by the man who gets the blow in first. If he offers to sell at a named price on the terms stated on the back and the buyer orders the goods purporting to accept the offer on an order form with his own different terms on the back, then, if the difference is so material that it would affect the price, the buyer ought not to be allowed to take advantage of the difference unless he draws it specifically to the attention of the seller. There are yet other cases where the battle depends on the shots fired on both sides. There is a concluded contract but the forms vary. The terms and conditions of both parties are to be construed together. If they can be reconciled so as to give a harmonious result, all well and good. If the

differences are irreconcilable, so that they are mutually contradictory, then the offending terms may have to be scrapped and replaced by a reasonable implication.

The only weakness in this otherwise admirable statement is that it does not tell us when or why these various divergent answers may be given. The most the law can offer is a set of general principles as to what constitutes a valid contract – in particular, here, the requirements of offer and acceptance. How those principles will apply to a given set of facts depends entirely on those facts, and the possible complications and variations from one case to the next are of course infinite.

Before we consider the facts of *Butler*, perhaps the foremost English authority on the subject, let us look at the earlier and simpler issue posed in *British Road Services v Crutchley*, 1968. BRS delivered a consignment of goods to Crutchley's warehouse. The BRS driver handed over a delivery note stating that the goods were left on BRS's terms. Crutchley's warehouseman overstamped the note to the effect that they were received on Crutchley's terms. The driver made no objection, and nor did BRS. Subsequently a dispute arose between the parties, and the question was, whose terms prevailed?

The court decided that BRS's delivery note was an offer and Crutchley's stamp a counter-offer. By its silence BRS was deemed then to have accepted the counter-offer, and so Crutchley's terms carried the day. The case therefore represents a straightforward example of the first of Lord Denning's answers, and in practice the one most commonly applied, that of victory for the man who fires the last shot.

Butler v Ex-Cell-O was more complicated, however. Machinery sellers quoted a price to the buyers. On the back of the sellers' quotations were various provisions including a price variation clause and the following statement: 'These terms shall prevail over any terms in the buyer's order.' The buyers placed an order using their own form. This contained no price variation clause but included a tear-off acknowledgment slip requiring the sellers to agree: 'We accept your order on the terms and conditions stated thereon.' The sellers signed and returned the acknowledgment but sent with it a letter saying they were fulfilling the order in accordance with their own original quotation. Costs increased after lengthy delays, and in due course the sellers charged some £3000 more than had been agreed, which they said they were entitled to do under the price variation clause.

Several important issues arose. The sellers fired the first shot. They said that the contract was to be made on their terms alone. Lord Denning seems to suggest that in that event they should win the day, but what significance should be attached to their returning the acknowledgment slip? Should compliance with such clear wording have no effect at all? Against that in turn is the fact that by their accompanying letter the sellers simultaneously seemed to reintroduce, if they ever lost, the advantage of their own original terms.

At the trial the judge thought the sellers should win because the terms of their quotation made the price variation clause the basis of all subsequent dealings. In the Court of Appeal this view was unanimously rejected. With the exception of Lord Denning, who agreed on other grounds, the judges thought that the issue could be resolved by asking simply 'Who offered?' and 'Who accepted?' The sellers offered, but by returning the acknowledgment form they then accepted the buyers' counter-offer. The wording of their accompanying letter was held only to identify the machinery and refer to the price first quoted, so in the event it was no help to them.

But what would the decision have been if the sellers' letter had in fact invoked all their original terms of supply, and in particular the provision overriding the buyers' terms? Presumably the letter would then both have cancelled and been cancelled by the acknowledgment slip, leaving the buyers' and sellers' original forms irreconcilably opposed. One side or the other might then withdraw without fear of breach of contract, since there could be no contract in existence at that point. But if the sellers went on to deliver the goods, clearly the existence of a contract would have been recognised. The buyers would have to pay for the goods, but it is very doubtful whether they had accepted or would be bound by the price variation clause.

Typically then, the kind of conduct proving acceptance of the other's terms is delivery of goods by the seller or payment for them by the buyer. But such actions do not always have that effect. The need for caution is well illustrated in the Canadian case of *Tywood v St Anne Co*, 1980. Tenders were invited by a buyer. The seller offered a quotation on his own standard form. The buyer accepted the quotation on his own form which for the first time required the parties to the contract to submit any dispute to arbitration. The seller did not note or appreciate the significance of this new provision but in reliance on the buyer's acceptance went ahead and delivered the goods.

Later on a dispute arose over the goods and the question was whether the seller was bound by the arbitration clause. The fact that he had delivered the goods might suggest he had accepted this particular counter-offer, but equally his conduct was consistent with the view that since the original forms made no reference to this issue he was entitled to assume the terms would not be changed at a later stage. The court held that delivery of the goods did not establish beyond doubt that he knew of or agreed to the new provision, and therefore that he was not bound by it.

This Canadian decision seems a very sensible one. Mechanical application of the 'last in time' rule could obviously cause injustice. It would be all too easy for one of the contracting parties to take advantage of the other by adding another clause at a late stage to what had already been agreed and hoping it would not be noticed. So when we ask whether there has been an acceptance of an offer or counter-offer, we must judge the conduct in question according to what was actually known or in the circumstances ought realistically to have been known by the party who is said to have accepted.

It should be understood in any case that the 'last in time' rule can only apply while the parties are still bargaining and before they have reached final agreement. Once agreement is reached it cannot be varied by one side's attempt to add in some new provision without the consent of the other. In *Evans v Merzario*, 1975, for example, certain longstanding shipping arrangements were to be changed by putting the goods in containers. The owner of the goods agreed to the change only on condition that his goods would be shipped in containers between decks. By an oversight one consignment was put on deck and washed overboard in a storm. When the owner sued he was referred to the standard form of shipment which he had earlier received, which entitled the shippers to put the goods where they thought fit and disclaimed any liability for loss. The court held that this standard form had no effect in the light of the concluded agreement to the contrary.

A similar point is that if the terms of a standard form are misrepresented in any way by the person putting them forward or if the customer does not read them because he is advised not to worry about them then again the form will probably be nullified: *Curtis v Chemical Cleaning*, 1951. That should be so even if the customer signs the form, though normally of course signature is binding: *L'Estrange v Graucob*, 1934. And if the terms in question are exclusion clauses they must in any case be read subject to the Unfair Contract Terms Act (see chapter 4).

We must add that these conclusions are not all equally acceptable elsewhere. Trading overseas brings further uncertainties. In America for example the basic rule in the Uniform Commercial Code is that a definite expression of acceptance of an offer constitutes acceptance of that offer *even though* the acceptor seeks thereby to introduce new or different terms. This rule applies unless his acceptance was clearly stated to depend upon the other's agreement to the new terms. Otherwise the new terms become part of the contract, subject to these three vital provisions. First, the offeror's original terms may make it clear that any subsequent amendment is of no effect (thus reaching the opposite conclusion to that in *Butler v Ex-Cell-O*); second, if the new terms 'materially alter' those proposed, that of itself ensures they are not binding (thus contradicting the BRS conclusion); and third, the offeror's express objection within a reasonable time of receipt of the new terms will likewise nullify them. It follows that under the American system, unlike ours, the man who fires the *first* shot should always win.

The American answer may have more to commend it than ours. It recognises that a person who opens negotiations on the basis that his terms of sale or purchase alone will govern the transaction probably means what he says and ought to be allowed to rely on his foresight in making that provision, rather than be deemed by subsequent silence, nothing if not understandable in the circumstances, to have agreed to precisely the opposite. Whether or not such prior provision is made, the idea of implied assent to terms incompatible with one's own borders on the absurd. We could at least put the onus on the offeree to prove agreement on his own new proposals rather than on the offeror to show he has rejected them.

OBLIGATIONS AND REMEDIES

CONDITIONS, WARRANTIES AND INNOMINATE TERMS

We turn now to the obligations imposed by the contract, the way they are classified by the law, and the consequences of breaking them. Knowledge of these classifications is particularly important for any understanding of the Sale of Goods Act (see chapter 3), but the classifications and their effects are of general application.

Contractual obligations are sometimes divided into 'conditions' and 'warranties', as for example by s.11 of the Sale of Goods Act (see appendix 1). According to this classification a condition is a basic term of the contract, breach of which is said to justify the innocent party in repudiating the contract (on the grounds that he has not received anything like the benefit he contracted for) and/or claiming damages. A warranty is a less important term, breach of which does not entitle the innocent party to repudiate the contract (because he has received more or less what he asked for), but enables him to sue for damages for the shortfall. In practice buyers often demand repair or replacement of defective parts, but these are remedies not yet recognised by law. If agreed, they are in effect settlements or compromises reached in lieu of the exercise of legal rights. Once a buyer accepts a settlement of this kind he is unlikely to be able to go back on it and demand return of his money. In any case the right to reject goods is lost once the buyer 'accepts' them, a difficulty discussed in chapter 3.

This classification of terms into major and minor, with remedies accordingly, may seem clear and comprehensive, but as we shall see when we come onto the Sale of Goods Act and similar legislation in chapter 3 it generates problems. The judges have therefore begun to move away from this relatively rigid approach and prefer now to decide the appropriate remedy by reference not to any prior classification but to the seriousness or otherwise of the consequences of breach of contract. The leading case here is *Hong Kong Shipping v Kawasaki*, 1962. It involved a 24-month hire of a ship. One of the terms of hire was that the ship should be seaworthy. On the face of it this requirement was fundamental and therefore a condition, so that in theory any breach would justify the hirers in repudiating the agreement. But the Court of Appeal observed that there were many very different reasons why a ship might not be seaworthy, some serious, some trivial; some taking months to put right, others curable almost immediately. That being so, said the Court, it would be absurd to give one and the same remedy in all cases. If the consequences of the breach were trivial then damages would suffice. If they were serious, or potentially so, repudiation would be justified. In this particular case the hirers' grievance concerned structural faults in the ship which kept it out of use for nearly four months, but the Court decided the hirers could not repudiate because they still got 20 months' use out of 24, which was nearly what they had asked for. Damages were therefore the appropriate remedy. The actual decision is debateable but depends of course on the hirers' needs as laid down in the contract.

When as in the *Hong Kong* case it is impossible to say beforehand whether a term in a contract is a condition or a warranty it is called an 'innominate' or 'intermediate' term. Although this approach has much to commend it, in the sense that the law's remedies are or ought to be tailored to what actually went wrong, the effect may be to leave the parties in some doubt as to the precise significance of the terms they have agreed on. There are for example many decisions by the courts on the importance of time clauses – time of delivery or time of payment, or the time within which to make a complaint or claim – from which it is difficult if not impossible to establish any general principle. Section 10 of the Sale of Goods Act says that other things being equal time of payment is not 'of the essence' but that the effect of other provisions as to time depends on the construction of the contract as a whole and commercial necessity in particular. It seems to be agreed that in the shipping context dates of availability, loading and delivery, and possibly payment, are crucial – *Bunge v Tradax*, 1981 – but otherwise uncertainty prevails. We may contrast *Mardorf v Attica*, 1977, a shipping case where it was held that one day's delay in payment brought into effect an acceleration clause in a commercial contract (under which the whole debt became immediately repayable), with *Amherst v Walker*, 1983, where a landlord's contractual right to demand a rent review by the end of December was held still to be open to him in May of the following year.

The problem often arises in instalment contracts. If one instalment of goods is defective or delivered late, or conversely if the buyer is late in making an instalment payment, is that a breach of contract serious enough to justify repudiation by the other side? There can be no definite answer, if only because the nature of and reasons for the breach may vary so considerably, including mistaken but not blameworthy belief in legal right: *Woodar v Wimpey*, 1981. Again, there is a world of difference between being a month late with the first instalment and a day late with the last: *Maple Flock v Universal Furniture*, 1934. But we can safely say that the law will not permit repudiation unless persuaded of its necessity or of a clear contractual right in the circumstances.

If the parties wish to avoid this kind of uncertainty they are free to adopt for themselves the kind of approach exemplified by the Sale of Goods Act and specify in advance which terms are important and which less so, and what the remedies shall be if they are broken. The only remaining question then is whether the judge will accept that the parties meant what they said. If they seem to have agreed that one side or the other can bring the contract to an end on some essentially trivial ground the judge would have to be quite satisfied that that was indeed what the parties intended and not the result of inadvertence, eg by using the words 'condition' and 'warranty' in their ordinary non-legal sense. *Schuler v Wickman*, 1974, was a case of this kind in which a German machine tool manufacturer agreed with an English agent that the agent should call on a specified number of clients at least once every week. This was stated to be a condition of the contract, and it was provided that any 'material breach' of the contract entitled the manufacturer to end it forthwith. The agent failed to call as agreed on certain occasions and so the manufacturer repudiated the contract. The judge said that the parties could not have intended a right to repudiate for any and every failure however small or unavoidable or unintentional, and so awarded damages to the English agent on grounds of the manufacturer's wrongful repudiation of the contract. Not all breaches of 'condition', in other words, are necessarily 'material'. Alternatively or additionally the parties may use anti-technicality clauses to ensure that claims are not made too readily, eg by requiring the buyer of goods to give the seller the opportunity to remedy defects before exercising his right to repudiate.

PENALTY CLAUSES

Two particular types of term affecting liability under commercial contracts should be noted. The first is the exclusion or exemption clause, whereby the seller seeks to avoid liability for defective or non-conforming goods or late delivery. This very common practice is now subject to detailed regulation by the law, notably the Unfair Contract Terms Act. We consider the issues separately and at length in chapter 4. The second important provision is the so-called penalty or 'liquidated damages' clause. These clauses are usually inserted for the benefit of buyers. They are attempts to hold sellers to their word by laying down in advance how much they will have to pay for breach of contract. Penalty clauses are enforceable so long as they represent genuine pre-estimates of the loss likely to be suffered by the buyer. In that event all the buyer has to do is to prove the breach, and he will then be awarded the sums specified in the penalty clause, the 'liquidated (= fixed) damages', without having to establish in detail how much he has lost. Conversely he cannot claim more than the clause provides, even though his loss turns out to be much greater. If on the other hand the penalty clause is indeed 'penal', ie if it attempts to compel the seller to carry out his contract by threatening to make him liable for a quite disproportionate sum if he fails, then it is unenforceable. That in turn means that the buyer has to prove his losses like any other party suing for breach of contract, and so, curiously enough, he might then succeed in claiming more than was originally agreed (though this point has not yet been settled).

It is difficult to predict whether or not the court will enforce a penalty clause, and the utility of such clauses is correspondingly doubtful. A leading case is *Dunlop v New Garage*, 1915, which emphasised that the question was not simply whether the contract described the clause as being for liquidated damages or a penalty, but whether at the time the contract was made 'the sum stipulated for is extravagant and unconscionable in amount in comparison with the greatest loss which could conceivably be proved to have followed from the breach'. A clause which requires the same penalty to be paid for various different kinds of breach, some important and others less so, will probably be regarded as unenforceable.

ASSESSMENT OF DAMAGES

In the absence of a valid penalty clause then we have to consider how damages at large are assessed following a breach of contract. Our remarks are applicable equally to breach of express terms and of those implied by law, as described in the next two chapters. The basic purpose of the claim is to put the plaintiff where he would have been if the contract had been performed, but this is easier said than done – partly because it is often difficult to calculate losses precisely, but very largely because of the common law rules as to 'remoteness of damage'. The law does not attempt to compensate for every loss caused by breach of contract, but only for those physical injuries or economic losses which are, putting it shortly, reasonably foreseeable.

In this context the most important case is *Hadley v Baxendale*, 1854, which still states the fundamental principles of predictability. According to this case damages for breach of contract will be given for losses which are either 'such as may fairly and reasonably be expected to arise naturally, ie according to the usual course of things, from such breach', or 'such as may reasonably be supposed to have been in contemplation of both parties at the time they made the contract as the probable result of it'. Liability is thus imposed either for the kind of losses which *usually* arise in a particular situation or for those *exceptional* consequences of which the defendant had special knowledge and for which expressly or by implication he had agreed to take responsibility. The first test is objective, the second more subjective.

Important illustrations include *Victoria Laundry v Newman*, 1949, where the defendant's failure to supply the laundry with a new boiler in the time agreed resulted in the laundry suffering general loss of profits and also loss of a particularly lucrative government contract which it was offered after ordering the boiler but was unable to take up because of the lack of extra capacity which the boiler represented. The court held the defendants liable for the laundry's loss of normal profits but not for the exceptional or 'windfall' loss which neither side had contemplated at the time the contract was made.

Another illuminating example is *Parsons v Uttley Ingham*, 1978. The contract here was for the supply of a pig food hopper. The hopper was installed defectively so that the food went mouldy. Many pigs died through a rare disease resulting from eating the mouldy food. It was held that the natural and foreseeable consequence of the defective installation was that the food would go mouldy and that the pigs would suffer accordingly. Since some form of harm was likely it made no difference that the actual damage was both more serious and more extraordinary than might have been expected. The owner of the pigs therefore recovered their value, but not the additional profit he might have made on resale, this latter loss being regarded as too remote. Generally loss of resale profit will only be compensated if the seller knows the buyer wants the goods in order to resell them: *Czarnikow v Koufos*, 1969.

It can be seen from *Parsons* in particular that apparently minor breaches of contract, or breaches which seem minor because the price of the goods or services is so small, may have quite disproportionately expensive results. The seller of a fire extinguisher, for example, could theoretically be liable for the destruction of a complete building and for the injuries of people escaping from the fire if the extinguisher failed to work at the vital moment, if and in so far as these were the reasonably foreseeable consequences of the defect – which would in turn depend on the type of building, need for other extinguishers or fire escapes, etc. Still more clearly might a car or aircraft component seller be liable to his buyer for the total cost of an accident caused by a hidden fault in the component. Such extensive and possibly ruinous liability might be avoided or reduced by insurance and/or by clauses to that effect in the contract of sale, subject once again to the Unfair Contract Terms Act (see chapter 4).

We might observe that many contracts purport to deal with these problems by dividing the losses which might arise from breach into 'direct' and 'consequential'. Liability might then be accepted for direct loss but rejected for that which is consequential. A car warranty for example might undertake to supply new parts to replace those found defective, but refuse liability for injuries caused thereby. It will be seen that this division is not in accordance with the 'foreseeability' rules of common law, and any attempt to override the rules in this way would probably be struck down by the Unfair Contract Terms Act.

Another basic rule on the assessment of damages, but one we need not pursue in detail, is that the law expects the victim of a breach of contract to do his best to reduce or 'mitigate' his own losses. If a seller fails to deliver goods, his buyer who wishes to use them for profit must try immediately to obtain similar goods elsewhere, and if a buyer refuses to accept delivery the seller must try to find another buyer. Inaction will reduce any damages which might otherwise be awarded. But if reasonable attempts to mitigate loss only make matters worse the further expense is recoverable.

Finally we should mention the problem of 'anticipatory breach'. This occurs where one party to the contract makes clear before the due day that he has no intention of carrying out his promise. The innocent party then has a choice. He may either 'accept' the repudiation, refuse to carry out his own obligations and claim damages for the loss he has *suffered at the date of repudiation*, subject to his duty to mitigate his loss, or treat the contract as still in being and claim (probably more substantial) damages for the loss he sustains *at the time it should have been carried out*. The difficulty arising from this choice is that the second course of action flatly contradicts the duty to mitigate, as illustrated in *White and Carter v McGregor*, 1962. According to this case a buyer who has second thoughts and cancels his order immediately after making it may still be liable to the seller for the seller's total loss of profit on the transaction, a surprising and indeed alarming conclusion! In *Hounslow LBC v Twickenham Garden Developments*, 1970, however, the rule was said not to apply where the innocent party needed the other side's 'co-operation', eg where the object of the contract was that the innocent party should do some work on the land of the 'wrongdoer' but the wrongdoer changed his mind and refused entry. Clearly the innocent party could not then force his way in and do the work regardless. The argument was taken a stage further in *Clea v Bulk Oil*, 1984, where the question was said to be simply whether continued performance of the contract by one side against the wishes of the other was reasonable in the circumstances. In this case a ship chartered for two years needed major repairs after the first year. The charterers rejected the ship but the owners insisted on repairing it, which took six months. The owners' conduct was held to be unreasonable and they were unable to claim hire-charges for this period.

FRUSTRATION

There is only one major exception to the general rule that blameworthiness or otherwise does not affect one's liability for breach of contract. That exception is in the doctrine of frustration. The doctrine applies and the contract is set aside when circumstances change so completely as to make it impossible or impracticable to perform the contract. Impossibility includes subsequent illegality. We must stress that a contract is not frustrated merely because in the changed circumstances there will be loss instead of profit, eg through inflation or devaluation, or because the seller is let down by his supplier. In the leading case of *Davies v Fareham UDC*, 1956, a builder contracted with the local authority to build certain houses for a fixed price. Because of delays beyond his control the costs of labour and materials rose so much that he would have made a substantial loss if held to the fixed price. He tried to escape from this provision and charge a higher price by arguing that the contract had been frustrated. The court held that he could not escape because strictly speaking it was still possible or practicable for the houses to be built. The lesson here is that a prudent businessman would include a price variation clause in his contract. Many contracts do in fact provide for delays and other such problems beyond the parties' control, eg by 'force majeure' clauses. These clauses take effect only if their wording covers the kind or extent of disruption which actually occurs: *The Penelope*, 1926.

If a contract is held to be frustrated – a rare event – it is void from that moment. The consequences will probably be those laid down by the Law Reform (Frustrated Contracts) Act, 1943. Shortly, the Act provides that money paid is returnable and money owing ceases to be so. But expenses are recoverable from sums already paid or due, and payment must be made for 'valuable benefits' received under the contract before it was frustrated, eg goods delivered or work done in partial performance of the contract.

The 1943 Act excludes certain types of contract from its provisions. The excluded categories are contracts for the carriage of goods by sea, insurance contracts, and contracts for the sale of specific goods which through no fault of seller or buyer and before the risk has passed to the buyer are frustrated through the perishing of the goods. In these cases the loss lies where it falls, eg upon the buyer who has paid for goods before delivery. The parties are free to make their own arrangements to cover these contingencies.

SUMMARY

We use the word 'contract' to signify a legally enforceable agreement. It is not always easy to say exactly when a contract is made or what its terms are. Broadly however there are four main 'ingredients' of enforceability: the parties' apparent intention to make a legally binding agreement; certainty or ascertainability of terms; offer and acceptance and valuable consideration. The latter requirement involves reciprocity of obligation or action undertaken in return for the promise which the plaintiff seeks to enforce. As a rule writing is not necessary but is valuable as evidence of agreement.

In deciding which commitments to enforce the courts

distinguish between commercial puffs which are of no legal effect at all, representations – statements of fact inducing a party to make a contract but not necessarily forming terms of that contract, and the terms themselves which may be express or implied. Basic obligations are classed as conditions and less important ones as warranties. If a basic term is broken, or if the consequences of breach are serious, the innocent party can repudiate the contract and claim damages. If a minor term is broken, or the consequences of breach do not strike at the root of the contract, the only remedy is damages. Damages are assessed according to the likely consequences of the breach. Alternatively the contract itself may contain a penalty clause which will be enforced if it is a genuine pre-estimate of loss.

Blameworthiness or otherwise does not usually affect liability for breach. Exceptionally however the law recognises that a party may be unable to fulfil his obligations for reasons entirely beyond his control and in that case the doctrine of frustration may relieve him of all further liability.

2 Express Terms and Guarantees

Usually when an aggrieved buyer asks 'What does the guarantee say?' he has in mind a written promise of after-sales service by the manufacturer. For present purposes however we shall extend the meaning of the word to cover both spoken and written assurances given by either seller or manufacturer as to the quality of their goods as well as after-sales service. Although such promises are very often made their legal effectiveness is surprisingly uncertain. There are many possible reasons for doubt, some merely circumstantial, others of a more legalistic and technical nature, but essentially the question is *'was the promise part of a contract?'*

As between buyer and seller the problem is likely to turn on the distinctions between 'puffs', representations and actual terms of contract (described in chapter 1). Puffs are of no legal significance at all and representations are always doubtful in their effect. Strictly speaking only promises which can be proved to be terms of the contract can be relied upon. Consider for example the facts of *Routledge v McKay*, 1954. The seller wanted to sell his motor cycle. Taking his information from the registration book he told the buyer on October 23 that the machine was a 1942 model. On October 30 a written contract of sale was agreed, which made no reference to the machine's age. Later the buyer found that it had been made in 1930 (perhaps an interesting reflection on advances in British design). He claimed damages to recover his overpayment. He lost his case because of the time lapse between the seller's original statement and the final contract, which the court took to show that the statement was not intended to be binding.

But a week or so's delay is not necessarily fatal. There are other questions to be asked: how important was the seller's statement? How far did the buyer depend on his expertise? In *Routledge* both parties were private individuals and neither had greater knowledge than the other as to the date of manufacture. In *Schawel v Reade*, 1913, a man selling his horse naturally knew more about its condition than the buyer and so was held liable on his statement three weeks before sale that no examination was necessary because the horse was perfectly sound. The House of Lords held that despite the delay the circumstances were such as to make the promise an express term of the contract, and thus directly enforceable as described in chapter 1. In contrast we should recall from chapter 1 the case of *IBA v EMI*, illustrating the proposition that even the clearest of promises may not be binding if circumstances of time and place indicate that it was not made with contractual intention.

CONSIDERATION

The more specifically legal issue, however, concerns *consideration*, which as we said in chapter 1 is essential for the enforcement of promises under English law. Let us now enlarge upon this point. We have seen that consideration is defined in the cases as something of economic value which must be given or done or suffered or undertaken by one person in return for a promise made to him by another. Typically the promisee gives a promise in return for a promise: 'If you will sell me your car I will give you £X for it.' That element of mutuality or 'bargain' makes both promises enforceable by English law.

In effect then the law decides which promises to enforce, apart from the purely social, according to whether or not consideration has been given. But the presence or absence of consideration may be quite fortuitous, and there is scope accordingly for sharp practice on the one hand and disappointment on the other. Other legal systems, the nearest of them the Scottish, do not have this rule. They look instead at all the surrounding circumstances, including consideration, but also whether the promise was in writing and whether it was or should have been relied upon by the promisee, in order to decide whether there is good reason for enforcement. What other people regard as only an item of evidence, in other words, is in our own system an essential prerequisite of enforceability.

For the purposes of English law therefore it is not enough to show that one person has made a promise which another has believed and acted upon. *Reliance* on a promise is not the same as giving or doing something *in return for* a promise, which is what the consideration rule requires. So if a businessman promises money to a charity and then changes his mind the charity has no claim against him even though it may have incurred expenditure in anticipation of the gift by taking on new staff or beginning new building. It follows, as a point of passing interest, that when Englishmen have gone round the world proclaiming 'an Englishman's word is his bond' our legal system has all the time been saying that that simply is not so.

But there are exceptions to every rule, including this one. Promises made in deeds, agreements under seal, are enforceable because of their formality and without the need for the promisee to undertake anything in return. Very few commercial contracts are made in this way. Again, a 'unilateral' contract may be enforceable, though the word tells us there is no reciprocal obligation. A unilateral contract is one in which only one side makes and is bound by a promise. The promise becomes binding when the promisee fulfils its terms. A simple example is a promise to pay a reward for return of a lost dog. Promotion schemes, sponsored walks, etc come within the same category, and so may guarantees. The terms of the offer do not bind anyone there and then to find the dog, buy goods, swim the Channel or walk to Land's End, but anyone who does the required act at the appropriate time becomes entitled to his reward. It also appears that once he has begun upon performance of the act he prevents the promisor from withdrawing his promise: *Errington v Errington*, 1952.

If we now apply these various rules to sellers' and manufacturers' guarantees we see the doubts and difficulties they create. A guarantee is a promise. That promise can only be enforced by someone who has given consideration for it. If a buyer can show he bought goods knowing they were guaranteed, all well and good. His purchase is regarded as consideration given in return for the promise and so it becomes binding. But what if the guarantee or other such promise is given only after the sale is completed, or if as commonly happens the buyer only comes upon it when he takes his purchase home and finds the guarantee card at the bottom of the box?

We shall consider these possibilities in turn: first, the nature and effect of prior knowledge of the guarantee. The best known case here is *Carlill v Carbolic Smoke Ball Co*, 1893. The company advertised that it would pay £100 to anyone who used their medicament but nonetheless caught influenza – a form of guarantee of its effectiveness. Mrs Carlill did as they suggested, caught 'flu, and claimed her £100. The company refused to pay, saying that the advertisement was too vague, only a 'puff', and that in any case one party could not be contractually bound to another without knowing of that party's identity. It was held that the terms of the advert were clear and factual and amounted to a unilateral contract. The advert said in effect: 'If you will do this' (ie use the medicament) 'we will do that' (ie pay £100 if you catch 'flu). Mrs Carlill gave consideration by using the medicament as required and so brought reciprocal rights and duties into being. And although the company's argument that one could not make a contract without knowing of the other's identity must normally be correct, in this case the terms of their offer showed that identity was unimportant, just as it is when an owner promises to pay a reward to anyone who returns his lost dog. That being so the law could and did enforce the company's promise.

COLLATERAL CONTRACTS

In *Andrews v Hopkinson*, 1957, a used car dealer told a prospective customer that a particular car was 'a good little bus' and that he would 'stake (his) life on it'. Thus rashly encouraged the customer decided to take the car on hire purchase. The hp contract itself was then made between the customer and a finance company to which the dealer sold the car. The car turned out to be dangerously defective. The customer's rights against the finance company were not clear and so he sued the dealer instead for breach of his glowing promise. His claim was successful. The court held that the customer had given consideration for the dealer's promises by entering into the hp agreement with the finance company. It was as if the dealer had said: 'If you make a contract with the finance company I promise the car is in good condition.' Once the customer had acted on the dealer's promise it was then enforceable as a collateral contract, ie one 'alongside' the main hp contract. The judge in this case went on to suggest that whenever dealers introduce customers to hp companies they should be deemed to enter into *implied* collateral contracts as to the fitness of the goods in question. This suggestion has not had much support, but was adopted in *Robotics v First Co-operative Finance*, 1983.

It will be seen that the interpretation and enforcement of manufacturers' guarantees depends very largely on this collateral contract theory. If essentially the guarantee says 'If you buy our goods from a retailer we promise to provide such and such services' then the courts will enforce it once the customer has responded by making his purchase. Notable cases showing how far this principle can be taken include *Shanklin Pier v Detel Products*, 1951, and *Wells v Buckland Sand*, 1965. In the first of these the owners of the pier made inquiries as to the most suitable paint for restoration work. The defendants, paint manufacturers, assured them that their paint was best. Relying on this assurance the owners required their contractor to use the defendants' paint. The paint proved unsuitable and the work had to be done again. The owners could not sue the contractor, who had only done what they had told him to do, and so they turned to the manufacturers. The court held that in extolling their paint the manufacturers had not merely made a bare or unenforceable promise but had entered into a binding contract with the owners. As in *Carlill* and *Andrews* the contract was unilateral. In effect it was: 'If you require your contractor to use our paint, we promise it is the best for the job', and as in those cases it became enforceable once the promisees, the pier owners, acted on it in the way expected of them.

Similarly in *Wells*, a flower grower inquired as to the best sand for his chrysanthemums, and the defendants assured him theirs was most suitable. He then bought some from a retailer, only to find it unsatisfactory. The retailer could not be liable, since he supplied only what he was asked for, but the plaintiff succeeded in his claim against the producers. Once again the court accepted that their sales talk was meant to encourage him to buy their goods and had contractual effect when he did so.

WHAT DOES THE GUARANTEE PROMISE?

It goes almost without saying that a guarantee cannot be enforced unless its terms are reasonably certain. So in *Carlill* the company tried to avoid liability by pointing to the fact that their alleged guarantee did not say how long might elapse between taking the medicine and catching 'flu. Nor did it say how long the offer itself was open, and common sense tells us that sooner or later such an offer must lapse through passage of time. But as we have seen the judge found that the basic promise to pay was quite unambiguous, and so felt able to resolve the doubts by the standard of 'a reasonable time'.

A similarly strong line was taken in the Canadian case of *Hallmark Pool v Storey*, 1983. A householder was contemplating purchase of a garden pool. He saw an advert for one particular pool which showed a reproduction of the company's guarantee. The reproduction prominently displayed a 15-year durability guarantee, but the rest was unreadable without a magnifying glass. Duly impressed by the 15-year commitment, the householder bought the pool. Eventually it became unusable and the householder tried to enforce the guarantee. In reply the company pointed to the small print which excluded liability for the defects in question. The judge said that as the details could not be read the 15-year commitment was clear and apparently unqualified and therefore binding. Since the householder bought the pool in response to this promise the company would still have been liable even if he had received the guarantee after the sale and read the details then. On the other hand if the details had been clear beforehand they would have been binding even though unread, and however limited their terms: in *Adams v Richardson*, 1969 prior promises as to after-sale dry rot treatment which Lord Denning thought better described as a 'non-guarantee' were nonetheless enforceable.

Lambert v Lewis, 1980, is an important and interesting case pointing in the opposite direction and showing how difficult it may be to hold a manufacturer strictly to the terms of his sales literature. The manufacturer here made caravan towing hitches which he advertised widely as 'foolproof', requiring 'no maintenance' and 'locking, positively and absolutely'. A consumer bought one from a retailer and fitted it to his car. He noticed some time later that the hitch had become defective, but went on using it. The hitch finally broke and in the resulting accident people in an oncoming car were killed. In the Court of Appeal the buyer was held 25 per cent to blame and the manufacturer 75 per cent. The Court found the retailer in breach of s. 14 of the Sale of Goods Act (see pp.48-54) for selling unfit goods and ordered him to indemnify the buyer. The retailer then sought to recover this loss. If he had been able to he would have sued the wholesaler, to hold him in turn liable under s.14. Unfortunately for the retailer however he had forgotten where he bought the hitches, and so had no alternative but to sue the manufacturer. His object then was to prove that he had a contract with the manufacturer, since the alternative of proving negligence in a non-contractual claim, as discussed below and in the following chapter, is always more difficult.

The retailer therefore argued that he had only bought the hitches because of the manufacturer's advertisements and that following *Carlill* and *Shanklin Pier* that meant there was a collateral contract between himself and the manufacturer. The Court did not believe that the advertisements had influenced him as much as he said, but even if they had the terms of the alleged contract were far from clear. More particularly, was the promise of safety a promise to compensate anyone injured in any way, directly or indirectly, if by chance something went wrong, which was of course what the retailer said? The Court distinguished the present case from the precedents. *Carlill* and *Shanklin Pier* involved express warranties for which the consideration was the procurement of a particular contract. But these cases were 'no authority for holding that the manufacturers (here) were saying to the suppliers: "If you acquire our product we promise it is safe and merchantable and if it is not we will pay you such damages as the law requires" '. In the Court's view no promise to indemnify retailers at large could be extracted from the manufacturer's sales literature, and the claim was rejected accordingly.

Having failed in his contractual claim the retailer tried the alternative of a claim in tort. In chapters 5 and 6 we discuss at length the meaning and effect of this area of civil liability which arises independently of any contractual relationship. We need only say here that under *Hedley Byrne v Heller*, 1964, a person who by negligent advice causes another person to suffer financial loss may be liable to compensate that other. Whether he will be so liable depends in part on whether there is a 'special relationship' between them, a relationship arising where the adviser knows that the advisee relies upon him and is likely to suffer loss unless the information or advice is given carefully and accurately. This degree of dependence may arise even though there is no contract between the parties. Might there not then be a special relationship between manufacturer and retailer, or anyone else who reads his advertisements, such as to make the manufacturer liable for negligent statements as to the safety of his goods?

In *Lambert v Lewis* the Court rejected this aspect also of the retailer's claim.

> We cannot regard the manufacturer and supplier of an article as putting himself into a special relationship with every distributor who obtains his product and reads what he says or prints about it and so owing him a duty to take reasonable care to give him true information or good advice... We consider that cases of liability for statements volunteered negligently must be rare and that statements made in such circumstances as these are not actionable at the suit of those who have not asked for them. To make such statements with the serious intention that others will or may rely on them... is not, in our opinion, enough

to establish a special relationship with those others or a duty to them.

This last proposition in particular may be found somewhat surprising, if not indeed quite extraordinary. If a person makes a statement intending another to rely on it why should he not be liable if he makes that statement negligently and causes loss? There is no doubt that if the direct and foreseeable result of the advice were physical injury, the adviser would be liable. Is there any obvious reason why the answer should be different when the injury is only financial?

Certain aspects of *Lambert* may therefore seem obscure or unsatisfactory. In a way it could be said that all these issues are only of academic importance, because a further appeal was made to the House of Lords and their Lordships took a different view. They decided that the retailer was absolved from all liability by the buyer's continued use of the hitch knowing it was faulty. The question of the retailer's rights against the manufacturer therefore fell by the wayside. It was unnecessary for their Lordships even to express any opinion about the Court of Appeal's reasoning. We are left therefore with the lines of argument described above which have been neither confirmed nor denied, but would surely be referred to in any subsequent case on the enforceability of guarantees. The Court's rulings are thus still very significant, even if not conclusive.

It will be recalled that all these cases, from *Carlill* to *Lambert*, have one thing in common, namely that the buyer or user of the goods knew of the guarantee before he bought or used them. But in everyday consumer transactions that situation is more likely to be the exception than the rule. If that is so – if as we put it the buyer only finds the guarantee card when he unpacks the goods at home – it is obviously difficult if not impossible for him to argue that he bought the goods in response to the promise. That in turn means that he cannot show consideration for the promise, which thereby becomes unenforceable.

An early example of the problem was *Roscorla v Thomas*, 1842. A buyer bought a horse. The seller then assured the buyer that the horse was 'sound and free from vice'. Unfortunately it was not, and the buyer sued for breach of promise. He lost his claim because he could not show he had bought the horse *in return for* that promise. The promise was in effect an optional extra, given at the seller's discretion after the contract had been made and not forming part of it. So today a car seller might complete a sale and then in a burst of enthusiasm promise the buyer that as a favoured customer he would have the benefit of a 10 per cent discount on service charges. That promise likewise would be unenforceable.

The same conclusion should apply to guarantees the buyer was unaware of at the time of sale. In this situation however the buyer might possibly argue that he *assumed* the goods were guaranteed on the basis of common commercial practice, even though he did not know the details, or that he had given consideration for the manufacturer's promise by sticking a stamp on the guarantee card before returning it. Or if the guarantee purports to give certain specific rights of redress instead of more general legal rights, the buyer might secure these specific rights by giving up other rights in return, a form of detriment the law regards as consideration. None of these arguments can be advanced with complete certainty since none have been upheld in as many words by the courts, and certainly the scope of the last one has been very much reduced by the Unfair Contract Terms Act (see chapter 4), but all seem to meet the consideration requirement.

We should note that even where a guarantee is enforceable, either because its existence was known before the sale or some form of consideration was given for it afterwards, it cannot usually benefit anyone except the buyer. As a general rule only the buyer could be said to give anything in return for the manufacturer's promise, and so only he could enforce that promise. So for example a passenger could not claim under a car manufacturer's guarantee. But again there are exceptions. The terms of a guarantee may expressly confer buyers' rights upon subsequent owners, a rare event but by no means unknown. There seems no legal objection to such express assignment of contractual rights. It may even be possible for someone who merely uses goods to claim the protection of a guarantee, but only if the guarantee purports to protect users as distinct from buyers or subsequent owners. It will be recalled that this was the effect of *Carlill*, where compensation was offered to all who used the product unsuccessfully, whether or not they were also the purchasers. Such provision is most unusual, however.

CONSUMER COMPLAINTS

All these difficulties of legal principle were summarised as follows in 1962 by the Molony Report, a Royal Commission enquiry into consumer protection:

> Whatever obligations a manufacturer accepts by virtue of his guarantee, it must be observed that he assumes this burden voluntarily, for he is not a party to the contract of sale, although in exceptional circumstances a court might hold a collateral contract to exist.

The Report observed at large that when manufacturers choose not to be benevolent

> and the consumer is required to bear all or part of the cost of rectifying the defects, it is hardly surprising that he feels deeply wronged. He has spent good money for an article which has broken down for reasons which, if divulged at all, are shrouded in such a technical fog that he can neither understand nor verify them, and which have arisen in the course of careful and reasonable use. As far as he is concerned, he has been badly treated in the first place, and he finds he is also being denied what he regards as his legitimate redress, denied by the manufacturer whose judgments in his own cause command little respect. It is difficult to avoid the conclusion that the procedures we have been describing are somewhat arbitrary in their working; that if some consumers receive more than their entitlement, there are others who receive less. To the extent that the latter were induced to purchase the article by the offer of a guarantee holding out the promise of fair treatment, they may regard themselves as victims of deliberate deception.

The Report was unable to put forward any positive proposal to deal with this form of deception by limiting or banning of guarantees. Despite the statutory developments noted immediately below it could not yet be said that the law is wholly satisfactory, and still less the practice.

The Office of Fair Trading noted in 1977 that local authorities had received over a thousand complaints about guarantees in the first half of that year. Complaints included cases where the guarantee was in the name only of the purchaser and could not be transferred, or had expired before the goods could be repaired, or was subject to unreasonable conditions such as return in the original packaging or instant return of the guarantee card.

Different solutions might be offered, taking effect at different levels. On an individual level consumer complaints to Trading Standards Departments or direct to the OFT might eventually lead to action under Part III of the Fair Trading Act 1974. The Act enables the Office to demand undertakings of good behaviour from anyone guilty of such sharp practice, if it involves actually breaking the law, and breach of an undertaking is a form of contempt of court which can be severely punished. Another possible answer lies in manufacturers committing themselves to codes of practice specifying their after-sales services. Many codes in existence today have been recently negotiated between trade associations and the OFT and although not directly enforceable there is certainly considerable pressure upon association members to observe their terms, if only because of the threat of legislation if they fail.

From the long-term point of view, legislation is no doubt the most effective solution. If manufacturers' guarantees were to be given general legal effect that would have to be done by overriding the consideration and privity rules. Parliament could of course do that if it wished, and has indeed taken that step in various other contexts such as life insurance. Other countries have given us a lead in this respect, notably America and Canada, and nearest to hand Ireland, whose important Sale of Goods and Supply of Services Act 1979 is reported in chapter 7.

STATUTORY PROVISIONS

The furthest Parliament has in fact gone to meet the criticisms above and modify the common law position is in the following two rules: the first in s.5 of the Unfair Contract Terms Act 1977 and the second in the Consumer Transactions (Restrictions on Statements) Order 1978.

The Unfair Contract Terms Act is discussed at length in chapter 4 and set out in appendix 3. Its purpose is to prevent abuse of contract clauses which limit suppliers' liabilities for injury, loss or damage caused by defective goods or services. Section 5 deals specifically with manufacturers' guarantees. These are defined as 'anything in writing [which] contains or purports to contain some promise or assurance (however worded or presented) that defects will be made good by complete or partial replacement, or by repair, monetary compensation or otherwise'. The section is concerned only with guarantees of consumer goods, defined as 'goods of a type ordinarily supplied for private use or consumption'. It provides that where loss or damage arises from goods proving defective in consumer use – use which is not exclusively for business purposes – and results from the negligent manufacture or distribution of the goods, liability for such loss or damage 'cannot be excluded or restricted by reference to any contract term or notice contained in or operating by reference to a guarantee of the goods'.

The meaning and effect of this section can only be understood in the light of certain other provisions of the Act, notably ss.2, 6 and 7. Section 2 annuls any contract term or notice excluding liability for death or injury caused by negligence, but permits terms or notices excluding liability for damage to property or other economic loss if reasonable in the circumstances. The combined effect of ss.2 and 5 therefore is to prevent manufacturers and distributors of consumer goods from excluding liability for negligence not only causing death or injury but also any other loss or damage.

This prohibition of guarantees which take away more substantial rights than they give may seem strangely limited by the proviso in sub-s.3 of s.5. This sub-section says that s.5 does not apply at all 'as between the parties to a contract under or in pursuance of which possession or ownership of the goods passed'. It does not apply, in other words, if the relationship between the parties is not that of manufacturer and user but seller and buyer or owner and hire purchaser. That may seem to make the rule quite meaningless, but ss.6 and 7 provide the explanation. As we shall see in chapter 4 these latter sections cover the relationship of seller and buyer, owner and hire purchaser and lessor and lessee of goods and give all requisite protection. The end result therefore is that if and in so far as manufacturers' guarantees do have legal effect they cannot be used to defeat any kind of non-contractual or negligence claim.

We refer lastly to the Consumer Transactions Order of 1978. The Order applies to consumer sales, hp agreements and redemption of trading stamps, but not to sales by auction or competitive tender or contracts for the international sales of goods. First it endorses s.6 of the Unfair Contract Terms Act, above, by making it a criminal offence for a seller to exhibit any written statement denying liability under the Sale of Goods Act or equivalent legislation (see chapter 3). Then with regard to guarantees the Order forbids sales of goods which are accompanied by written statements as to buyers' rights, whether or not legally enforceable, unless 'in close proximity' there is another 'clear and conspicuous' statement that consumers' statutory rights are not affected thereby. Because of this Order therefore manufacturers' guarantees now end with the message that 'these rights are in addition to the buyer's rights under the Sale of Goods Act', or words to that effect.

SUMMARY

A seller is bound by any express promise he may make to the buyer as to the quality or fitness of his goods, if and insofar as his promise appears as part of the contract of sale. The position is less clear where the promise comes from the manufacturer. The difficulty arises because under English law promises are not binding unless consideration is given in return. As a general rule the buyer's consideration – his promise to pay, or his payment – is given to the seller, not the manufacturer. Strictly speaking therefore manufacturers' guarantees of after-sales service, or any other statements about their goods, are only 'optional extras', and not enforceable at law. But if the buyer can show he knew of the guarantee before he bought the goods his purchase or use of them may be seen as consideration, as also where he returns a guarantee card afterwards.

Guarantees of consumer goods which exclude liability for personal injury or damage to property caused by manufacturers' negligence are void. This provision does not of itself help the injured buyer to sue the manufacturer, since his primary rights are against the seller. Guarantees must state that these primary rights are unaffected.

3 Terms Implied by Law

The primary obligations of the seller are those he expressly agrees with the buyer in the contract of sale. Often enough however the parties do not reach express agreement on every detail of the contract, perhaps because they take a point for granted or perhaps because it does not occur to them in the first place. In that case one side or the other will ask the law to fill in the gaps and add terms into their agreement.

Terms may be implied either by common law or statute. Generally the judges are reluctant to intervene and make the kind of provision which they think the parties ought to have made for themselves. They will not add terms in simply to make a contract more fair or reasonable, but only if they are based on trade custom or, more commonly, are necessary to enable it to make sense. By reference to this test of necessity judges have decided, for example, that in the absence of agreement to the contrary work must be completed within a reasonable time and a reasonable price paid. What is reasonable is decided by the judge on the facts of each case.

Much more important are the terms implied by Act of Parliament, affecting all transactions of a particular type. Usually the terms apply only in the absence of agreement between the parties, but sometimes Parliament lays down minimum standards of fitness or fairness as the case may be and so enforces them regardless of the parties' wishes.

So far as product liability is concerned the standards with the widest application are those implied by the Sale of Goods Act 1979, the Supply of Goods (Implies Terms) Act 1973, dealing with goods supplied on hire purchase and on redemption of trading stamps, and the Supply of Goods and Services Act 1982 regulating hiring and rental agreements and goods provided under service or repair contracts. Premium offers and free gifts are not controlled by statute. It should also be noted that drugs supplied by doctors' dispensaries and by chemists on prescription are not regarded as goods sold but as services provided: *Appleby v Sleep*, 1958.

The obligations under these Acts are in virtually identical terms, and are nearly all classified as either conditions or warranties. As we mentioned in chapter 1, a condition is a basic term whose breach entitles the innocent party to repudiate the contract, unless he has accepted the goods, and/or to claim damages, while a warranty is a less important term breach of which only entitles the innocent party to claim damages. We shall see shortly that this apparently simple but in practice rigid classification of duties and remedies creates difficulties. If what might appear as a minor breach of contract is in fact classified by the Act as a breach of condition the resulting 'all or nothing' solution may seem clumsy or even self defeating. Judges are naturally reluctant to set aside contracts on essentially trivial grounds, but on the other hand the Act may preclude any other remedy. Proposals for reform are noted later in this chapter.

THE SALE OF GOODS ACT

The Act of 1979, reproduced in appendix 1, is largely a restatement of the first Sale of Goods Act of 1893. The most important difference is that sales are now subject to the Unfair Contract Terms Act 1977 (see chapter 4) and sellers' powers to opt out of the liabilities we are about to examine are thus very much reduced.

It should be understood that the word 'seller' refers equally to manufacturers, distributors, retailers and private individuals if and in so far as they enter into contracts of sale. Section 14 of the

Sale of Goods Act applies only to business sales, but otherwise all are bound to their buyers by the same terms of the same Act. So far as retailers and distributors are concerned we should observe that they are almost always in business on their own account and thus personally or corporately liable on their contracts. They may well be described in the sales literature as 'manufacturers' agents' or 'franchised dealers', but that does not make them agents in law. Only where one person genuinely contracts for and on behalf of someone else does he make that other liable for his own breach of contract.

TITLE

The first of the relevant rules in the Act is s.12, but it requires only brief mention for present purposes. The section says there is an implied condition in all contracts of sale that the seller has a right to sell the goods, and implied warranties of freedom from prior rights over the goods and of quiet possession of them except in so far as any limitations are disclosed before sale. Thus a seller is liable for infringement of a third party's patent rights, deliberate or inadvertent: *Microbeads A G v Vinhurst*, 1975

DESCRIPTION

Section 13 says that in sales by description there is an implied condition that goods will conform with their description, ie that the buyer will get what the seller promised. In sales by both sample and description the bulk of the goods must also correspond with the description.

The key question is as to the meaning of the word 'description'. The word clearly does not encompass everything said or written by the seller about his goods. Nor on the other hand does it presuppose a spoken or written statement. Many goods 'describe themselves' by the way they are packed or displayed. The judges have held that 'description' is confined to those express or implied statements which actually identify the goods or are otherwise part of their essential attributes; the sort of thing one might write on a sales or receipt note to define one's purchase. If the goods do not conform with these particulars then s.13 enables the buyer to reject them and demand his money back, subject always to the question of acceptance noted in chapter 1 and below.

Difficulties naturally arise in distinguishing between essential and inessential attributes. 'New', for example, is an essential element while 'in good condition' probably would not be because it is merely a question of degree. Even then the precise meaning of 'new' is open to argument. In *Phillips v Cycle Corp*, 1977, a motor cycle sold as new was held to be so even though it was five years old, because it had not previously been sold by retail. This was surely a quite incorrect test in the circumstances. Conversely if the goods are indeed 'new' or otherwise as specified the fact that they are defective does not of itself prove breach of s.13. So in *Grenfell v Meyrowitz*, 1936, the buyer ordered a particular kind of safety glass which then broke and injured him, but he had no claim under s.13 because he got the type of glass he asked for. Presumably there is a point at which an article is so defective that it cannot properly be given the same description as if it were in working order, but such situations must be rare.

Normally therefore the scope of s.13 is limited to situations where the buyer orders 'A' but is delivered 'B'. If 'A' is delivered but found defective the buyer's remedy if any is usually in the quality and fitness requirements of s.14. We shall see that these requirements are necessarily matters of degree, and so should bear in mind the possibility of using s.13 to define quality and avoid the doubt which might otherwise arise. This can be done only by the use of very precise language which as we have said identifies or defines the goods. A good example is *Tradax v European Grain*, 1983, where the buyer ordered a consignment of animal feeding stuffs with 'maximum 7.5 per cent fibre content'. On delivery the consignment was found to have up to 9.25 per cent fibre content. It was held that the statement as to fibre content was part of the description of the goods, and the buyer was thus enabled to reject the goods under s.13 without having to argue questions of suitability or fitness under s.14.

As a rule then the judges attach much weight to precise specifications of this kind. In *Arcos v Ronnaassen*, 1933, for instance, $1/2''$ staves were ordered but staves of $9/16''$ supplied. The buyer was held entitled to reject them even though they could still be used for his intended purpose. This very strict approach is of course open to abuse. It may give a buyer who has changed his mind about the wisdom of his purchase a gratuitous and quite unnecessary opportunity to renege on his contract. More recently the courts have asked simply whether the seller's deviation from contractual requirements is of any real significance: *Cehave v Bremer,* 1975: *Reardon Smith v Hansen Tangen,* 1976. So if there is only a very minor shortfall or excess in quality or quantity, the buyer's claim will probably be rejected. In contrast with the *Tradax* case above is *Tradax v Goldschmidt,* 1977, where a contract for the sale of barley allowed for up to 4 per cent impurity but the barley delivered contained 4.1 per cent of foreign matter. The buyer was not allowed to reject the goods on this pretext.

One last point about s.13 is that the more the buyer examines the goods and satisfies himself they are what he wants, the less he can claim to rely on the seller's description of them. There may be no 'sale by description' at all, or none at least in respect of those aspects of the description his examination was intended to confirm. In *Beale v Taylor,* 1967, two halves of cars were welded together; the buyer tested the car but was still protected by s.13 because his examination was not directed towards this structural shortcoming. It should follow that when goods are sold 'as seen' or 'as is' s.13 should apply only to hidden faults: *Cavendish Woodhouse v Manley,* 1984.

QUALITY AND FITNESS

For product liability purposes the most important duties imposed by the Sale of Goods Act are those in s.14. The rules are set out in full in appendix 1, so here we need do no more than summarise and then illustrate them. Their main provisions are that where goods are sold in the course of business they must be of *merchantable quality* and *reasonably fit for their purpose.*

These requirements of quality and fitness are both *conditions,* which as stated above means that if goods fail to meet these standards the buyer can reject them and recover his money, together with compensation for any personal injury or economic loss directly caused by the goods. The right to reject goods is lost once the buyer has accepted them – ss.11 and 35 (see below) – and in that event he has only a claim for damages.

BUSINESS OR PRIVATE SALE?

It is of interest first of all that these rules as to quality and fitness apply only to business sales, whereas ss.12, 13 and 15 apply to all sales including those between private individuals. It follows that if Mr A sells his own car to Mr B and it then breaks down completely, Mr B has no redress under s.14 of the Sale of Goods Act, nor, unless there is fraud or negligence, under any other rule of law. As between private individuals the policy of the law is still summed up in the maxim *caveat emptor*: let the buyer beware. A person who buys goods from his neighbour must satisfy himself of their worth, or have only himself to blame. Since the law will not help him he must help himself, and the most useful way of doing that, apart from having an expert examine the goods, is to extract some appropriate and preferably written promise from the seller as to their quality or quantity before purchase. This promise, so long as it is factual and not mere sales talk, then becomes an express term of the contract and if broken can be sued upon according to the general principles of law discussed in chapter 1. Failing any express contractual commitment a private seller could only be liable on grounds of negligence; in other words that he knew or ought to have known that the goods were likely to cause injury or loss. In a private sale the buyer might well find it difficult if not impossible to prove the seller at fault in this way.

Because private sellers are not liable to the same extent as business sellers, the latter sometimes try to hide their identity. In the 'small ads' columns of newspapers, for example, it may be very tempting for the business seller to masquerade as a private individual and thus escape the burdens of s.14. The purpose of the Business Advertisements (Disclosure) Order 1977 is accordingly to compel advertisers selling in the course of business to state that fact. Failure to do so is a criminal offence. Sales by auction or competitive tender are outside the

Order, as are sales of agricultural produce gathered or produced by the seller.

There may occasionally be difficulties in deciding whether a particular sale is indeed in the course of a business. The Sale of Goods Act defines business to include a profession and the activities of public authorities, so it is not merely a question of seeking to make a profit. It is certainly not necessary to be a manufacturer of the goods in question, nor even to deal frequently in such goods, as where for example a coal merchant sells his lorry. There is no single test, whether of intention or frequency or any other element. An overall objective view is necessary. Two recent cases indicate the possibilities. In *Blackmore v Bellamy*, 1983, a postman had a hobby of buying, improving and then selling old cars. Since it was his hobby he neither sought nor made any significant profit. He was prosecuted for breach of the 1977 Order, above. The magistrates accepted his evidence that his activities were no more than a hobby, and acquitted him. Another case of interest is *Davies v Sumner*, 1983. A self-employed courier used his car almost entirely for the purposes of his job. He likewise was prosecuted when he sold it, and he also was acquitted because the sale was not in the course of his trade or business.

If a private person sells through a business agent, eg an auctioneer, then under s.14(5) the conditions of merchantable quality and reasonable fitness bind the business agent unless he makes it clear to the buyer that the seller is not acting in the course of business.

MERCHANTABLE QUALITY

We observe first that this basic requirement in s.14(2) does not apply as regards defects pointed out to the buyer before sale, nor to faults the buyer should have seen in any examination of the goods he may have carried out. He is not obliged to examine the goods beforehand, and indeed very often cannot do so, eg because they are sold when in transit.

In practice the most difficult question arising under this sub-section is to decide what the expression 'merchantable quality' actually means. There is a definition of sorts in sub-section 6:

'Goods are of merchantable quality if they are as fit for the purpose or purposes for which goods of that kind are commonly bought as it is reasonable to expect, having regard to any description applied to them, the price (if relevant) and all the other relevant circumstances.'

This definition is nothing if not vague. It is also circular, in the sense that merchantability is defined in terms of reasonable fitness, the requirement in sub-s.3, which is not itself defined. What is aimed at however is the *norm* of performance or fitness or appearance, rather than perfection. Whether goods reach a norm, the generally acceptable standard, depends on the nature of such goods. It is usually easy enough to decide whether an article with only one or two functions, eg an electric kettle, is working properly, but very much more difficult where multifunctional and extremely complex products such as cars are involved. Buyers' reasonable expectations also depend of course on whether the goods are new and if so whether expensive and said to be of good quality, or cheap and therefore perhaps less reliable and durable, or secondhand, and if so on their age and appearance and the reduction in price.

Let us illustrate the problems a little further. 'Merchantable' must mean 'saleable'. But then the questions arise, saleable to whom and as what? In *Sumner Permain v Webb*, 1922, the buyer bought goods he intended to export to Argentina. Unknown to him the Argentine government had prohibited the import of such goods. But the fact that he could not sell them there and the object of the contract thus defeated so far as he was concerned did not mean they were not saleable. He was still able to sell them elsewhere, though at lower prices. Similarly, in *Buchanan-Jardine v Hamilink*, 1983, an enforced delay in the exercise of the buyer's right to resell goods was held not to affect their merchantability.

If goods can only be resold at a lower price that does not of itself prove them unmerchantable under their original description, but that depends of course on the extent of the reduction and the reason for it. There is always the possibility of the market dropping in the meantime, or the goods may be usable for some other more economical purpose than that originally intended: *Brown v Craiks*, 1970. Conversely a resale price only just below the price first agreed does not necessarily prove the goods merchantable, as we see immediately below. Variables such as these led the Law Commission in 1983 to observe that 'merchantability' was no longer a suitable test, envisaging as it did goods bought by merchants for resale rather than by consumers for use, and to suggest a redefinition in the interests of consumers. The Law Commission's proposals on this and other problems of sales of goods are noted later.

If the question is indeed one of consumer acceptability then how much importance should the law attach to scratches or blemishes or other purely cosmetic defects? A person given a choice of, say, washing machines, all identical except for one with a scratch or dent, clearly would not buy that particular one, at least at the full price. It should follow that an article may not be merchantable because of very minor and superficial faults and even though otherwise in good working order. But could that article likewise be rejected by the buyer after he has taken delivery of it?

The Canadian case of *IBM v Shcherban*, 1925, is instructive here. The buyer ordered a $300 computer scale. It was delivered with a broken dial glass which would have cost only 30 cents to repair and which did not affect the working of the machine in the slightest. The court held the machine unmerchantable and the buyer therefore entitled to reject it. Whether or not one agrees with the decision it is obviously very much on the borderline. No commodity is perfect. There must come a point when a scratch or mark, particularly on industrial rather than consumer goods, is so trivial that no reasonable buyer would take account of it and a court would certainly refuse to acknowledge it. And even if one of these very minor cosmetic faults is sufficient to justify rejection at the moment of delivery, it is hard to see how it could continue to do so thereafter.

The problem is to discourage shoddy workmanship while at the same time preventing buyers from behaving unreasonably. That seems to mean that very minor or cosmetic flaws could usually justify rejection only in consumer sales, and that any such right would be lost within a very short time after delivery. In business contracts sellers may avoid difficulties of this kind by specifying tolerances within which their goods are sold, or using 'anti-technicality' clauses giving them the right to repair before the buyer exercises any right to repudiate.

REASONABLE FITNESS

Merchantability is not of course confined to the kind of trivial faults we have just considered, but anything more substantial and affecting the working order of goods will more probably be considered under sub-s.3 of s.14: the requirement of reasonable fitness for purpose.

As with merchantability so the requirement of reasonable fitness depends on certain qualifying factors. We have mentioned one of the most important already, that the sale must be in the course of business. The buyer must also have informed the seller expressly or by implication of the purpose for which the goods are required. As a rule this presents no difficulty because the purpose of most goods is self evident: clothes for wearing, cars for driving, and so on. It is only necessary for the buyer to state his needs expressly when they are in some way more specialised or demanding than the normal purposes or uses of the goods. The case of *Teheran Europe v Belton*, 1968, however, reminds us that the seller's awareness of the buyer's plans, in this case to export goods to Iran, does not of itself oblige him to ensure their fitness for that purpose.

Another prerequisite of sub-s.3 is that the buyer has relied upon the seller's skill and judgment in selecting his goods. Reliance is normally presumed and does not have to be proved. 'A buyer goes to the shops in the confidence that the tradesman has selected his stock with skill and judgment': *Grant v AKM*, 1936. But this presumption may be displaced by evidence, eg of the buyer's own expert examination of the goods, or that they were made to the buyer's design, in which case, depending on the extent of reliance upon his expertise, the seller may be answerable only for the quality of the materials he uses and not the overall success of the design: *Cammell Laird v Manganese Bronze*, 1934; *Dixon Kerby v Robinson*, 1965. In the very unsatisfactory case of *McDonald v Empire Garage*, 1975, the seller escaped liability because of the buyer's expert examination of the goods, even though the fault could not have been found on any reasonable examination.

Subject to these provisions sellers must ensure that their goods are reasonably fit for their purpose, or, if not, take them back and return the price. The standard of fitness is again not one of perfection but depends entirely on normal usage, and in particular on the complexity of the goods and their age and price. This question of degree is perhaps best illustrated by a number of cases on new and secondhand motor vehicles.

The first of these cases is *Farnworth Finance v Attryde*, 1970. This was a contract of hire purchase rather than sale, but involved the same issues of fitness and quality. The machine was a new Enfield motor cycle. It developed a series of lethal defects: a pannier fell off and made the machine slide about the road; the headlight failed at night and at speed once because the dip switch was corroded and twice more because the terminals came off the wires; the chain broke and the lubricating system was faulty. In the Court of Appeal their Lordships agreed this was a 'most formidable list of defects', making the motor cycle 'thoroughly unsatisfactory' and 'not really a workable machine on the road'. It was accordingly held to be neither reasonably fit for its purpose nor of merchantable quality and the hire purchaser was able to repudiate the contract and recover all he had paid. In view of the inconvenience he had suffered he was not obliged to make any allowance for the 4000 miles he had in fact driven on the machine.

One could scarcely doubt the rightness or obviousness of this decision, but the important point is that it clearly identifies *danger* as a breach of condition, not, of course, *any* danger however trivial or remote, but a real risk of serious injury.

With this landmark before us we turn to the Scottish case of *Millar v Turpie*, 1976, which concerned a new Ford Granada. The day after taking delivery the buyer noticed a leak of oil from the power assisted steering box. He took it back to the dealer. In due course the dealer told him he had mended it and the buyer took the car home again. Next day he found another leak from the same source. At that point he evidently decided he could trust neither car nor dealer and told the dealer to take the car back and return his money.

The question was therefore whether two oil leaks made the car unfit and unsaleable, since that is what s.14 of the Sale of Goods Act and the equivalent hire purchase rules require. Our only guide so far is that of imminent danger. How dangerous is an oil leak from the steering box? Opinions may differ, but certainly the judge thought there was no immediate likelihood of any serious risk, if only because so much oil would have to be lost before any risk at all could occur that the driver would have been bound to see it and have the car properly repaired. Although the dealer had failed to do the job on the first occasion, the fact remained that this was a minor fault, easily and cheaply remedied. That being so, said the judge, there was clearly no breach of s.14. And that in turn meant that the buyer had no redress at all.

Millar's case raises in passing the interesting question whether a buyer of defective goods can reject them straightaway if the fault is serious enough, or whether he must first take them back to the seller and give him the chance to try to mend them; and, if so, how many times has the seller the right to try but fail? On the face of it goods must be reasonably fit and of merchantable quality *at the time of sale* and for whatever period is appropriate thereafter. If the buyer had a legal duty to return goods for repair before he could think about rejecting them that would mean the goods were only required to be fit after that time, and that any kind of trial run was always at the buyer's risk. That would seem absurd, and the Canadian case of *Friskin v Holiday*, 1977, makes it clear that such is not the law.

On the other hand the judgment in *Millar* makes it equally clear that the buyer was wrong in not giving the dealer another chance to mend the leak. If the fault had been one the dealer and perhaps another independent expert had both tried but somehow failed to remedy, then and only then might the buyer have succeeded. In effect he would have proved that the defect was not as we said above easily and cheaply remediable. But that seems to be the same as saying that the buyer *does* have a duty to return goods for repair before he can reject them, so how can the arguments be reconciled?

The answer may be that except as regards immediate dangers some goods, such as cars, are sold 'subject to service', ie on the basis that work remains to be done on them. In that case the buyer has no alternative but to return the goods to the dealer to find out exactly what is wrong with them. Unless he does that it may be difficult if not impossible to say whether the fault is serious or trivial and repairable or not. In practice then, if not expressly in law, the buyer must behave reasonably and the seller will often get another chance to put things right. This conclusion is supported by *Leaves v Wadham Stringer*, 1980, where the buyer complained about the brakes on his new Leyland Princess. The dealers accepted that if a brake fault rendered the car unroadworthy the buyer was entitled to reject it. But an independent engineer found later complaints unjustified, and the judge held on the facts that there were no significant defects in the brakes *after their repair.*

The main points we have sought to establish so far however are the limits of the seller's liability. If his goods are so defective in normal use as to represent a real danger to life and limb the buyer can reject them and recover his money (subject to the problem of 'acceptance', below). But conversely if faults appearing after delivery are 'normal' or do not substantially affect the value of the goods or their safety then the buyer usually has no remedy at all.

We come now to what is probably the commonest problem area, that of goods whose faults put them somewhere in the middle of this spectrum of liability, with little or no element of danger but frequent failures in operation or many minor faults or blemishes.

One of the most interesting and important cases in this connection is *Spencer v Rye*, 1972, and nonetheless so despite the fact that it was never officially reported. The plaintiff was however kind enough to let the present writer have a copy of the judgment. The vehicle in question was a new Triumph Vitesse. 'There was trouble from the start.' The day after it was delivered the throttle cable came adrift and running repairs were necessary. When the buyer took the car back to the dealers to have the cable repaired he remarked also that the temperature gauge was above normal and the engine seemed to run hot. There was also a rattle, leaks in the convertible hood and elsewhere, a knock from the back on acceleration and 'fierce vibration' at speed. Some of the faults were cured in ensuing weeks; others appeared, such as wind whistle, the first signs of rust and collapse of a boot support strut. Periodically the car filled with exhaust fumes. The overheating suddenly became much more serious. After the car had done 2500 miles the radiator boiled over four times in the course of the following 400 miles. There was also excessively high petrol consumption: some 10 miles to the gallon.

Mr Spencer took the car back to the dealers with these

problems 10 or 12 times. Most of the faults were eventually cured, more or less to his satisfaction. But try as they might, and no complaint was made against them in this respect, the dealers were quite unable to discover what made the radiator boil over or to stop it from doing so. They called in independent experts and the manufacturers themselves, but all were equally powerless to cure the fault. Four months after he bought it therefore Mr Spencer returned the car for the last time to the dealers and demanded return of the purchase price.

The judge said: 'If this car had been exhibited for sale with a label saying it was liable to boil on and off every 100 miles for a reason which nobody could discover, I do not see anybody buying it except somebody interested in motor car research or for its scrap value.' The car was a 'freak' and 'unserviceable'. It was therefore neither merchantable nor fit for its purpose and so Mr Spencer won his case. The dealers' counter-claim for the cost of storing the vehicle pending the trial was shortly rejected.

None of this may seem at all remarkable. A new car whose engine seizes up every 100 miles or so is obviously useless and one could not really doubt that the buyer must be able to recover his money. The more important and remarkable part of the decision lies in what the judge said about all the *other* defects we have listed: 'I think that all the other complaints, although they were reasonable to make and must have been most irritating to experience in a brand new car, *were not such as to justify rejection* . . . . They were all capable of adjustment or being put right without too much trouble' (author's italics). Had it not been for the trouble with the radiator, in other words, Mr Spencer would have had no claim at all.

To the consumer at least this conclusion may seem hard to justify. How can a vehicle which has to be taken back 10 or 12 times with so many defects, even excluding the radiator, with all the consequential inconvenience and expense of finding alternative means of transport, be said to be reasonably fit? The answer, though not advanced in so many words by the judge, depends on the general level of performance and acceptability of the class of goods in question. The law requires cars to be reasonably fit, which is as we have said a standard short of perfection. A car is reasonably fit if it meets the normal standards of performance, for better or worse. Most new cars have teething troubles, some more than others. Mr Spencer's car had teething troubles; perhaps more than most, but not so exceptional (apart from the radiator) as to make it wholly abnormal and unusable.

This is no doubt how the judge interpreted and applied the law. It may still be suggested that in his application of the law to those particular facts he accepted depressingly and unnecessarily low standards of workmanship and performance. At the same time we should bear in mind that the decision was confined to the facts of the case, and that next time a buyer tries to return his car he will have a different set of complaints which may have to be considered in a different light. As and when this occurs we may find that standards of reasonable consumer expectation have risen. There are in particular several Canadian cases to which the judge's attention might be drawn, setting standards somewhat higher than our own apparently very basic requirements.

In *Lightburn v Belmont*, 1969, for example, the plaintiff bought a new Cortina, which he had been assured would meet his requirements as to economy and reliability but which he found – as the judge said – he could not rely on 'from one hour to the next'. The car had to be towed back to the seller's garage twice and returned a total of 17 times in the eight months following sale because of continuous trouble with the electrical system. It never started easily, and the battery frequently went flat. The battery had to be recharged three times in one week and on one occasion the engine 'died' while the car was moving. There were other miscellaneous troubles such as a cracked oil pump and oil leaks, which were cured. The judge ordered rescission of the contract with no allowance for depreciation despite the eight months' use of the vehicle in the course of which the plaintiff had driven some 8000 miles, and laid down a standard of fitness apparently in advance of that required in England. 'I conclude that the defendant was in breach of a fundamental term of the contract to purchase a motor car of workable character capable of giving a *sustained reliable performance throughout the year*. . . . It can hardly be said (the plaintiff) had reasonable use of the motor vehicle for its continued operation was uncertain and a steady cause of worry' (author's italics). It will be seen and should be emphasised that the plaintiff's claim was upheld primarily because the vehicle was *unreliable* rather than dangerous.

The facts in *Gibbons v Trapp Motors*, 1970, were very similar. 'The plaintiff purchased a new automobile (a Pontiac convertible) and by no means a low cost one and was entitled to enjoy from it a performance typical of a new car from an established manufacturer. Instead of such a performance he in fact acquired a running fight with a chronically defective car.' Over 30 hours repair time was required in the first 10 months, followed by a period of 10 days during which the car was to be brought once and for all to reasonable running order. But even that lengthy treatment failed to deal with its many (unspecified) weaknesses in 'steering and roadability (and) reliability'. The judge held that all these various defects together constituted a breach of condition. Although the question was partly one of safety it seems clear from his Honour's words that repeated loss of use and unreliability were the main factors. 'Such use was not free from justified worries on his part, inconveniences and restrictions on what I choose to term serene possession of a reliably performing car' – a strikingly apt and agreeable phrase indicating again a higher standard than that in *Spencer* or *Farnworth Finance*. His Honour held that the fact that the defendant had tried to repair all the defects as they appeared at his own expense did not compel the plaintiff to accept the car. The judgment was that the car be reconveyed to the defendant, who was ordered to return the purchase price less half the plaintiff's cost of hiring replacement vehicles.

A more recent example where persistent starting trouble was held to justify repudiation was *Finlay v Metro Toyota*, 1978. On the basis of these Canadian cases it may now be argued that the proper test of the fitness of goods is whether they should be satisfactory for a reasonable buyer, not simply whether they meet the most basic requirements of safety or utility. This is evidently the view of the Law Commission, as noted below.

USED GOODS

With regard to secondhand goods there are several interesting cases, one of which is *Bartlett v Marcus*, 1965. The dealer here sold a used Jaguar car for £950, warning the buyer that minor clutch repairs might be needed. They became necessary almost immediately and cost the buyer £45. His claim for damages was rejected because the car was 'in usable condition even though not perfect. . . . It was fit to be driven along the road in safety'. Secondhand cars are likely to need repairs, and expensive cars need expensive repairs. But it is all a question of degree, as illustrated in *Crowther v Shannon*, 1975, which also concerned a Jaguar. The car was sold for £390 with 80,000 miles on the clock. After the buyer had driven it 2000 miles in the following few weeks the engine failed completely and had to be renewed for another £400 or so. The Court of Appeal distinguished this case from *Bartlett*. In *Crowther* the defect was such that the car was not fit for the road, and on the basis of evidence that Jaguar engines were supposed to last for some 100,000 miles the buyer had got very much less than he was reasonably entitled to expect. His claim succeeded accordingly.

Feast v Vincent, 1974, is an instructive New Zealand decision. A company specialising in heavy road building equipment needed another engine for one of its road rollers. The right type of engine could not be found but eventually the company came across another one in the hands of a small dealer which it was thought might be suitable. The engine was bought without a test and for about one third of its price when new. It ran for two days and then seized up and became completely unusable. It was held that the buyer had no redress, partly because of his greater expertise and corresponding absence of reliance on the seller's skill and judgment and partly also because this was very much a speculative purchase, leaving the seller with no ground for complaint if things went wrong.

DURABILITY

Pending acceptance of the Law Commission's proposals (see p. 64) English law has little to say on the relationship between fitness of goods and their durability. If and when statute law expressly recognises an obligation as to durability, now only tentatively acknowledged by the common law, it will still only be possible to say that goods must remain fit for a reasonable time after purchase. That in turn will depend entirely on the normal life expectancy, age, price and quality of the particular product, as illustrated in *Crowther*, above.

A similar problem is whether goods should be regarded as unfit if no adequate repair service is provided. This may happen for example because a new model is produced and spare parts for the old become unobtainable. Many so called consumer durables are thus made virtually worthless. Certain Canadian Acts on sales of agricultural machinery oblige dealers and/or manufacturers to carry spare parts for up to 10 years after sale, but there is no comparable English requirement on the point and none is proposed. There are however one or two codes of practice to the same effect such as that relating to domestic electrical appliance servicing. The DEAS Code says that manufacturers should stock spare parts for between five and 15 years, depending on the item.

SALE BY SAMPLE

Section 15 of the Sale of Goods Act should be briefly noted. It provides that in contracts of sale by sample there are implied conditions that the bulk of the goods shall correspond with the sample in quality, that the buyer shall have a reasonable opportunity of comparing the bulk with the sample, and that the goods shall be free of any defect making them unmerchantable which would not be seen on reasonable examination of the sample. The only significant point is that for a sale to be by sample an express or implied term of the contract to that effect is necessary (s.15(1)), and accordingly the fact that a product is used for purposes of demonstration or illustration by the seller does not of itself bring the sale within s.15. The section will help the consumer only in cases where off-cuts of cloth, carpet, etc are produced to 'speak for themselves': *Drummond v Van Ingen*, 1887.

ACCEPTANCE

A plaintiff loses his right to reject goods for breach of express condition or one implied by ss.12, 13, 14 or 15 if he 'accepts' the goods. His only claim then is for damages. This rule is laid down by s.11 of the Sale of Goods Act, and acceptance is defined by s.35. It takes place if (i) the buyer tells the seller he will keep the goods, or (ii) after taking delivery and having a reasonable opportunity for inspecting the goods, the buyer acts in a way inconsistent with the seller's continued ownership of them, eg by reselling, or (iii) he retains them for more than a reasonable length of time without notifying the seller of his rejection. To put that another way, the longer the buyer holds on to goods the more difficult it must be for him to say they are not what he wanted. The trouble is that defects in consumer durables in particular may not appear for some considerable time after they have been bought and used. The question then arises whether the idea of 'acceptance' is meaningful unless it involves both knowledge of the defects and the intention to keep the goods despite them. Lord Denning said in *Guarantee Trust of Jersey v Gardner*, 1973, that that was indeed the position: 'A person cannot be said to affirm a contract unless he has full knowledge of the breach and deliberately elects to go on with it.' But it is not clear how far this represents the decided view of English law.

The courts do however seem less inclined than they once were to treat almost any use of the goods as an affirmation of the contract and hence as a bar to rescission. While retention and use by the buyer naturally tend to suggest acceptance, the parties' rights can only be determined by looking at the precise sequence of events and the reasonableness of the buyer's conduct after discovering the defects. He could not expect to return a motor car immediately because of only one or two trivial faults. It is their cumulative effect which is important, and this might not be known for many months.

In *Lightburn v Belmont*, above, rescission was ordered even though the buyer had driven his car 8000 miles in eight months. The judge explained the considerations which weighed with the court: 'Mr Lightburn was endeavouring to give (the car) a reasonable chance to perform and I do not agree that delay in finally repudiating his contract can be attributed to that period of time or the mileage that was covered. He was not acting as a capricious buyer who had repented the purchase and sought to get out of his contract at an early time on a frivolous basis.' Most recent English decisions are to the same effect. In *Spencer v Rye* three months' possession and intermittent use was no bar, nor were four months' and several thousand miles' driving in *Farnworth Finance*. In *Laurelgates v Lombard*, 1983, the buyer purported to reject a new Jaguar after eight months' continuous and serious complaints, but then gave the manufacturers the opportunity to try to make it fit to drive. They failed. The judge nonetheless allowed the buyer to reject: he had acted reasonably to avoid litigation and had shown commendable patience.

On the other hand in *Lee v York Coach*, 1977, the court held that after five or six months' limited use with knowledge of the faults it was too late for the plaintiff to return the car. Similar decisions have been given in certain hire purchase cases, eg where the hirer has continued to pay instalments despite knowledge of major faults: *Charterhouse Credit v Tolly*, 1963; *Jackson v Chrysler Acceptances*, 1978; but *Robotics v First Co-operative Finance*, 1983, is to the contrary. These cases make it very difficult to predict the outcome of any particular set of facts. The former decisions seem very much preferable, however, in the sense that they gave adequate relief where it was necessary while still obliging consumers generally to try to 'make a go' of the contract; a requirement which is essential in view of the value and complexity of the goods and the market's overall need for stability.

STRICT LIABILITY

In the rules examined above we find one of the most important principles of English sales law. It will be recalled that under s.14 of the Sale of Goods Act goods sold in the course of business *must be reasonably fit*. How or why they fall short of this standard is immaterial. The seller may be no more than a conduit for goods made and packed by others over whom he has no control, but he must still guarantee to the buyer their reasonable suitability and safety. He remains liable, in other words, whether the defect is known or unknown, and whether or not he tries or is able to remedy it. So in *Spencer v Rye*, above, the car dealer had to take back the car and return the purchase price because he was unable to prevent the car radiator from boiling over every 100 miles, however hard he tried, and in *Frost v Aylesbury Dairy*, 1905, the defendants were liable for selling milk with typhus germs though at the time quite unable to detect the presence of the germs.

The primary liability for the fitness of goods is thus upon the seller and not the manufacturer, a basic rule of English law remarkably little known even in commercial circles. The rule is very much in the buyer's interest since the seller is probably close to hand and the more responsive to threats of legal proceedings and attendant bad publicity. And conversely it seems right that a person who makes his livelihood out of selling should take some responsibility for what he sells. The seller might of course argue that it is unfair to blame him for defects which are the manufacturer's fault, but the immediate answer is that he can sue the distributor or manufacturer under the same section of the same Act for an indemnity. His claim may then depend on the validity of any exclusion clause there may be in the contract between them, as explained in the next chapter.

This form of liability without fault is called strict liability. But strict liability is by no means the same as absolute liability, under which a seller would be responsible for any and every injury caused by his goods. The effect of strict liability is to require redress only for injuries which are the reasonably likely consequences of the defects proved, but which the buyer could not be expected to predict or guard against for himself. So where detergents or dyes or clothes safe for everyone else cause dermatitis in one or two individuals because of wholly abnormal and undisclosed susceptibilities, the seller is not to blame: *Board v Hedley*, 1951; *Griffiths v Conway*, 1939. There is of course no precise answer as to the number of people who have to be injured before goods will be regarded as unsafe, nor as to the requisite seriousness of injury. The more serious the harm, the fewer the number who need suffer it before a product is condemned. So in *Kendall v Lillico*, 1969, the judge said: 'I should certainly not expect food to be held reasonably fit if even on very rare occasions it killed the consumer.' But conversely a seller is not bound to be liable even when his buyer suffers a most serious injury. In *Heil v Hedges*, 1951, for example, the plaintiff suffered trichinosis after buying raw pork chops infected with worms. She sued the butcher for selling her these injurious goods, and lost. The court said that as raw meat the chops were in a normal condition and it was for her to cook the meat properly to eliminate this normal risk. There are many such cases in which the buyer might be injured through failing to carry out his own responsibilities under the sale, eg where he buys a car but does not bring it back to be serviced, or where he sees or ought to see the goods are not fit for use and so should stop using them: *Lambert v Lewis*, 1980. The seller is then most unlikely to be liable for any resulting injury.

HIRE PURCHASE

The same conditions laid down by sales law as to title, description and quality of goods are applied also to hire purchase transactions by ss.8/10 of the Supply of Goods (Implied Terms) Act 1973, with the same consequences in terms of strict liability. Depending on the form of credit, however, the responsibilities may fall on different parties. If the dealer himself provides credit facilities then he remains liable as if he were the seller. But if as more commonly happens credit is provided by a finance company, it is the company as owner of the goods which is responsible for passing good title to them and ensuring their quality and fitness. The dealer's function then is essentially that of intermediary. He displays the goods and acts as credit broker, ie enables the consumer to make a hire purchase contract with the finance company, and having done that his responsibility is usually at an end: *Drury v Buckland*, 1941.

As we saw in chapter 2, there may be exceptions to this general rule. It may be recalled that in the case of *Andrews v Hopkinson* a dealer expressly promised a customer that the car in question was 'a good little bus' and that he would have no trouble with it. In response the customer took the car on hire purchase from a finance company. The court held that he thereby gave consideration for the dealer's promise and so could enforce the promise against him. It is not yet clear whether the dealer might alternatively be liable for breach of an *implied* promise. The judge in *Andrews* suggested that he should be, because the transaction was so like a sale that the common law should imply obligations akin to those in the Sale of Goods Act. This argument was adopted in *Robotics v First Co-operative Finance*, 1983, but seems not yet generally accepted.

In the absence of any express undertaking by the dealer therefore the position may still be as decided in *Drury*, above. For the consumer this is less agreeable than the sale situation. He may well think he has contracted with the dealer who supplied the goods, who is as we said responsive to threats of legal action and bad local publicity, only to find that he must make his complaints to a finance company probably at the other end of the country and correspondingly less interested in his problem. One might then have expected the Consumer Credit Act 1974 to impose additional liability on dealers but instead it went in the opposite direction and strengthened consumers' rights against finance houses.

Manufacturers involved in giving credit to finance the purchase or hire purchase of their goods should take very careful note of ss.56 and 75 of the Consumer Credit Act. Both apply only to regulated agreements, ie where credit up to £15,000 is given. Section 56 makes the creditor liable to the consumer for anything said or done by the dealer in the course of negotiations leading up to the making of a hire purchase, conditional sale or credit sale agreement. 'Negotiations' include advertisements and 'any other dealings'. Even though a dealer is usually an independent party he is regarded for the purposes of this section as the creditor's agent. So in *Andrews*, above, the consumer could now sue either dealer or finance house or both, and leave them to sort out their liability between themselves.

Section 75 affects what are usually called 'connected lending' transactions, where a creditor lends money to a debtor to enable him to *buy* goods from a third party supplier under pre-existing arrangements between creditor and supplier. Purchases with credit cards are within this section, unless as with American Express and Diners' Club cards prompt repayment in full is required. The object of the section is to give the debtor the same protection as if he had obtained the goods on hire purchase, and the rationale is that the creditor here has much the same kind of continuing interest. It provides accordingly that whatever rights the debtor might have as buyer against seller he can exercise equally against the creditor. The creditor thus becomes responsible for any misrepresentation by the seller or his breach of an express promise or implied condition as to title or description or fitness under the Sale of Goods Act. In the Scottish case of *UDT v Taylor*, 1980, a debtor/buyer returned a defective car to the seller and under s.75 was also held able to rescind the finance agreement with the creditor. The section gives the buyer a useful alternative remedy where the seller denies liability or is insolvent or goes out of business. As with s.56 the present rule does not apply to leasing agreements. Unlike s.56 the scope of s.75 is limited according to the cash price of the goods. It applies only where the cash price is between £50 and £30,000.

SERVICE AND HIRE CONTRACTS

Until recently there has been no equivalent of the Sale of Goods Act or hire purchase legislation to define consumers' rights in relation to goods supplied not by way of sale or hire purchase but under contracts for services or on lease or hire. These various different types of contract were regulated only by the somewhat uncertain standards of the common law. The object of the Supply of Goods and Services Act 1982 was accordingly to bring the law in this area more clearly into line with existing legislation. The Act is printed in full in appendix 2. It does not apply in Scotland.

Sections 1 to 5 of the 1982 Act concern goods supplied under contracts for services, eg installation or repair contracts, and ss.6 to 10 those supplied on hire or loan. The obligations imposed on the supplier are essentially the same as those under ss.12 to 15 of the Sale of Goods Act and ss.8 to 10 of the Supply of Goods (Implied Terms) Act. Standards of quality and fitness for purpose are therefore strict, as illustrated in *Myers v Brent Cross Service*, 1934, where a garage was liable for an accident caused by fitting a component with a hidden defect in the course of a car repair. But as we have said before strict liability is no guarantee of perfection. A burglar alarm, for example, might still be reasonably fit for its purpose even though it can be wrenched off the wall and silenced: *Davis v Afa Minerva*, 1974. In any case liability is strict only in relation to the other contracting party and not, as in a car case for example, to his or her passengers or other road users. Their only claim could be for negligence, which in a case like *Myers*, they would be unable to prove against the garage: *Sigurdson v Hillcrest Service*, 1977 (Can).

Liability can be avoided or reduced if the consumer does not or in the circumstances should not rely on the supplier's skill or judgment. This might happen where for example the consumer specifies exactly the type of material or product to be used, in which case the supplier does not warrant fitness for purpose but only the quality of the goods: *Young v McManus Childs*, 1968.

The new Act also covers contracts for services which do not necessarily involve transfer of ownership or possession of goods. The most important provision is s.13, which says that in contracts for the supply of services in the course of business there is an implied term that the services will be carried out with reasonable care and skill. The duty thus imposed in relation to services is different from that affecting goods. A supplier of goods must ensure they are reasonably fit, whereas a supplier of services undertakes only to act in accordance with the normal standards of his trade or profession, for better or worse. He may nonetheless find the duty quite far reaching, as in *Taylor v Kiddey*, 1968, where a garage was held liable for failing to check a wheel under the terms of a service contract specifying attention only to steering.

Another rule worth noting is in s.14, requiring that if no time is fixed for the performance of a contract it must be performed within a reasonable time, depending of course on the type and scale of the work to be done. Examples of the common law coming to the same conclusion include *Charnock v Liverpool Corporation*, 1968, where a garage was held liable for taking eight weeks over repairs which should have taken five, and thus had to pay for three weeks' car hire; and *Stanners v High Wycombe Borough Council*, 1968, where the local authority was held responsible for a delay in completing building work which enabled thieves to break into a warehouse next door.

REFORM

While working our way through the conditions implied by law in contracts of sale, hire purchase and lease we have noted various difficulties in their interpretation and application. These issues were recently examined by the Law Commission whose report on Sale and Supply of Goods was published in 1983. We list here the Commission's proposals to indicate likely developments in this area of law.

So far as the Sale of Goods Act was concerned, the Commission recommended that the condition of merchantable quality should be replaced by a new provision which did not use the word 'merchantable' but was couched in general terms of 'consumer acceptability' or 'suitability' or the like and also specifically referred to the goods' fitness for normal purposes, state or condition, appearance, finish, and freedom from minor defects, suitability for immediate use, durability, safety, any description applied, and their price if relevant. This new provision together with the existing ones on description, fitness and sample should be classed simply as 'terms' and not conditions, thus permitting greater flexibility in the remedy. It was proposed that the consequences of breach of these terms should be stated in the Act. In consumer sales the buyer should be entitled to reject the goods and recover his money unless the seller could prove the breach was trivial and that it was reasonable for the buyer to accept repair or replacement of goods (which would be the first recognition of this remedy in English law). Where repair or replacement was delayed or unsatisfactory, the buyer should be entitled to reject, as before. In all cases damages should be awarded for injury or loss. In non-consumer sales the buyer should be entitled to reject except for trivial faults, and to claim damages.

The rules as to acceptance and loss of the right to reject should remain substantially unchanged, but the Commission thought it should be made clear that attempts to cure defects did not constitute acceptance and that goods could not be rejected unless in much the same condition as when delivered, unless the change in condition was caused by the breach of contract. In consumer sales the buyer should not lose his right to reject unless he had reasonable opportunity to examine the goods, and what was a reasonable time for rejection should depend largely on when and how the defects appeared. The right should not be lost through resale or other such 'inconsistent act' (s.35 Sale of Goods Act, above), except possibly in non-consumer sales.

The Commission proposed the same changes in relation to other contracts for the supply of goods, by hire purchase, etc, with these provisos. As an alternative to a claim for damages the consumer might recover whatever he had paid under the contract, subject to a deduction for use, depending on which yielded the larger sum. In consumer hire contracts the hirer should not be obliged to continue payments while the goods were being repaired or replaced, but the Commission was uncertain whether this rule should apply also in hire purchase contracts. The same remedies should be available to the innocent party in a 'trading in' contract.

OWNERSHIP AND RISK

We end this chapter with a few words on a rather different aspect of sales law, one not directly related to the quality or fitness of goods but possibly causing some confusion in that connection and certainly important in itself. The issue is that of ownership, and the first short point is that the buyer's right to reject goods for breach of condition does not depend on his or the seller's rights of ownership over them. There are nonetheless many other very good reasons for wanting to know the precise moment in time when ownership passes from seller to buyer. Whoever owns goods usually carries also the risk of their accidental loss or theft or damage, but has also the right to keep the goods in the event of insolvency. It is not simply a question of possession, because of course one may own goods without physically possessing them, and vice versa.

Rules to determine when ownership passes are laid down in ss.16 to 20 of the Sale of Goods Act. Section 16 says that ownership, which the Act calls 'the property in the goods', cannot in any case pass until the goods are ascertained, ie until a particular article is identified as the subject matter of the sale. Once we know which goods we are concerned with – 'this car' rather than 'a car of this type' – then under s.17 the parties are free to decide for themselves when ownership passes. Commercial contracts often provide that ownership passes on delivery, generally a sensible and straightforward provision. If there is no express term of that kind the parties' intentions may be inferred from other aspects of the agreement. Thus a clause enabling the seller to retain documents of title may suggest that he is still owner, whereas an obligation on the buyer to insure the goods from a certain point in time indicates that he becomes owner then. But if there is no clue one way or the other as to the parties' wishes, the Act itself decides the outcome according to the provisions of s.18.

Section 18 rule 1 provides that in contracts for the sale of specific goods – goods identified and agreed upon at the time of sale – which are ready to be delivered as per contract, ownership passes *when the contract is made*. Terms delaying payment or delivery do not of themselves affect the rule. This may seem a somewhat surprising provision, though not unknown in other legal systems, and it is certainly one the parties should take account of. Its effect is simply illustrated by the old case of *Tarling v Baxter*, 1827. The buyer bought the seller's haystack, but left the stack on the seller's land until he could come back and collect it. In the meantime it was burned down in an accidental fire. The court held that the buyer still had to pay for it, though he received nothing in return. In theory the same would be true today where for example a buyer left a piece of furniture he had bought in the store pending delivery, and it was destroyed overnight by accident and without negligence on the store's part. On the other hand the store would probably be insured against such losses and so might not find it necessary to sue the buyer. And if there were any continuing uncertainty about the terms of the contract judges nowadays would probably prefer to say that the requirements of rule 1 were not fulfilled and so avoid the possible unfairness of holding the buyer liable. 'In modern times very little is needed to give rise to the inference that the property in specific goods is to pass only on delivery or payment': *Ward v Bignell*. 1967.

We have said also that rule 1 only applies to goods ready to be delivered in accordance with the contract, or 'in a deliverable state', as the rule puts it. This might seem to suggest that ownership of defective goods can never pass to the buyer, but that is evidently not so. If the buyer accepts delivery, for example, there is no reason why the goods should not be held at his risk until such time as he discovers their faults and rejects them, whereupon ownership reverts to the seller. In effect then 'deliverable' means only that nothing remains to be done to the goods under the contract. An example is *Head v Showfronts Ltd*, 1970, which concerned a contract for the sale and laying of a carpet. The carpet was delivered to the buyer's premises but stolen from there before it could be laid. Whoever owned the carpet at the time of theft had to stand the loss. It was held that the carpet still belonged to the seller because it was not yet 'deliverable', ie had not been laid.

The next two rules in s.18 make much the same point. Both refer to contracts for the sale of specific goods. Rule 2 provides that where the seller is bound under the contract to do something to the goods to put them into a deliverable state, ownership does not pass until he has done that thing and he has notified the buyer. Rule 3 says that if the seller has to weigh, measure or test the goods to establish their price, they do not belong to the buyer until that act has been done and he has been told so.

Rule 4 of s.18 affects goods delivered on approval or on a sale or return basis. They become the buyer's when he 'signifies his approval' to the seller or in some other way 'adopts the transaction', eg resells them or does something else which prevents him returning them. The contract may expressly preserve the seller's title, to protect his rights against third parties, but he may nonetheless lose the goods if he appears to authorise the buyer to dispose of them.

Rule 5 of s.18 is very important. It concerns goods which are *not* identified and agreed upon at the time of sale, and tries to determine that point in time *after* the contract is made at which they become the buyer's. It says that in the absence of agreement to the contrary ownership of unascertained or future goods (meaning goods not yet made or not yet in the seller's hands) can only pass to the buyer when goods as described in the contract and in a deliverable state are unconditionally appropriated to the contract by either seller or buyer with the other's express or implied agreement.

The crucial question then is as to the meaning of 'unconditional appropriation'. Suppose for example that a seller has several identical goods in store, all answering the same contractual description, eg a particular type of washing machine. What does he have to do in order to appropriate one of the machines unconditionally to the order of a particular buyer, and thereby make that buyer owner? Would it be sufficient to label the machine with the buyer's name and address? Would the buyer necessarily have agreed, expressly or even by implication, to the labelling of that machine, if, for example, it was not in quite such good condition as the others?

As usual it is easier to pose questions than to answer them but the case of *Federspiel v Twigg*, 1957, provides at least a partial answer. An overseas buyer ordered some bicycles from an English manufacturer. The manufacturer crated them, addressed them to the buyer, registered them for consignment and ordered shipping space in a named ship. Before they could be sent to the port from which they would be shipped abroad the manufacturer went into liquidation and his receiver refused to deliver them. The problem for the buyer was whether he could claim the cycles as his own at that time. If not, he would have only a worthless claim for damages for breach of contract against the insolvent manufacturer. The court held that the cycles still belonged to the manufacturer. They had been 'appropriated' to the contract, but not 'unconditionally', in the sense that even at that late stage the manufacturer could have changed his mind, readdressed them and sent them elsewhere.

Appropriation must therefore be 'irretrievable' to be effective. When goods are sent by sea that last decisive act usually occurs when they are loaded across the ship's rail, but only if separately addressed and distinct from any other similar goods on board. Delivering goods to an independent carrier or sending them by post is regarded as unconditional appropriation, though that still begs the question whether the buyer agrees to that particular selection of goods.

Section 19 says that whether a contract is for the sale of specific goods or for goods subsequently unconditionally appropriated to the contract under s.18 the seller may still reserve rights of disposal of the goods until certain conditions are fulfilled, and if he does so he remains owner until they are fulfilled. In practice conditions of sale agreed betwen businessmen often provide that despite delivery to the buyer the seller shall remain owner of the goods until the buyer has paid for them, or paid off any other debts he may have to the seller.

These retention of title clauses are known as *Romalpa clauses* from the case of *Aluminium Industrie v Romalpa Aluminium*, 1976, where, surprisingly enough, the complexities and consequences of these provisions in British law were first examined. Romalpa clauses are not intended to prevent buyers of goods subject to such clauses from dealing with them; indeed the purpose of the sale is usually to enable the buyer to carry on business by reselling the goods, as they stand or processed in some way, and so to pay the seller out of his profits. Thus although the buyer does not become owner of the goods until he has paid for them he resells them as principal and not as the seller's agent. As principal he can pass ownership immediately, or even subject to his own Romalpa clause, to his subsequent purchaser. Most Romalpa clauses therefore seek to protect the seller's claim to 'mixed' goods and provide that upon resale he shall become entitled to the proceeds of sale, and that these sums must be kept where they can be traced in a separate account.

Difficulties may arise over the appropriate wording and 'reach' of these clauses. They are very unsatisfactory from the point of view of the buyer's creditors, particularly because they do not have to be publicly registered unless they create a floating charge over a company's assets. It is not altogether clear either how proceeds of sale can be measured when the buyer mixes the goods with others to make a new product, or how in such cases the claims of competing sellers, all using retention of title clauses, might be resolved. No particular form of wording can be guaranteed to 'do the trick' and protect the seller against all conceivable contingencies, but readers interested in this specialist subject might usefully refer to John Parris's recent book on Retention of Title where the possibilities are explored in detail.

Lastly s.20 explains the main effect of the three preceding sections. It says that unless otherwise agreed goods are at the seller's risk until ownership passes. When that happens they are held at the buyer's risk whether or not he has taken delivery.

'Risk' refers only to loss or damage caused by accident for which no one is to blame. If delivery is delayed through the fault of one party the goods are at that party's risk in respect of any accident which might not otherwise have occurred. So where a buyer of apple juice was late in taking delivery and in the meantime the juice went bad it was held that he had to stand the loss: *Demby Hamilton v Barden*, 1949. In any case whichever side has custody of the goods must take reasonable care of them.

SUMMARY

Terms may be added into contracts at common law and by Act of Parliament. Generally the judges will only add terms into particular contracts to express a trade usage taken for granted by the parties, or if it is necessary to do so because otherwise the contract would be wholly one-sided or lack business efficacy. Terms added by Parliament on the other hand are intended to lay down minimum standards of performance or fitness for all contracts of a particular type. Such statutory terms are most important in contracts of sale and hire purchase of goods if the parties themselves fail to specify their requirements in detail. So far as product liability is concerned the key provision is in s.14 of the Sale of Goods Act and its equivalent in legislation for hp and service contracts. In effect the section requires business sellers to guarantee the reasonable quality and fitness of their goods. If this implied condition is broken the buyer can reject the goods and recover his money. The seller's liability in this respect is strict, which means that he is liable for breach of the condition even though he may be in no way personally to blame for it. But the seller can then sue his own supplier to recoup his losses, and so on back up the line until the manufacturer carries the responsibility.

The right to reject faulty goods or as the case may be to claim damages is unaffected by the question of ownership, but the passing of ownership in turn decides who bears the risk of accidental loss or damage or of insolvency on one side or the other. These issues also are regulated by the Sale of Goods Act failing agreement to the contrary between the contracting parties.

4 Exclusion Clauses

We have looked at length at sellers' contractual liabilities, and in following chapters we consider manufacturers' liabilities in the absence of contract. Before we go on, however, we should take account of the opportunities open to both sellers and manufacturers to avoid these burdens. It is still common practice on the part of trade sellers in particular to insert clauses in their contracts avoiding or limiting responsibility for breach, whether by late delivery or poor quality or other causes. Sometimes such terms seem to defeat altogether the basic purpose of the contract. Are they then enforceable? Manufacturers likewise may seek to avoid liability to the ultimate users of their goods by means of warning notices, instructions and the like.

COMMON LAW RULES

Our subject therefore is the exclusion (or exception or exemption) clause and its non-contractual equivalent the warning notice. It is important to understand first of all that there are two completely different sets of rules about exclusion clauses and notices; those of the common law, developed by judges over the last century or so, and those in Acts of Parliament, notably the Unfair Contract Terms Act of 1977. When we have examined them each we shall say a little more about how they interrelate. In the meantime we might distinguish between them by saying that the rules of common law in this connection are essentially rules of 'construction' or 'interpretation' whereas those in Acts of Parliament are matters of substantive law. That means that the common law does not control or prohibit exclusion clauses as such. Its attitude towards them is essentially neutral. It is concerned only to resolve the doubts and ambiguities they create; to decide exactly what meaning to attach to any particular clause and determine its effect on the relationship between the parties. To do this it invokes the various tests or standards of validity we now consider.

NOTICE

The first test is whether the buyer or consumer had reasonable notice of the existence of the clause. A clause is ineffective unless the supplier can show he took reasonable steps to bring it to the consumer's attention. This does not oblige him to ensure that the consumer reads or understands the clause, but only that he has a fair opportunity and good reason to do so. In practice this requirement seems to work very arbitrarily. In *Richardson v Rowntree*, 1894, for example, the plaintiff was given a steamship ticket folded in such a way that it could not be read without being opened. He knew there was writing on the ticket, but not what it was about. The court decided that he was not bound by a clause there purporting to limit the company's liability for loss of luggage. On the other hand a train ticket saying on one side 'For conditions see over' and on the other referring to rules and regulations published in the company's timetable, for which a charge was made, was held to give sufficient notice of the existence of an exclusion clause in *Thompson v LMS Railway*, 1930.

It is fair to say that more recent cases suggest that the obligation to give reasonable notice is somewhat more onerous. So in *Mendelssohn v Normand*, 1969, Lord Denning said that notices at reception desks and the like could not be effective 'unless brought home so prominently that (the plaintiff) must be taken to know of and agree with (them)'. What has to be done in this direction may depend upon the scope of the exclusion clause. It may perhaps be necessary to establish not only that the clause is 'visible', but that it clearly appears as an exclusion of liability. 'Some clauses which I have seen would need to be printed in red ink on the face of the document with a red hand pointing to it before the notice could be held to be sufficient,' said Lord Denning in *Spurling v Bradshaw*, 1956.

The second rule, really only an aspect of the first one, is that the document or notice containing the exclusion clause must appear as part of the contract. If it seems for example no more than a formal receipt which might properly be thrown away, the court may say it has not been brought sufficiently to the consumer's attention. So in *Chapelton v Barry UDC*, 1940, a deckchair ticket was held to have no contractual effect and in *Burnett v Westminster Bank*, 1965, the same was said of conditions printed in a cheque book. In *Parker v SE Railway*, 1877, on the other hand, the provisions printed on a 'left luggage' ticket were held binding because the depositor knew he had to keep the ticket and should have appreciated that it stated the terms on which he could recover his luggage.

Thirdly, another way of looking at the same problem, the courts say that the clause must not be added after the contract has been made. So, for example, if a hotel wishes to exclude liability for theft of guests' belongings it must do so at the reception desk and not by a notice exhibited only in the hotel bedroom: *Olley v Marlborough Court*, 1949. But difficulties may still arise in deciding exactly when the contract was made, or what its terms are. A ticket or receipt for money might quite possibly refer the consumer to some other document which he is to be sent at some later date, and which is said to contain the terms of the contract. In the past this practice has been accepted; but now it appears that only a commercial party accustomed to dealing on such terms would be deemed to have adequate notice of them. Alternatively it might be said that additional terms can be incorporated into a contract by the course of dealings between the parties. If in *Olley*, for example, the guest had been to the hotel before and knew of the notice in the bedroom the notice could eventually be regarded as part of the terms of his occupancy. Many cases discuss what constitutes a sufficient course of dealing for these purposes, but each turns on its own facts and provides no guide for the solution of any subsequent problem.

MISREPRESENTATION

The fourth rule is that an exclusion clause provides no protection against fraud or misrepresentation. In particular it will be invalid if it tells a lie, eg by saying falsely that the consumer examined the goods beforehand: *Lowe v Lombank*, 1960; or if its effect is misrepresented or varied by the supplier, orally or otherwise, before or after the clause is put to the consumer. In *Curtis v Chemical Cleaning Co*, 1951, a laundry assistant told a customer that the ticket she was asked to sign referred only to certain kinds of damage, when in fact it excluded all liability. Ticket and signature were thus invalidated. Rephrasing this proposition we may say that where a standard form contradicts an oral agreement the latter is likely to prevail: *Evans v Merzario*, 1976.

AMBIGUITY

Next is the *'contra proferentem'* rule. If a clause is ambiguous or obscure it will be interpreted in the way least favourable to the party relying upon it, the supplier. Thus where a contract denied the buyer the right to repudiate goods it was held he was still free to claim damages: *Ashington Piggeries v Hill*, 1971. In particular if the clause does not make clear exactly what type of liability is to be excluded, the courts will assume that the clause refers only to breach of contract. Accordingly if the supplier is also under a tortious duty of care to the consumer (chapter 5), he may still be liable for negligence. But if the clause specifically excludes liability for negligence or excludes liability for loss or damage 'howsoever caused' or by other such all-embracing language then liability for negligence can effectively be excluded: *White v Blackmore*, 1972.

SIGNATURE

If an exclusion clause is clear and unambiguous a consumer who signs a contract containing it will be bound by it at common law, subject perhaps to the 'red hand' argument advanced above and questions of misrepresentation: *L'Estrange v Graucob*, 1934.

THIRD PARTY RIGHTS

The seventh rule is that normally an exclusion clause can only benefit the person putting it forward, and affords no protection to anyone else. Where because of the terms on her ticket an injured passenger was unable to sue the shipping company, she was nonetheless able to sue individual members of the crew for their negligence: *Adler v Dickson*, 1955. As a matter of principle, however, there is no reason why an employer should not contract on behalf of his employees or agents so as to enable them to escape liability, nor even why a person should not act as intermediary to benefit some completely independent party in the same way, so long as the latter promises or undertakes some act or forebearance which constitutes consideration for the consumer's promise to limit liability and so makes it binding upon him. This was illustrated in *NZ Shipping v Satterthwaite*, 1974, where goods were shipped under a contract limiting the carrier's liability and that of his agents or contractor. The stevedores who unloaded the ship, and damaged the goods, were held to have brought themselves within the protection of the clause by undertaking the unloading.

FUNDAMENTAL BREACH

Until quite recently there was said to be another common law rule on exclusion clauses; one which had perhaps more immediate effect than all the others put together. This was the 'doctrine of fundamental breach'; the proposition that no clause however comprehensively worded could enable a supplier to disregard entirely the terms of his contract and supply goods or services totally different from those promised. The doctrine was undoubtedly beneficial to the consumer, but had many drawbacks including unpredictability of operation. The courts often had to distinguish between goods which did not work at all, to which the doctrine applied and so nullified the exclusion clause, and those which were merely faulty, to which the doctrine did not apply and so left the clause unaffected. This was a fine and eventually unsustainable distinction. The doctrine of fundamental breach was also criticised on the ground that while it might help consumers it was unnecessary as between businessmen negotiating on more or less equal terms. It was moreover used as a rule of substantive law, in effect a prohibition of certain types of clauses, which was out of line with the overall approach of the common law, that of reliance upon rules of construction.

Within the past few years the doctrine of fundamental breach has been examined several times by the House of Lords; notably in *Suisse Atlantique v NV Rotterdamsche Kolen Centrale*, 1967, *Photo Productions v Securicor*, 1980, and *Mitchell v Finney Lock*, 1983. All three cases involved commercial contracts. The first was a contract for the charter of a ship. It provided for payments in the event of delay in loading and unloading, but the delays which in fact occurred were said to be far beyond those contemplated by the contract, and so the charterers argued that the doctrine of fundamental breach nullified the demurrage clause and allowed them to claim loss of profit. In *Photo Productions* the defendants contracted to provide security services for the plaintiffs' factory, but their watchman deliberately started a fire there and the factory was destroyed. A clause in the contract excluded the defendants' liability for damage done by employees except in so far as such damage could be attributed to the defendants' own negligence. Another clause limited their liability in any event to £25,000. Very understandably the plaintiffs argued that since the whole object of the contract had been defeated they should not be bound by the clause limiting the defendants' liability. In *Mitchell* seed merchants sold a certain type of cabbage seed to a farmer. The crop proved worthless because the seeds were neither as described nor of reasonable quality. The conditions of sale excluded all express or implied conditions or warranties as to fitness and limited liability for defective seeds to their original cost. The farmer said that the total failure of the crop enabled him to override the exclusion clause and claim all the costs he incurred in cultivating the crop, plus the profits he should have made.

In each case the House of Lords rejected the fundamental breach argument, and except in *Mitchell*, for other reasons, below, upheld the exclusion or limitation clauses as they stood. Their Lordships conclusively decided that the doctrine of fundamental breach was not a rule of law but at most a rule of construction, and perhaps not even that, but just an expression describing a breach of contract which deprives the innocent party of substantially all he has bargained for.

This response confirms what we describe above as the common law's neutral attitude towards exclusion clauses. Its effect as a rule of construction is that when confronted with a contractual provision whose meaning or scope is uncertain the judges will if possible interpret it in such a way as to give effect to what appears as the basic purpose of the contract. They will presume on the parties' behalf that they did not intend both to make and at the same time to nullify a contract by enabling one side to disregard his obligations to the other without giving some form of redress. A less strict approach will therefore be taken if the clause restricts rather than excludes liability. But the presumption only applies in cases of doubt or ambiguity. Since as we now know there is no rule of law against fundamental breach it follows that a sufficiently clear and comprehensive exclusion clause could indeed defeat the whole apparent purpose of a contract and yet be upheld by the courts. The only proviso is that the effect of the clause must not be to nullify the contract completely. If there is no contractual commitment at all then the clause becomes meaningless and unenforceable.

That at all events is the common law position. It may seem a somewhat unhelpful one, but was justified by their Lordships on several grounds: first the inherent uncertainty of the fundamental breach rule; second that it was not the law's job to rewrite commercial contracts and redistribute risks; and third that since 1973 consumers have been much more effectively protected by statute. The most comprehensive protection is now given by the

Unfair Contract Terms Act 1977, to which the rest of this chapter is devoted.

THE UNFAIR CONTRACT TERMS ACT

The text of the Act is set out in full in appendix 3. Part I, ss.1 to 14, applies to England; Part II, ss.15 to 25, applies the same provisions appropriately to the law of Scotland and Part III, ss.26 to 32, affects the United Kingdom as a whole. Schedules 1 and 2 contain definitions and exceptions. By way of introduction to this far-reaching measure we might note that its title is a little misleading, in some respects too broad and in others too narrow. It does not affect every different kind of unfair clause but only exclusion clauses, while on the other hand it controls also the use of warning notices and the like which seek to avoid liability in non-contractual contexts. Although mainly concerned with contractual liability therefore its provisions should be borne in mind when we discuss questions of negligence in chapters 5 and 6. The method of the Act is to identify certain kinds of exclusion clauses as particularly objectionable and declare them void, while others are permitted if and insofar as the supplier can prove them reasonable in the circumstances. We shall list the various provisions in turn and then consider the guidelines and cases which tell us something of the meaning of reasonableness for present purposes.

The Act's first objective is to prevent or restrict avoidance of liability for negligence; ss.1 and 2. Section 1 defines negligence as breach of any contractual or legal duty to take reasonable care. It says also that the Act applies only to exclusions of *business* liability, with one minor exception noted below. The Act applies whether the breach of duty is deliberate or accidental and whether the fault is personal or vicarious (chapter 6). 'Business', a troublesome concept as we noted in chapter 3, is defined in s.14 to include a profession and the activities of any government department or local or public authority.

Section 2(1) declares null and void contract terms or non-contractual notices excluding or limiting liability for death or personal injury caused by negligence. But liability for other forms of loss or damage – economic loss or damage to property – can be excluded if the contractual term or notice is reasonable in the circumstances: s.2(2). This key concept of reasonableness is enlarged upon in s.11 and Schedule 2 and discussed below. Section 2(3) says that a person's awareness of or apparent agreement to a term or notice excluding liability for negligence does not of itself prove acceptance of risk. To this extent therefore the Act overrides *L'Estrange v Graucob* (see p. 75).

In commenting on these provisions, except with regard to the question of reasonableness which we pursue later, we should observe that not all injury, loss or damage is necessarily caused by negligence. Injuries may be caused by natural hazards and inherent risks. Notices warning of such dangers are clearly not invalidated by the Act; indeed it might well be evidence of negligence if no warning were given. Likewise there can be no objection to notices excluding liability for loss or damage in circumstances where the danger is unavoidable or there is no duty of care in the first place. 'Owners' risk' notices in car parks, for example, are usually unobjectionable because the car owner pays only for space, not care: *Ashby v Tolhurst*, 1937. Negligence in these circumstances is only likely to become an issue when one person actually takes another's goods into his possession, eg when the key must be left with the attendant: *Mendelssohn v Normand*, 1969.

The case of *White v Blackmore*, 1972, is an interesting example of problems left unresolved by the Act. A charity sponsored a car race. The organisers displayed a notice at the entrance to the track saying that as occupiers they accepted no liability for injury howsoever caused. Through their negligence a competitor was killed. The notice was held sufficient to relieve the charity of all liability. It seems likely that the same answer would be given today since on the face of it a charity is not a business.

We should observe also that although the Act invalidates terms or notices excluding liability for negligence it does not actually forbid them. An unscrupulous dealer might therefore go on using clauses of this kind, indeed many do, and hope thereby to dissuade injured parties from legal action. The Office of Fair Trading is aware of this practice and has recommended that it be made illegal to use these clauses, as is already the law in relation to consumer transactions under s.6, below.

Section 3 applies as between contracting parties where one of them deals as consumer (s.12, below) or on the other's written standard terms of business. The section limits the rights of the party who is not a consumer or who as the case may be relies on his own written standard terms. It says that this (stronger) party cannot by reference to any contract term (a) exclude or restrict his own liability for breach of contract, or (b) claim to be entitled to perform the contract in a substantially different way from that reasonably expected, or (c) claim to be entitled not to fulfil the contract or some part of it, except in so far as any such term is reasonable in the circumstances.

The importance of the alternative situation covered by s.3, where the buyer is not necessarily a consumer but must accept the other's written standard terms, is that it protects the small businessman against abuse of bargaining power by larger businesses upon which he is dependent. This in turn means that when a retailer is held strictly liable for selling defective goods contrary to s.14 of the Sale of Goods Act (see chapter 3), he has a reasonable prospect of recovering his loss from his own suppliers.

Many different types of exclusion clauses are covered by s.3. Under subheading (a) for example are laundry terms which purport to limit liability for loss of or damage to clothing to a certain sum of money. Under (b) are travel agency booking forms, so worded as to enable the agency to provide different accommodation or different forms of transport or other services without any redress by the customer. Subheading (c) covers among other examples contracts for delivery of goods by a certain date, accompanied by a term excluding liability for failure to deliver or late delivery. All these clauses must now be reasonable if they are to be upheld (s.11, below).

The next section, 4, strikes at unreasonable indemnity clauses, and invalidates them accordingly. One might find such a clause for example in contracts for hire of machinery, under which the hirer is required to indemnify the owner against liability for injury or damage caused by the machinery or by the owner's employee in charge of it: *Phillips v Hamstead*, 1982.

Section 5 goes some way to ensuring that manufacturers' guarantees are of positive value and do not take away more rights than they confer. The section does not apply as between buyer and seller, however. Details are given in chapter 2 on retailers' and manufacturers' guarantees.

The next two sections are probably the most important rules in the whole Act so far as the consumer is concerned. Essentially s.6 re-enacts rules introduced by the Supply of Goods (Implied Terms) Act 1973 to prevent or restrict avoidance of liability under the Sale of Goods Act and hire purchase legislation. We saw in chapter 3 that s.12 of the Sale of Goods Act requires sellers to pass a good title, while s.13 ensures conformity of goods with their description and s.14 provides that goods must be of merchantable quality and reasonable fitness for purpose. Similar obligations are imposed on finance houses supplying goods on hire purchase. With regard to these various implied duties s.6 of the Unfair Contract Terms Act first declares void any attempt to exclude or restrict the duty to give a good title. The possibility of excluding the remaining obligations as to description, quality and fitness then depends on whether the transaction in question is between businesses or with someone dealing as consumer (s.12, below). Any purported exclusion or limitation of ss.13 and 14 ('No refund', etc) in a consumer contract is *void*, and is also a punishable offence under the Consumer Transactions (Restrictions on Statements) Order 1978. Between businesses however terms excluding ss.13 or 14 of the Sale of Goods Act are *valid if reasonable* (ss.11 and Schedule 2, below).

The underlying principle is that while consumers need more protection than businessmen, there may still be abuses in the business context which need to be regulated, albeit less strictly. Although sales by private individuals are otherwise outside the Act s.6 also requires a private seller to pass a good title and provide goods conforming with their description. Sale of goods 'as seen' by either business or private seller might possibly prevent the description rule from arising, and 'with all faults' seems to preclude any contractual claim as to unfitness, but both may be illegal under the Consumer Transactions Order: *Hughes v Hall*, 1981 and *Cavendish Woodhouse v Manley*, 1984.

Section 7, amended by the Supply of Goods and Services Act 1982, makes the same provision as s.6 for title and fitness of goods passing under contracts which are not governed by the law of sale or hire purchase but are supplied on lease or under contracts for services, eg repair.

In s.8 a provision introduced by the Misrepresentation Act of 1967 is restated, making terms intended to avoid liability for pre-contractual statements – 'representations', as explained in chapter 1 – valid only if reasonable. Proof of reasonableness is upon the person relying on the term. As we said in chapter 1 many standard form conditions of sale exclude liability for non-compliance with advertising or other pre-sale statements. The application of s.8 will depend on the buyer's familiarity with standard forms, the clarity of the term in question and other aspects noted below with regard to Schedule 2. Wording which seeks to deny the existence of any representation in the first place, eg 'The accuracy of these statements cannot be guaranteed', will not be allowed to defeat the purpose of the Act: *Cremdean Properties v Nash*, 1977.

Section 9 declares that the reasonableness or otherwise of a contract term may still be decided, and effect given to it accordingly, whether or not the contract as a whole has been broken or repudiated. Conversely if the injured party decides not to exercise his right to repudiate he may still argue that the exclusion clause is unreasonable. Section 10 prevents a person evading liabilities by means of a secondary or collateral contract.

Guidance as to the meaning of reasonableness in the present context is given partly by s.11 and partly by Schedule 2. Section 11 says that where a person by contract term or notice tries to restrict liability to a specified sum of money account must be taken of his resources and how far he might be expected to cover himself by insurance. This section also clarifies the burden of proof. It is for the party claiming that a term or notice satisfies the test of reasonableness to show that it does.

CONSUMER TRANSACTIONS

We have seen that the effect of certain sections depends on one of the parties to a contract 'dealing as consumer'. This requirement is defined in s.12. A person deals as consumer if he does not act in the way of business while the other party does and if the goods in question are of a kind normally supplied for private use. The definition excludes sales by auction or competitive tender. The onus of proving that a transaction was not for consumer purposes is upon the supplier.

Sometimes goods may be used for both business and domestic purposes, and if so it may be very difficult to predict how the Act will apply, eg in *Symmons v Cook*, 1982. The question neatly posed here was whether a city firm of chartered surveyors who bought a Rolls Royce partly to impress clients and partly for private use did so as consumers. Was the car bought in the course of their business? That might in turn depend on whether we mean by that 'bought for business purposes', or, 'bought by a business whose integral or necessarily incidental purpose is the buying of such goods'. If the former definition is accepted then no expertise in the buying of these particular goods can necessarily be expected. As a layman *in this respect* it could be said that the buyer is entitled to protection as a consumer. That at all events was the somewhat controversial conclusion reached in *Symmons*, and a term in the contract of sale excluding liability for defects in the car was annulled accordingly.

We should refer briefly also to ss.13 and 27. Section 13 explains that when the Act forbids exclusion or restriction of liability it thereby forbids terms which admit liability but subject to onerous or restrictive conditions, or which restrict any right or remedy or impose any prejudice on a person seeking to enforce his rights. Clauses requiring complaints to be made within a very short time of delivery, or making the supplier's decision final, would fall within this prohibition: *Green v Cade*, 1978, below. On the other hand s.13 makes it clear that a written agreement to submit to (independent) arbitration is permissible. Lastly s.27 records that the Act does not apply where parties who would not otherwise be bound by the law of the United Kingdom have voluntarily made it the law governing their contract, but that the Act *is* effective where another country's law has been adopted only in order to avoid it.

EXCEPTIONS

These then are the main provisions of the new Act. We have seen that the statute has a very extensive coverage, making it as we have said of incalculable benefit to the consumer and even in some respects to the small business. There are however several significant exceptions to its scope. Firstly, various important sections, notably ss.3, 4, 5, 6 and 7, make special provision for consumers and to that extent leave non-consumer transactions less well provided for. Secondly, s.29 declares that the Act does not affect contract terms authorised or required, expressly or by implication, by statute or made under an international agreement to which the UK is party. Further, a term satisfies the test of reasonableness, below, if incorporated in a contract or approved by a competent authority exercising any statutory jurisdiction or function and not itself a party to the contract. A competent authority is defined as any court, arbitrator, government department or public authority. Codes of practice approved by the Office of Fair Trading might therefore confer certain limited immunities which would otherwise be forbidden but are seen to be necessary in particular cases.

More specific exceptions, all of great commercial significance, are created by Schedule 1 of the Act. Sections 2 to 4 are here stated not to apply to any contract of insurance, any contract relating to the creation, transfer or ending of an interest in land or a patent, copyright or other intellectual property right, or one relating to the formation or dissolution of a company or partnership or to its constitution or the rights or duties of its members. Contracts of marine salvage or towage, charterparties of ships or hovercraft, and contracts for the carriage of goods by such means are covered by s.2(1) (avoidance of terms excluding liability for death or injury caused by negligence), but otherwise ss.2, 3, 4 and 7 only apply to these particular contracts in favour of consumers. Section 2(1) and (2) does not extend to contracts of employment, except in favour of employees.

REASONABLENESS

Finally we must take special account of Schedule 2 of the Act, giving guidance as to the reasonableness or otherwise of contract terms within ss.6 and 7, ie those excluding or restricting liability in business transactions for defective title to goods, non-conformity with description, unmerchantable quality or unfitness for purpose. The most important factors are the relative bargaining power of the parties; the availability of other sources of supply; whether the customer received an inducement (such as a lower price for a greater risk) to agree to the terms; whether other suppliers offered similar contracts without excluding liability; the customer's knowledge of the existence and/or extent of the exclusion clause; whether any precondition of liability (eg notification within seven days) could practicably be complied with, and whether the goods were made or processed to the customer's own requirements. The same or similar factors are clearly relevant to all the other sections in the Act turning on reasonableness.

The test of reasonableness has been illustrated in a number of important cases including *Mitchell v Finney Lock*, mentioned above in connection with the doctrine of fundamental breach. The House of Lords held the seedsmen's exclusion clause valid at common law but unreasonable under provisions in the Supply of Goods (Implied Terms) Act identical to those now in Schedule 2 of the 1977 Act. The evidence was that a similar limitation of liability had been included in the terms of trade between seedsmen and farmers for many years and although the limitation clause had not been negotiated between representative bodies, neither had the National Farmers' Union objected to it. These factors were as one of their Lordships put it 'equivocal'. More significant was the fact that when anything went wrong the seedsmen usually negotiated settlements in excess of their strict contractual liability, apparently recognising that their terms were not fair. Two further pointers were that the supply of the wrong seed was due to negligence, in so far as the seedsmen knew that the kind they delivered could not be grown in the buyer's area, and that seedsmen could insure against the risk of crop failure without materially increasing their prices. In these circumstances the court decided 'without hesitation' that it would not be fair or reasonable to allow them to rely on the contractual limitation of liability.

In *Green v Cade*, 1978, another dispute over seeds, terms of sale had been agreed between seed merchants and farmers' trade association. All complaints were to be made within three days, and damages if any were limited to the contract price. The court rejected the three-day limit as plainly unreasonable but upheld the damage limitation clause, partly because it had been collectively agreed and partly because seeds certified free of disease were available at a higher price. Failure to provide such an alternative service, more expensive but more reliable, led to rejection of another exclusion clause in *Woodman v Photo Trade*, 1981.

The dispute in *White Cross Equipment v Farrell*, 1982, concerned a waste compactor sold to a salvage disposal operator. There was a six-month guarantee and an exclusion of all liability thereafter. The machine developed defects a little beyond the guarantee period and the buyer sought redress. The judge rejected his claim on the following grounds, reported here as a clear and helpful statement of the issues.

> These parties were very much at arms' length. I have no doubt that the defendant could have bargained away the plaintiff's terms had he so wished. If the plaintiffs had not been willing to give up (this) condition the defendant could undoubtedly have gone elsewhere. It is to be noted, secondly, that the plaintiffs do undertake to replace parts or the entire machine if necessary and, apart from that, to repair or replace parts which are defective, due to workmanship or design, subject to certain safeguards. That undertaking is good for six months which should, in the ordinary course of events, be ample time for any major deficiency to emerge. Thirdly, once a compactor is in use, it can be subjected to an almost infinite variety of conditions of use and abuse,

both as to the waste which is fed into it, the operators who are using it, and the conditions under which it is being used. Those considerations, in my view, amply justify the plaintiffs saying to a purchaser: 'After six months you are on your own as far as defects of design or workmanship are concerned.'

I have borne in mind carefully that this is not a case where the parties could easily insure and, indeed, insurance against breaches of the implied condition of suitability or a representation as to performance would not be a practical proposition at all. So I have viewed this matter simply as a question of allocating risks between two commercial parties of equal bargaining power; and having taken into consideration all the circumstances, I find that the requirements of reasonableness are in fact satisfied.

OTHER STATUTORY PROVISIONS

Apart from the Unfair Contract Terms Act there are several statutes controlling the use of exclusion clauses in certain more limited circumstances. So for example the Consumer Credit Act makes void any term in a consumer credit or hire agreement or a related agreement which is inconsistent with any provision in the Act or regulations made under it for the protection of the debtor or hirer. The Defective Premises Act 1972 imposes duties of good workmanship upon builders which by s.6 cannot be excluded. A group of Acts concerned with domestic and international transportation should be noted. These are the Road Traffic Act 1960, which makes void any provisions in a contract to carry a passenger in a public service vehicle which purport to restrict liability for his death or injury. The Carriage by Railways Act 1972 and the Carriage of Passengers by Road Act 1965 have similar effect regarding the international carriage of goods. The Carriage of Goods by Sea Act 1924, which gave effect to the Hague Rules, invalidates any clauses relieving the carrier of liability for loss of or damage to goods caused by his negligence. Similarly a carrier by air cannot escape his liabilities under the Carriage by Air Act 1961 (enforcing the Warsaw Convention), but such liabilities are subject to financial limits.

COMMON LAW AND STATUTE

In sum therefore exclusion clauses are now very largely and effectively regulated by statute. At the same time however we should not overlook the element of doubt created by the requirement of reasonableness in certain sections of the Unfair Contract Terms Act, still less those many situations outside the Act altogether. In either event it may be helpful to refer back to the common law. All exclusion clauses are still subject to the rules of common law examined earlier, whether or not the Act applies. If the Act does not apply then they remain as the only form of protection available. If the Act does apply the rules of common law serve as hurdles which must be overcome before the effect of the Act can be considered. So for example a consumer might argue that he did not have reasonable notice of the existence of an exclusion clause, and on that common law ground alone should not be bound by it. If his argument were successful it would not then be necessary to look at the Act at all. The questions posed by the Act, whether the clause is classified as void or valid only if reasonable, or, if the latter, whether it is in fact reasonable in the circumstances, simply would not arise for decision.

SUMMARY

Business contracts usually contain clauses excluding or limiting sellers' liabilities for breach of contract. To a lesser extent manufacturers subject to non-contractual liabilities also seek to avoid responsibility for injury by warning notices. The effect of exclusion clauses and other disclaimers is regulated in two entirely different ways, first by common law rules of construction, imposing in particular requirements as to due notice; second by Act of Parliament. The Unfair Contract Terms Act declares void clauses or notices excluding liability for personal injury caused by negligence and others affecting fitness of goods in consumer transactions. Various other types of exclusion clause or notice will be upheld only if the supplier can prove them reasonable in accordance with standards laid down in the Act. Contracts relating to insurance and intellectual property rights are among those outside the Act and so regulated only by common law.

5 Negligence (1) The General Principles

Apart from the exceptional 'guarantee ' cases discussed in chapter 2 English law denies any contractual connection between retail buyer and manufacturer. Usually the buyer is none the worse off for this because he has his strict contractual rights under the Sale of Goods Act against the seller, as described in chapter 3, and so has no occasion to wish to sue the manufacturer. But if the seller has gone out of business, or lacks the resources to meet a very large claim for damages, who else should the buyer sue for his injuries? And if the person injured by the product was not a buyer but some subsequent user such as an employee or member of the buyer's family, or someone else inadvertently brought into contact with the goods, who should be liable then?

The answer given by our own legal system, and most others, is that in the absence of a contractual right an injured person must prove *negligence* before he or she can be awarded compensation. We shall see that the concept of negligence or 'fault' is both complicated and nebulous. It may be very difficult to say that anyone at all is to blame. Or, depending entirely on the facts of the particular case, the party at fault may be the manufacturer, or one of his component suppliers, or perhaps an importer, distributor, or retailer. Another possibility is that

BURDEN OF PROOF

The need to prove negligence somewhere along the line makes a profound difference to the injured user's claim. The point may be illustrated by a domestic example. Suppose first of all that a husband buys some such item as an electric hedge cutter from a local store, and suffers an electric shock while using the cutter in the proper fashion. Under the Sale of Goods Act the seller must ensure that the cutter is reasonably fit for its purpose, which it is proved not to be by the fact that this accident happened. He is liable accordingly. But if it is the wife who is injured when using the goods in exactly the same way her case becomes much more difficult. The seller's duty under the Act is owed only to the buyer. Since a husband does not usually buy as his wife's agent, the wife in this example has no contractual relationship with the seller. She can therefore only succeed if she can prove negligence against someone. On the facts before us that someone is very unlikely to be the seller. He has in all probability no reason to suspect there is anything wrong with this particular cutter, nor to unpack or test every cutter in the shop to make sure there is no danger. If anyone is to blame for the wife's electric shock, it is almost certainly the manufacturer. The result is that because the wife did not buy the goods she has to sue manufacturer instead of seller, and the burden of proof upon her is entirely different from that which would face her husband.

Negligence is not proved by the mere fact that an accident has happened. In theory at any rate the manufacturer in our hypothetical case could escape liability by showing he had taken all reasonable care in the design and production of the cutter, or by showing that the accident was caused by a defective part supplied by a sub-contractor, a problem touched on again below, or by some intermediate use or misuse. And if the cutter had been made abroad then for all practical purposes the wife might as well abandon her claim altogether, unless perhaps she could pin liability on the importer or distributor – another possibility discussed below. There are however certain exceptions to the burden of proof rule in negligence cases. The first is the result of a rule of evidence rather than law. If the circumstances of an accident seem incapable of explanation on any ground other than that of the defendant's negligence, the judge may invoke the maxim *res ipsa loquitur* ('the thing speaks for itself' – though if so why does it not speak in English?) to reverse the burden of proof and require the defendant to *disprove* negligence. In theory he should then be able to show he took all due care by supervision of workers and tests of products to avoid the risk, but in practice the fact of the accident might be taken as conclusive proof that he had failed in his duty.

The point is illustrated in *Grant v Australian Knitting Mills*, 1936. The plaintiff bought a pair of underpants. They contained excess sulphites, which caused severe dermatitis. He sued both seller and manufacturers. In seeking to disprove negligence the manufacturer's established that they had a very modern factory and had sold more than a million pairs of underpants without complaint. The court held:

> If excess sulphites were left in the garment, that could only be because someone was at fault. The (plaintiff) is not required to lay his finger on the exact person in all the chain who was responsible, or to specify what he did wrong. Negligence is found as a matter of inference from the existence of the defects taken in conjunction with all the known circumstances.

In *Daniels v White*, 1938, on the other hand, lemonade manufacturers escaped liability for carbolic acid in their bottles by proving they had a 'foolproof' method of cleaning and filling bottles. This conflict may perhaps have been resolved by *Hill v Crowe*, 1978, where it was emphasised that proof of a 'perfect' system – ie discharge of the manufacturer's personal duty of care – did not rule out liability for employees' negligence. This issue of *vicarious liability* is discussed on p. 126.

It follows that if the judge cares to say that the *res ipsa* rule applies, the injured plaintiff is in a very strong position. The fact remains that the rule is invoked very rarely, as it was eg in *Steer v Durable Rubber Co*, 1958, where a hot water bottle burst after only three months' use and scalded the plaintiff. It is certainly not employed in many circumstances where one might think it could be. The burden of proof was not reversed in the famous case of *Donoghue v Stevenson*, for example, discussed below, nor was it suggested that it should be in the Thalidomide cases.

One or two statutory provisions relieving the plaintiff of the burden of proving negligence should also be noted. The Consumer Safety Act 1978, described in detail in chapter 9, entitles anyone injured by a manufacturer's failure to comply with regulations made under the Act to claim against the manufacturer without proving negligence. The scope of the Act is to be much enlarged, as noted on p. 176. Under the Employers' Liability (Defective Equipment) Act 1969, an employee injured by defective equipment can claim against his employer even though the latter could not have discovered the defect by any reasonable inspection. The employer can then seek reimbursement from the manufacturer, or whoever sold him the equipment. Employers are strictly liable under the Factories Act for the safety of lifts and certain other items of equipment. Finally a person injured in the limited circumstances covered by the Vaccine Damage Payments Act 1979 is entitled to a small recompense from the Department of Health, again without proof of negligence.

REASONABLE CARE

To define the issues involved in proving negligence we must refer first to the case of *Donoghue v Stevenson*, 1932, the starting point of English law on this subject. The facts were very simple. The plaintiff was bought a bottle of ginger beer by her friend. The bottle was opaque and sealed. After opening the bottle and drinking some of the contents the plaintiff poured out the remainder into her glass, and found a decomposed snail floating there. She suffered severe gastroenteritis. Who should she sue? There was no statutory provision to help her, so she had to rely on common law. The basic problem was that she had no contract with the seller, or anyone else. She had to fight the case all the way up to the House of Lords which, after the greatest difficulty and by a majority of only 3 to 2, reached the painfully obvious conclusion that it was the manufacturer who should be liable for the contents of this bottle. Their Lordships laid down a general rule of liability in all such non-contractual cases, namely that suppliers of goods must take *reasonable care* to ensure the safety of the goods for those likely to use them – their 'neighbours', as Lord Atkin put it.

This is in fact just one instance of the duty we are all under, individually and corporately, legally and morally, to try to avoid harming each other. We could equally well say, for example, that employers owe a duty of reasonable care to their employees, vehicle drivers to other road users, doctors to patients and so on. Sometimes, as under the Health and Safety at Work Act, this same duty is reinforced by the criminal law (see chapter 9), but normally in cases of unintentional injury it is enforceable only by claims for damages.

Our next task therefore is to see what is meant by 'reasonable care'. It will be understood that this expression falls well short of a guarantee of safety. The law does not demand the impossible, nor say that one person must *always* be liable whenever he harms another however indirectly and inadvertently, otherwise business would be impossible and unions illegal. When someone is injured by a product the question the judge asks himself is so far as possible an objective one: did the producer do what a reasonable man in his position should have done to try to avoid the injury? His answer will depend entirely on the facts put before him and on what seems to have been the proper course of action in the circumstances according to the standards we shall try to define. Judges naturally do not wish to appear only as wise after the event or to condemn manufacturers when they have undoubtedly done their best, even though what they did might subsequently seem mistaken. But the possibility remains that the manufacturer's best may not be good enough in the light of advancing standards in society at large and within that industry in particular.

A quotation from a case on employers' liability indicates the general approach, bearing in mind as we said above that we could substitute 'producer' or 'manufacturer' for 'employer'.

> It is the duty of an employer in considering whether some precaution should be taken against a foreseeable

risk to weigh on the one hand the magnitude of the risk, the likelihood of an accident happening and the possible seriousness of the consequences . . . and on the other hand the difficulty and expense and any other disadvantages of taking the precaution.

There are then a number of clearly identifiable factors which will determine whether a consumer's claim should be successful. In effect these are the 'ingredients' of reasonable care, or put another way they are the main elements of the 'safety checklist' against which every product must be tested.

ELEMENTS OF LIABILITY

LIKELIHOOD

First and foremost is the likelihood or otherwise of injury, on the common sense basis that the more likely an accident is the more one should do to avoid it. Conversely if the risk is very small or remote it might never occur to the reasonable man that it exists or is worth guarding against and on that basis he should not be liable if an accident occurs.

The judges ask themselves therefore whether the accident was reasonably foreseeable, which in the present context demands a consideration of who might be expected to use or come into contact with the goods in question and the circumstances in which they might do so. It is not easy to say what degree of probability or improbability will tip the balance one way or the other. As John Munkman, an eminent writer on employers' liability, once put it: 'Some learned judges are able to foresee very little; others, by taking a complex succession of events step by step, are able to foresee almost anything.' In particular we might observe that if an injury of some sort is reasonably foreseeable there will still be liability even though the consequences are far more serious than might normally be expected. In *Smith v Leech Brain*, 1961, for instance, an employee suffered a burn on his lip because of his employer's negligence. The burn later caused cancer. The employer was nonetheless held to blame for this disastrous development.

Sometimes the sequence of events begun by the defendant leads to an accident only because of some further incident such as the intervention of a third party *(novus actus interveniens)*. Liability still turns on whether such intervention was likely or not. In *Philco v Spurling*, 1949, an employer was liable for the negligence of his employee in delivering inflammable scrap to the wrong address and without notification, even though the passerby who was injured thereby had lit the scrap deliberately to see if it burned. This was held to be foreseeable in the circumstances and not a completely 'new departure' whose effect would be to sever the link between the employer's negligence and the ultimate injury.

SERIOUSNESS

Likelihood of risk must be weighed against a second factor: that of the potential seriousness of an accident. There are many industrial processes, for example, where accidents are very unlikely, but which if they occurred would be catastrophic. In such cases the gravity of the consequences would outweigh their improbability and all due precautions would have to be taken under this second heading.

OBVIOUSNESS

The third item on the checklist is the obviousness of the danger. A manufacturer can only guard against hazards of which he knows or ought to know, and so cannot usually be blamed for injuries caused by hidden or unexpected dangers. On the other hand he might well be held liable for dangers which would have been revealed by proper research or testing or information flow systems. The obviousness of the danger may be important for another reason. If the danger should have been as clear to the manufacturer as the injured user says, then presumably the user himself should have seen it and taken appropriate precautions. His failure to do so may cost him part or all of his compensation on grounds of contributory negligence or consent to run the risk. These defences are discussed further at the end of this chapter.

COST

Fourth is the question of cost; the economic factor. How much does the law require a manufacturer to spend on the safety of his product? It will come as no surprise to be told there is and can be no definite answer to this question in the form of a percentage of production cost or sale price. The law's task is simply to balance the producer's search for profit and society's need for the product against the reasonable safety requirements of the consumer. It rarely demands precautions so prohibitively expensive as to drive the manufacturer out of business, but might of course have to reach that conclusion if there is no other way of avoiding an imminent risk of serious injury.

INHERENT RISK

Lastly we take account of the inherent risk factor. Use of any commodity carries with it some unavoidable element of danger, perhaps not in normal careful use but certainly through carelessness or misuse. Even in normal careful use there may be hazards, as with disagreeable (as distinct from imminently dangerous side effects of drugs. If the product is to be used at all, this degree of danger must be accepted. No blame can then be attributed to anyone, except sometimes to the user himself, and so no compensation can be claimed.

These then are the main elements of the calculations judges must make in deciding whether or not reasonable care has been taken in any particular case. We shall see in the following pages how the calculations are made. But ultimately the significance attached to any given factor, or how one factor may be balanced against another, depends entirely on the judge's view of the facts of the case, and each case is new and unique. All too often the outcome must be entirely unpredictable. The injured consumer will derive little satisfaction from the judge's dilemma, and the manufacturer may well feel that clearer guidance would not come amiss.

We see below (p. 171) that Parliament has devised minimum safety standards for certain products, notably motor vehicles and the products regulated by the Consumer Safety Act, but in all fairness we could not expect it to lay down detailed rules for every conceivable item. Eventually, and subject to the reservations in chapter 8 as to the best way of compensating the injured, we must accept that safety is almost always a matter of compromise to be worked out case by case. If the judge agrees with the balance struck by the manufacturer; agrees, that is to say, that the risk of injury has been reduced so far as is reasonably practicable, then he will not hold the manufacturer liable if an accident occurs despite his precautions, eg when a tried and tested drug suddenly produces disastrous side effects.

Another way of expressing that proposition is by saying that in tort the manufacturer's duty is to *try* to ensure that his goods are reasonably safe, whereas under the Sale of Goods Act the seller's duty is to *succeed*; he must ensure that they are so. This is the essential difference between negligence liability and strict contractual liability. We should remember however that strict liability is not the same as absolute liability, as explained on p. 58, and mention again the evidentiary and substantive exceptions to the negligence rule noted on pp. 92-3.

We have stressed that the duty of care is a personal one, applying at every stage from design to distribution. Although in the nature of things there is usually no single person we could call the manufacturer but only a company, and even though he or the company must work through subordinates, employees and independent contractors, distributors and the like, nonetheless neither company nor individual can escape liability by delegating responsibility to others, however expert they may be. The duty remains, but its effect then is to require the manufacturer to take reasonable care in the selection of employees and contractors, providing them with appropriate designs, specifications and equipment and inspecting and testing their products so far as practicable. The effects of the duty as regards design, research, etc, are considered at length in the next chapter as are limitations on liability in relation to independent contractors and the possibilities of holding the contractors themselves liable.

DEFENCES

The main defence of a manufacturer, distributor, etc sued for damages for negligence is of course that he took all reasonable care in the design, construction and/or marketing of the product. We have indicated above the main issues raised by this requirement and in the next chapter consider its application in detail. Certain other possibilities should now be noted. The Law Reform (Contributory Negligence) Act 1945 enables the court to apportion liability according to the parties' respective degrees of fault. The judge may assess a plaintiff's share of the blame as say a third or a half and reduce his compensation accordingly. 'Fault' is measured more in terms of the effect of folly or carelessness than in failure to comply with any legal duty. The result may be that if the real cause of an accident is the plaintiff's own behaviour, eg his failure to read a clear warning or to inspect goods before use in circumstances where he could reasonably be expected to do so, any breach of duty by the defendant may be largely or even entirely disregarded. Examples of contributory negligence given in the next chapter include *Tearle v Cheverton & Laidler*, 1970, and *Goodchild v Vaclight*, 1965.

Another defence is that of consent. The lawyers' tag *volenti non fit injuria* expresses shortly the proposition that a person who agrees to run a risk cannot then complain if he is injured. The defendant has to prove both the plaintiff's knowledge of the risk and voluntary agreement to run it. Knowledge alone is not sufficient, as we shall see in *Rimmer v Liverpool City Council*, 1983. But in *Farr v Butters*, 1972, and *Allard v Manahan*, 1974, among other cases considered in the next chapter, the plaintiffs were deemed to have agreed to run the risk by disregarding known hazards or recommended safety precautions. Where consent is proved it defeats a claim altogether, unlike contributory negligence which involves only a reduction in compensation – even though the reduction may sometimes reach 100 per cent.

DAMAGES

So far as possible the object of an award of damages is to compensate the plaintiff for the extent of his loss; to put him back at least in financial terms where he was before the accident. In practice this objective is rarely if ever achieved. In the first place the law cannot compensate for all losses but only for those which are the most direct and likely consequences of injury, such as loss of earnings. Those more 'remote' will be disregarded. Even more clearly no amount of money can make up for the loss of an eye or an arm or a leg or other pain or suffering. Sums awarded for personal injuries can never be more than tokens. There will in any case be no agreement on the amount of the token, which depends entirely on the circumstances of the individual plaintiff. Only the judge can decide what is appropriate, reaching his conclusion by reference to awards in comparable cases. Current maximum awards for total permanent disablement are of the order of £350,000.

Most negligence cases involve physical injury or damage to property. Until very recently our judges have refused to give compensation for pure economic loss, ie financial loss not deriving from physical injury or damage. Compensation for loss of profit caused say by delivery of defective machinery has been seen as a matter for contract law alone, eg a buyer's claim against a seller. If the seller were insolvent there would then be no redress even though it was plainly the manufacturer's fault the machinery did not work.

An exception to this rule was made in 1964 when the House of Lords decided in *Hedley Byrne v Heller* that damages could be given for economic loss in isolation if caused by negligent advice or information and subject to the test of 'proximity', ie dependence on expertise and resulting likelihood of loss. In chapter 2 we noted the possible application of *Hedley Byrne* to advertisements and guarantees, as also its rejection in what might have seemed the likely context of *Lambert v Lewis*.

Junior Books v Veitchi, 1982, represents a further important development, though one whose limits are far from clear. A publishing company contracted with a builder to have a factory built. The builder sub-contracted with a flooring specialist. The specialist did the job badly and the floor cracked and could not be used. It was not dangerous, only defective. The company suffered loss of profit until the floor was rebuilt. The House of Lords decided that there was a sufficient degree of proximity between the sub-contractors and the company to make the sub-contractors liable for breach of duty of care to the company, but their liability was limited to the cost of relaying the floor. The company's claims for compensation for loss of use, disturbance, alternative storage requirements, etc, were all rejected. Liability for the negligent production of defective but not dangerous goods is evidently then confined to costs necessarily incurred in remedying such faults, but in any case depends upon there being a degree of reliance on the manufacturer's skill and judgment comparable to that of buyer upon seller. The primary liability remains that of the seller.

TIME LIMITS

Under the Limitation Acts 1939/80 an injured party must as a general rule begin legal action, ie issue a writ, within three years of the injury occurring. But if the injury is a disability or disease which may take many more years to appear he must sue within three years of knowing that he has a significant injury attributable to someone else's negligence. If there is no physical injury but only damage to property or economic loss the claim must be brought within six years of 'the date when the cause of action accrued'. The House of Lords held in *Pirelli v Faber*, 1983, a building case, that a cause of action 'accrued' when the faults occurred (here, when a chimney cracked), as distinct from either the date when the work was done or the date when the faults were actually discovered. This decision may have arbitrary and indefensible consequences. It may well be more than six years after the occurrence of a fault (whatever that might mean) before a person discovers that the goods supplied or work done was faulty. It seems that he will then lose his right of action before he knows he has one. In *Dove v Banham*, 1983, the judge evaded the *Pirelli* ruling by holding that the fault occurred and time began to run from the date when thieves broke through a defective security gate and not when the gate was installed. Reform is urgently needed nonetheless.

We should bear in mind finally that if a plaintiff fails to pursue his claim with all due diligence and allows delays to occur which seriously prejudice the defendant, eg through the difficulty of getting hold of witnesses or simply of remembering events long ago, the defendant may apply to the court to have the action struck out.

SUMMARY

This chapter has covered the general principles of liability for the tort or non-contractual civil wrong of negligence. Liability for negligence may be imposed by contract or arise in tort at the same time as in a breach of contract action, but normally arises in the absence of any contractual relationship between the parties. The basis of liability is a breach of one's duty of care to one's 'neighbour', who is anyone likely to be harmed by one's actions. Producers and distributors alike are bound by this duty in relation to the users of their goods. The precautions they must take are determined by the foreseeability and seriousness of risk, its obviousness to the user, the cost of avoiding or reducing the risk, and the dangers inherent in the enterprise. These principles are the common law's 'safety checklist', to be consulted and observed by executives at all levels in industry and commerce.

6 Negligence (2) Manufacturers' and Distributors' Duties

In the previous chapter we discussed the elements of liability for negligence. Our purpose now is to see how the rules actually work in different factual situations. For the sake of convenience we shall divide the cases under the four general headings of Materials, Design, Advice and Warning, and Workmanship. But these headings are not mutually exclusive, and we may often find that issues arising under one heading may be resolved by reference to another. We shall refer to these issues again in chapter 9 when we consider manufacturers' and suppliers' criminal liabilities under the Health and Safety at Work Act and other present and proposed legislation.

MATERIALS

The producer of raw materials faces immediately the problem that many of them are inherently dangerous and most if not all involve further hazards in extraction and processing. If we really wished to avoid these dangers we could simply forbid the use of the materials, but will more probably find that society regards the materials as necessary for its comfort or convenience and so decides that someone must be employed to run the risks. Precautions will be imposed but they will be essentially second best, requiring for example safe storage or handling, use of respirators or safety clothing or barrier cream. In his capacity as employer the producer will then have to do his best to ensure that his employees observe these precautions, and if not will be liable to them in damages. If he sells the materials for others to use, he must ensure they are packed as safely as reasonably practicable and that the user has adequate information as to their proper use. Only very occasionally do we accept that the risks are so great that the product must be taken off the market. An early example was the Factories Act prohibition of white phosphorous in match making, to avoid the disease of 'phossy-jaw' commonly found among matchmakers in the nineteenth century. More recently blue asbestos has been banned and restrictions imposed on other forms of asbestos which make its continued use almost impossible and provide the strongest incentive to find alternatives. Certain other carcinogenic products and various drugs with exceptionally severe side effects have also had to be withdrawn. The lead content of petrol is gradually being reduced.

These various points, apart from the question of warnings and advice to users discussed separately below, are illustrated in a number of leading cases. First *Pearson v NW Gas Board*, 1968, and *Hawes v Railway Executive*, 1952, discuss problems of inherent danger and social utility in relation to gas and electricity supply. In *Pearson*, a gas main, buried at the standard depth and so far as was known in good condition, was fractured by an exceptionally severe frost. The result was an explosion in which a house was destroyed, the husband killed and his wife severely injured. She claimed compensation for these losses from the Board, on grounds of negligence. On that evidence the court held that the Board had taken all the normally effective precautions and could not be liable for failing to predict or prevent this tragic accident. The cost element was crucial here. If the Board were to be held liable in this quite exceptional case it would then have to spend limitless sums of money reburying all its pipes all over the country to try to avoid such accidents recurring, though of course no one could say for sure how much deeper they would have to be to *guarantee* safety. Further precautions were therefore impracticable.

The facts of the *Railway Executive* case were that Mr Hawes, a railway ganger doing minor maintenance work on a stretch of electrified railway line, slipped or tripped and was electrocuted on the live rail. Clearly his widow could prove the elements of likelihood and seriousness of accident listed in chapter 5 as the main ingredients of liability. She could also establish an easy and effective way of eliminating what might otherwise appear as an inherent risk, that is, by turning the current off. The Executive defended the case simply by denying it was under any duty to turn the current off. The court argued that her claim, pursued to its conclusion, meant that every time anyone did minor maintenance work the current would have to be off, and since such repairs took place all over the system all the time the railways would be in a state of complete and permanent dislocation. This result would be quite unacceptable to society as a whole. The widow therefore lost her claim because the cost of taking effective precautions was far more than society would be willing to pay. That in turn involves recognition of the fact that electricity is extremely dangerous and that there are limits to what we can do to make it safe. Some countries such as Germany deal with this problem by imposing strict liability on public utility suppliers. It is interesting to see that in America, where the position is governed by common law rules of product liability, their answer seems to be the same as ours: *Harris v Northwest Natural Gas*, 1979.

Again we might ask in passing whether these apparently neat and logical common law conclusions represent acceptable ways of dealing with families which have lost their breadwinners. Society wants gas and electricity supplies; in a sense therefore it sentences to death or injury some of those who work on or use these products. Should it not then be society's responsibility to make sure that victims and dependants are adequately provided for, rather than left virtually destitute as may be the case at present? This is the question underlying all proposals for reform, to which we return in chapter 8.

If the hazard is one against which precautions are feasible, how far must the producer go in his capacity as employer to ensure they are observed? This issue was discussed at length in *Woods v Durable Suites*, 1953. The plaintiff was an experienced glue spreader working in the defendants' furniture factory. He knew and they knew that there was a risk of dermatitis in his work. His employers provided barrier cream and washing facilities, put up notices and told him personally about the dangers and the precautions he had to take. Unknown to his supervisors Mr Woods did not use the cream or wash his hands as often as he was supposed to, and so contracted dermatitis. He then sued his employers for their alleged failure to provide a safe system of work, ie to provide a level of supervision sufficient to ensure that he obeyed the rules. The judge rejected his claim. The level of supervision which Mr Woods seemed to want would have required someone set on to watch each individual employee, empowered perhaps to force him to wash his hands, which was obviously out of the question. It was held that once the appropriate equipment had been provided and the instructions given there was nothing more the employers could do. 'There is no duty at common law to stand over workmen of age and experience,' said the judge.

Another important case is *Stokes v GKN*, 1968. Mr Stokes had been a tool setter for many years. His job involved close contact with ordinary machine oil, which over the years frequently soaked through his overalls. He eventually died of scrotal cancer, caused by the oil. The carcinogenic properties of oil had been understood in medical circles before this time and warned against by factories inspectorate publications, but the danger had not previously been brought to the attention of the general public. GKN's doctor knew of the risk, but because the disease was very rare and because many employees could have been unnecessarily frightened by an all-out safety campaign he adopted a policy of 'soothing rather than alerting'. The judge held that the seriousness of the disease outweighed its rarity, and that the precautions which could have been taken at this time, in the way of washing, clean overalls, medical inspections and the like, might well have saved Mr Stokes' life. He therefore held the doctor negligent in the policy he had pursued, and under the doctrine of vicarious liability (p. 126) that made GKN liable. We note in passing that no claim was made against the original producers of the oil, because it was not sufficiently clear that they knew or ought to have known of this particular hazard.

Materials which pose more obvious risks than those

illustrated in *Woods* and *Stokes* may not require the same high level of precautions by the employer. In *Qualcast v Haynes*, 1959, for example, there was a danger of splashes from molten metal. It was held that the employer's duty was only to provide safety equipment and ensure that his employees knew it had been provided. The kind of all-out safety campaign necessary in the two previous cases was not required here, because its effect would have been only to tell the employee something he already knew perfectly well, that molten metal was dangerous, and that boots and goggles should be worn. One adult has no duty to another to tell him not to put his finger in the fire. Comparable conclusions may be drawn as to the nature of the manufacturer's duty to warn the ultimate users of his products of their inherent dangers (see below).

If however materials create real risks which cannot otherwise be controlled, then different considerations apply. In the light of these two factors the product will probably have to be withdrawn, at least in its present form, either to avoid criminal liability under some statutory provision, eg the Health and Safety at Work Act, chapter 9, or the certainty of liability in damages to anyone injured. The possibilities were explored in *Wright v Dunlop*, 1973. ICI made a product called Nonox S which they supplied to Dunlop for use in tyremaking. ICI discovered that the product carried a risk of cancer and took various steps including ultimately withdrawal of the product to safeguard their employees. The question then arose as to ICI's liabilities if any to Dunlop's employees as users of their product. The court held that ICI's duty was the same as that towards their own employees, at least if they knew how the product was being used and on the assumption that it was used as ICI intended, which was so here. ICI were then bound to

> take all reasonable steps to satisfy themselves that Nonox S was safe: 'safe' in the sense that there was no substantial risk of any substantial injury to health on the part of persons who were likely to use it or to be brought into contact with its use, the method of the use being such as was intended or contemplated or was at least reasonably to be expected as a normal and proper use.

The judge explained the possible courses of action as follows:

> It is obvious that the answer to the question: 'What are reasonable steps?' must depend upon the particular facts. It is obvious, also, that the duty is not necessarily confined to the period before the product is first produced or put on the market. Thus, if, when a product is first marketed, there is no reason to suppose that it is carcinogenic, but thereafter information shows, or gives reason to suspect, that it may be carcinogenic, the manufacturer has failed in his duty if he has failed to do whatever may have been reasonable in the circumstances in keeping up to date with knowledge of such developments and acting with whatever promptness fairly reflects the nature of the information and the seriousness of the possible consequences. If the manufacturer discovers that the product is unsafe, or has reason to believe that it may be unsafe, his duty may be to cease forthwith to manufacture or supply the product in its unsafe form.
>
> It may be that in some circumstances the duty would be fulfilled by less drastic action: by, for example, giving proper warning to persons to whom the product is supplied of the relevant facts, as known or suspected, giving rise to the actual or potential risk. Factors which would be relevant would be the gravity of the consequences if the risk should become a reality, and the gravity of the consequences which would arise from the withdrawal of the product.

In the event ICI were held liable for not telling Dunlop of the danger sooner and Dunlop were also to blame for not acting on the advice quickly enough.

DESIGN

From dangers created by the extraction or processing of materials we turn to those resulting from defective design or construction. The designer's objective is not to provide products incapable of causing injury, which as we stressed in chapter 3 is impossible, but only to ensure they are reasonably safe in the circumstances of their likely use. They must not in other words give rise to unnecessary risk of injury; specifically, those which the user cannot foresee and guard against for himself. The law asks therefore whether the designer or producer knew or ought to have known of the likelihood of his product being used in a particular way. If so, was injury a reasonably foreseeable consequence? And if so again, what if anything could he and should he have done to avoid or reduce that risk?

The practical limits of product liability are well illustrated in the context of such obviously dangerous products as aeroplanes or cars, or, if it comes to that, cigarettes or whisky. The law does not ban the product, nor require it to be totally safe. Car manufacturers are not expected to build crashproof vehicles nor those 'incorporating only features representing the ultimate in safety', as was said in an American case. But while it is not commercially viable to build cars which will withstand high speed impacts there is increasingly the view that cars can realistically be expected to be safe in 5 or 10 or possibly 20 mph crashes, and injuries caused by splintering glass or steering shafts can and should be prevented even at higher speeds.

This problem area was instructively examined in the Canadian case of *Gallant v Beitz*, 1983. There was a collision between a car and a Datsun lorry. The lorry driver's injuries were caused in part by his being forced up against an iron bar which the manufacturers installed behind the driver's seat for use in tyre changing. The question then was whether Datsun were responsible for these particular injuries. On appeal it was held that on principle there could be liability

> for negligently designing a vehicle that is not reasonably crashworthy. Since motor vehicle manufacturers know or should know that many of their vehicles will be involved in collision and that many people will be injured in those crashes, they must turn their minds to this matter during the process of planning the designs of their vehicles and they must employ reasonable efforts to reduce any risk to life and limb that may be inherent in the design of their products.

That being so it was for the trial court to decide whether the manufacturers should have foreseen the danger to occupants from the position of the bar. The answer on retrial might well have been in the affirmative, but unfortunately we have as yet no record of that final decision.

A manufacturer's duty is thus to provide goods which are reasonably safe *for what they are*. A cheap, light car or motorcycle is less safe than an expensive and well constructed vehicle, but that does not mean that light cars or motorcycles must not be built. Taking the cheaper product as it stands, the court asks whether it has unnecessary dangers and if so whether it is practicable to reduce them. Feasibility can only be measured by reference to other comparable products and practices and to the cost of the proposed improvements.

Some very helpful remarks on cost were made in *Turner v General Motors*, 1974, an American case. Speaking of an alleged defect in the design of a car the judge said: 'If a change in design would add little to safety, render the vehicle ugly or inappropriate for its particular purpose and add a small fortune to the purchase price then the court should rule that the manufacturer had not created an unreasonable risk of harm.'

The designer's or manufacturer's overriding concern in the light of these technical and economic considerations is as we have said to take whatever precautions are practicable against reasonably foreseeable hazards. Such hazards are not confined to those involving intended users or arising from proper or normal use. It is foreseeable for example that a defective car part might cause an accident and that the accident might involve passers-by or other car drivers or passengers. Brought thus involuntarily into contact with the product they are still 'users' and as such within the producer's duty of care. In *Lambert v Lewis*, 1980, a manufacturer of a dangerous caravan towing hitch was found 75 per cent to blame for an accident to an oncoming vehicle even though the immediate cause was the owner's continued use of it despite knowledge of the defect (for which he paid the remaining 25 per cent). Similarly in *Stennett v Hancock*, 1939, a car repairer was held liable to a passer-by injured when a part he had fitted came off the car.

Again the 'normal' if not the 'proper' use of goods includes certain predictable misuse or abuse of them. The designer's or manufacturer's responsibility does not of course extend to any and every conceivable form of misuse. He cannot for example stop people speeding or driving dangerously in the cars he designs or builds. He cannot stop a child burning itself on ordinary domestic heating pipes: *Ryan v Camden LBC*, 1982. Here as elsewhere it is difficult to draw the line and even the criminal law varies in its approach, as discussed further in chapter 9. Thus under the Health and Safety at Work Act designers and suppliers are criminally liable for supplying articles and substances for use at work which are not as safe as reasonably practicable – but only in relation to the proper use of such articles and substances. For the purposes of the Consumer Safety Act and the major amendments to it proposed in 1984, however, suppliers' criminal liabilities extend also to normal, as distinct from completely unreasonable, misuse.

Designers' and suppliers' civil liabilities are illustrated in cases such as *Williams v Trimm Rock Quarries*, 1965, and *Hindustan SS Co v Siemens*, 1955. In *Williams* manufacturers of a new type of drill were liable for injury caused when it moved and fell. The judge said:

> Before sending a machine like this out for demonstration and putting it on the market, the toolmakers should have guarded against the possibility of its rising up and toppling over, and should have investigated those possible sources of danger. Since this accident they have taken steps to that end and all is now well; but reasonable foresight would have discovered it before the machine was issued.

The *Hindustan* case concerned a ship's telegraph system so designed that 'full astern' could easily be misinterpreted as 'full ahead'. It was held that the manufacturers would have been liable for the resulting collision but for the fact that the ship's officers were now familiar with the problem and should have guarded against it themselves.

Certain employment law cases are also very helpful even though neither designers nor suppliers were directly involved in them. The employee in *Tearle v Cheverton & Laidler*, 1970, worked on a machine with a sloping control panel from which the starting button projected at waist height. Behind the control panel were the moving parts. The employee was instructed to adjust these parts. He stopped the machinery and intended to turn it off also at the mains, but unfortunately was distracted and forgot this further precaution. He then removed the guard on the machine and got on with the job of adjustment. While doing this he inadvertently pressed on the starting button with his body and injured his hands in the machinery. He sued his employers, not because of any failure to fence or isolate the machine itself, because that was not how the accident happened, but because of the position of the starting button. The judge held the employer liable for negligent failure to hood the button so as to prevent this foreseeable occurrence of someone pressing it on by accident and being injured as a result. It will be seen that exactly the same charge of negligence could have been made against the designer or supplier of the machine, with exactly the same outcome. In passing however we should note that the plaintiff lost two thirds of his compensation because of his own forgetfulness. Similarly in *Farr v Butters*, 1932, the plaintiff lost his claim altogether because he could see the machinery he was assembling was defective but nonetheless continued to use it.

As regards misuse of equipment the case of *Burns v Terry*, 1950, is instructive. An employee was instructed to clean a shelf. To reach the shelf he got a ladder and leaned it against a rotating shaft which ran across the top of the workroom. He climbed the ladder and was thrown off it by the movement of the shaft. He fell onto a nearby machine, which, though securely fenced against the user, was not fenced against the contingency of people coming into or onto it from above. He was therefore injured on unfenced machinery. Section 14 of the Factories Act 1961 requires that dangerous machinery be securely fenced. This is a strict duty, not qualified by reference to 'reasonableness'. In interpreting the duty our judges have nonetheless said that parts of machinery are dangerous if they represent reasonably likely sources of harm – introducing, in other words, the test of foreseeability of injury. In *Burns* it was held that injury caused in this particular way was entirely unforeseeable and so there was no duty to fence against it. Since the Factories Act places the primary liability for unfenced machinery upon the employer it follows that if *he* is not liable then the manufacturer, as a more distant party, must likewise escape liability, unless by chance he is or ought to be aware of some hazard hidden from the employer. *Burns* thus supports what is from the employer's or supplier's point of view the consoling proposition that guards on machinery must be 'foolproof' but not 'bloody foolproof'.

RESEARCH

We have stressed the manufacturer's duty to keep up to date. In effect he is obliged to conduct continuous research into safety aspects of his products; in particular to seek and respond to information from users as to operating hazards. In appropriate cases that will mean establishing feedback systems such as those agreed between doctors and drug manufacturers and between car dealers and manufacturers. It is most important that he should keep records of research findings, either to show he then took the necessary precautions or to avoid charges of destruction of evidence which if proved would be virtually conclusive of liability.

Reasonable care does not of course require a manufacturer to begin at the beginning and find out for himself all over again that which is already well established, as is recognised for example by s.6 of the Health and Safety at Work Act (see p. 166). He is entitled to rely on common knowledge within the industry. But how can we say what level of knowledge is or ought to be common within an industry at any given time? *Vacwell v BDH Chemicals*, 1971, is an illustration of the problem. Pharmaceutical manufacturers were held to blame here for marketing a new and possibly dangerous combination of chemicals, with disastrous results, without consulting all reasonably accessible literature on the subject. Conversely a Health Authority's treatment of a patient's minor hand and ankle disabilities with Butazolidin, which resulted in near blindness, was held after much conflicting evidence not to be negligent in the light of medical knowledge at that time: *Sheridan v Boots and Kensington AHA*, 1981.

The same question has often had to be considered by the courts in relation to the precautions employers must take to safeguard employees against industrial disease. Employers must keep abreast of information about safety published in the journals of the trades in which they are engaged and in current reports and notices of bodies such as the Health and Safety Commission and the Department of Employment. They would be expected to comply with British Standards Institute requirements so far as relevant. Conversely they cannot be expected to know of dangers not yet known even to the medical profession, or discussed only in research papers in medical journals. So in *Harman v Mitcham Works*, 1955, an employee who contracted chronic poisoning through handling beryllium oxide in the manufacture of fluorescent lighting tubes lost his claim because at that time the employer had no knowledge of the risk and no reason to suspect it. In *Graham v CWS*, 1957, the only evidence to show that an employer should have taken precautions against a risk of dermatitis from wood he had not previously used was a warning in the Chief Inspector of Factories' Report for 1935. Again the employer was not liable. All these observations and conclusions apply with equal force to manufacturers.

The manufacturer's duty is particularly stringent in relation to new drugs, perhaps the most vexed of all product liability issues. The trials necessary to meet the requirements of the Committee on Safety of Medicines are rigorous, but even followed to the letter still cannot eliminate the possibility of some totally unlooked-for or delayed reaction causing serious injury. The plaintiff's position in these cases is unenviable. There is as we have said no presumption in his favour however disastrous his injury, as illustrated by *Sheridan's* case above. From outside the industry he has to prove that the manufacturer failed to follow normal test procedures, and that these procedures would have revealed the risk in question. The manufacturer for his part will have his own battery of experts to say that all the right precautions were taken and no indications of danger appeared.

It is impossible to predict the outcome of such conflicts of evidence. All one can say with any degree of certainty is that the claim will be very hard fought, may take many years to reach final appeal, and may then result in defeat for the plaintiff who will have achieved nothing to compensate him for his loss but will probably be irretrievably ruined by legal costs. These were no doubt among the considerations facing the parents of children harmed by Thalidomide. Although the cause of the harm was clear the last thing the parents wanted to do was to go to court. In effect they fought for compensation with both hands tied behind their backs, and suffered accordingly delays of 12 or more years before public sympathy induced the manufacturers to offer reasonable sums in settlement. This tragedy became a mainspring for reform proposals, as we shall see in chapter 8.

Even if his product is approved by some independent authority the manufacturer's responsibilities are not necessarily at an end. The Canadian case of *Willis v FMC*, 1977, is an instructive example. The plaintiff was a farmer and turnip grower. He bought an insecticide and a new herbicide. The sellers made the insecticide themselves but were merely distributors of the herbicide. The herbicide had undergone limited trial use for one year, and then the manufacturers applied for and were granted Canadian government approval of their product for general field use. It was intended that both products should be used together. When the plaintiff did use them together, however, they interacted and damaged his crop. He sued the seller for breach of the Canadian Sale of Goods Act and the herbicide manufacturers for negligence. The seller was liable for the damage done by the herbicide. Although effective for its purpose it was still not reasonably fit since it could not be used with certain insecticides and carried no warning to that effect. The court also found the manufacturers liable in negligence. They were at fault in not allowing a longer period for the testing of the herbicide, because otherwise it might clearly cause a great deal of damage, and they could not escape liability by relying on government approval. On the one hand the duty to carry out proper tests was on them alone, and on the other there was always the possibility that the government's approval might itself have been given negligently.

The full significance of the *Willis* case may be put another way. It shows that when one acts in accordance with a government directive or licence or other guideline, eg one set by the Health and Safety Commission or BSI, that of itself does not rule out the possibility of negligence. Specific statutory duties do not necessarily absolve a producer or anyone else from his general common law duty of care.

NEW SAFETY DEVICES

In the course of research a manufacturer will sooner or later find a way of making his product safer than it has been in the past. He might for example invent a new safety device for it. What if any liability does this discovery or invention create in relation to his existing products already out on the market? Common sense suggests that if the product was reasonably safe when first put on the market there can be no continuing duty to recall and update it. Inevitably the older the product the greater the danger attached to its use. But the fact that the discovery is new does not of itself mean it should have no retrospective effect. Exceptional cases might arise where, depending on the extent of the danger which might now be averted, a recall or renovation programme might conceivably be both feasible and necessary.

Before further consideration of recall and renovation programmes we should note the case of *Birnie v Ford*, 1960. This was an unusual decision where employers were held liable to an injured employee despite the fact that it was not until several months after the accident that they devised precautions which would have prevented it. On the face of it this may seem to penalise the employer or manufacturer for the successful outcome of his research. But the problem, that of injury from razor-sharp car body panels, was a relatively simple one and it was clear that if the employer had applied his mind sooner and put a fully trained safety engineer on the job he would almost certainly have made the invention in time to prevent the accident. Essentially therefore it was a matter of holding the employer liable for failing to exert himself sufficiently to resolve a familiar but serious danger.

NEW HAZARDS

Research of other subsequent events may alternatively reveal or confirm previously unsuspected or insufficiently appreciated dangers. The proper response must vary with the circumstances, but may include at least a publicity campaign, quite possibly a recall programme and conceivably even a complete standstill if the danger is sufficiently great; eg the grounding of aircraft when a structural defect is discovered.

By way of illustration we refer first to *O'Connor v British Transport Commission*, 1958. The BTC, predecessor of British Rail, discovered through various accidents and incidents with which we are not here concerned that their carriage door handles were not as safe as they had thought, and in particular that they could be opened all too easily by children. What should they do then? Warning notices would be defaced or ignored. The only solution was to embark upon a long-term programme of modifying the door handles. While this programme was under way a child opened the door of an unmodified carriage and was injured. BTC was held not liable for his injuries because they had taken the only course of action open to them. There were thousands of carriages and the doors could not all be altered overnight. In the meantime there was a continuing risk, but since it was unavoidable no one could be blamed.

This answer is only valid if the necessary repairs or alterations are undertaken as soon as reasonably practicable. The consequence of delay is shown in the Canadian case of *Malat v Bjornson*, 1981, where a highway authority was held to blame for failure to instal a particular type of barrier, which had been available for 10 years, to meet a serious danger recognised for 13 years. A recent English example to the same effect is *Rimmer v Liverpool City Council*, 1983. The plaintiff injured himself falling against a 3mm glass panel, a standard fitment on certain types of corporation housing built in 1959. He had complained at the beginning of his tenancy that the panel was dangerous for children but had been told it was standard and nothing could be done about it. The judge found that although in 1959 the corporation architect had no code of practice to guide him on the safety of glass 'an intelligent reading of the 1966 and 1972 codes of practice would have called to the minds of the architects' department the risk of danger to anyone stumbling against that glass'. He held that the department was not relieved from reconsidering the position in the light of after-acquired information since they then knew that the flat contained this foreseeably dangerous and easily substituted panel. It is worth noting that the plaintiff's own knowledge of the danger did not affect his claim, because in the circumstances there was nothing he could do about it.

So far as recalls are concerned, there is a helpful statement of the position in *Walton v British Leyland*, 1978. The plaintiffs here were involved in a disastrous accident in 1975 after a wheel came off the Austin Allegro in which they were passengers. By the beginning of 1967 BL had received over a hundred reports of 'wheel adrift' problems on this model. They knew the risk was a real and serious one. A recall would have cost some £300,000 and of course damaged their image. Instead they instructed their dealers to fit larger washers, though without fully explaining the risk. Non-franchised dealers were told nothing at all about the problem. This particular car had been serviced by both franchised and non-franchised dealers. The plaintiffs claimed against the dealers, who all escaped liability since they were unaware of the dangers, and against BL. The judge held BL wholly to blame, not for use of the component which caused the accident, which was manufactured by a reputable third party and not in itself faulty, but for failure to give adequate public warning. The crucial passage in his judgment was as follows:

> The duty of care owed by Leyland to the public was to make a clean breast of the problem and recall all cars which they could, in order that the safety washers could be fitted. I accept, of course that manufacturers have to steer a course between alarming the public unnecessarily and so damaging the reputation of their products, and observing the duty of care towards those whom they are in a position to protect from dangers of which they and they alone are aware. The duty seems to me to be the higher when they can palliate the worst effects of a failure which, if Leyland's view is right, they could never decisively guard against. They seriously considered recall and made an estimate of the cost at a figure which seems to me to be in no way out of proportion to the risks involved. It was decided not to follow this course for commercial reasons. I think this involved a failure to observe their duty of care for the safety of the many who were bound to remain at

risk, irrespective of the recommendations made to Leyland dealers and to them alone.

In 1979 a Code of Practice for the Motor Industry was agreed between the Department of Transport and the Society of Motor Manufacturers. The Code does not and cannot specify exactly the nature or number of defects requiring action but obliges manufacturers, importers and dealers concerned about the number of faulty vehicles to tell the Department of the faults and resulting dangers and their proposed precautions. They must then take all suitable steps to inform vehicle owners, sending at least two letters if necessary, and recall the vehicles if that seems desirable. The Department may put forward its own proposals as to the appropriate precautions and publish such warning information as it thinks necessary. It will be seen that manufacturers' and dealers' obligations under the Code are broadly in line with those of the common law.

From time to time the Committee on Safety of Medicines withdraws its approval for the marketing of a drug when serious side effects are reported. Under the Code of Practice for the recall of such products a manufacturer who can prove he has taken all feasible steps to withdraw or recall his products when necessary will escape liability if in any particular case his efforts fail, for example because the distributor or user cannot be contacted or ignores the warning. If injury results from the continued prescribing of a disapproved drug liability seems almost inevitable, but there is always the possibility that as between immediate pain and suffering and continued use of the drug the latter might be upheld as the lesser of two evils. The doctor would of course have to advise the patient of the risks involved.

Very occasionally legislation might be introduced to prohibit use of a product made before a certain date unless modifications are made. Farm tractors were affected in this way by the Agriculture (Tractor Cabs) Regulations of 1974, requiring roll bars to be fitted to safeguard drivers against the increasingly widely recognised risk of tractors overturning on hilly ground.

We should also bear in mind the possibility of preventive action by the Health and Safety Executive or other such agencies. Certain types of farm machinery, notably hay balers, were regarded as reasonably safe when built but on subsequent use proved lethal without further fencing. The Executive put pressure on the manufacturers of one model to introduce new safety measures even after production of the model had ended. The manufacturers then asked dealers to contact purchasers and give them warning labels to be attached to the baler. Owners were advised to fit additional guards. Manufacturers of power-take-off shaft guards have likewise agreed with the Inspectorate that replacement guards will meet certain new BSI test procedures. These various informal approaches avoid the need for improvement or prohibition notices or for prosecution.

These last few examples indicate that a manufacturer who recalls his goods or modifies or even withdraws them does not *thereby* admit liability for them. He might for example have been prompted to take remedial action by some unforeseeable accident for which he would not be liable, and his action might serve only to demonstrate his anxiety to ensure that no such accident should happen again.

OBVIOUS DANGERS

We turn now to another aspect of design; the question of liability for injury caused by dangers which are or ought to be obvious to the user. There must of course be a point at which a risk is so obvious that there can be no ground for complaint, as when one hits one's thumb with a hammer or cuts oneself when shaving. American cases have observed that there is no need to warn against the unwisdom of landing on one's head on a trampoline, or of prematurely releasing a rubber exerciser: *Garrett v Nissen*, 1972; *Jamieson v Woodward*, 1957. But that is not the issue here. These products were, we presume, fit for their normal purposes and without any risk other than those plainly inherent in their use. What should the law's response be when the danger is obvious but not inherent?

An excellent illustration of the problem is provided by *Crow v Barford*, 1963. In this case a person using a motor mower with a large grass ejection aperture inadvertently put his foot in the hole and was injured by the rotating blades. He sued the manufacturer on grounds of negligent design. The judge rejected his claim, simply because the danger was so clear. One might very well doubt however whether this was the right answer. Surely the question ought not to be 'Was the danger obvious?' but 'Was it *necessary?*' Otherwise manufacturers could put on the market whatever shoddy designs they pleased and escape liability simply by pointing to their glaring imperfections.

American courts have had to deal with disputes of this kind, and have examined the issues perhaps rather more realistically. In *Wright v Massey Harris*, 1966, for instance, the judge in a similar sort of case cited this passage from an article on power lawn mower injuries in *The American Surgeon*:

> ... approximately 30 per cent of all power lawn mowers are made by companies whose primary objective is to turn out a lower priced, sometimes poorly constructed machine for a profit. These companies have given little or no consideration to safety features of their products and some do not bother to caution the buyer of the machine about its inherent dangers. The low cost of these mowers makes them attractive to the unsuspecting customer. On the other hand, some of the more reputable manufacturers have attempted to construct mowers which meet rigid safety standards. These also usually attach a card or booklet for instructions regarding proper operation of the machine and emboss special warnings at the danger points on the machine housing.

In the light of these considerations the judge directed the jury that the machine in question was one whose design disregarded the basic safety principles. The issues of contributory negligence and consent referred to at the end of chapter 5 must not be overlooked, but it may still be thought that such cases reflect safety needs more accurately than *Crow v Barford*.

DURABILITY

When we discussed the standard of reasonable fitness required by the Sale of Goods Act we asked how long goods were expected to last. The same question arises in the present context. 'A reasonable time' is not a satisfactory answer, but it is the best we can manage. Nobody expects manufacturers to produce goods which will never wear out, nor suffer from the consequences of wear and tear. What matters is whether the goods were reasonably safe when first sold and used. Passage of time and the possibility or proof of intermediate handling may suggest that the fault could not be the manufacturer's. In *Evans v Triplex Safety Glass*, 1936, the plaintiff lost his claim against the manufacturers for injuries received when his windscreen shattered for no apparent reason a year after he bought the car. The court rejected his claim because of the length of time between purchase and the accident, the possibility that the glass might have been strained when installed in the frame by the intermediate seller, and lastly because the breakage might have been for some reason other than a defect in manufacture. Again it appears that American courts might take a rather more rigorous view and assume fault upon the manufacturer in the absence of compelling evidence to the contrary: *Henningsen v Bloomfield Motors*, 1960. And even after several years it might still be possible to prove that the goods were defective in the first place.

PACKAGING

Design liabilities extend to the safety of packaging, eg provision of containers which do not break or leak or open too easily, particularly when they may be harmful to children or others ignorant of their contents. Manufacturers should take due note of recommendations made in November 1983 by a working party of MPs, doctors and health authorities that bleach, white spirit, oven cleaners, paint strippers and other potentially dangerous products should be available with child resistant lids or tops, as with certain medicines. The report proposed that if safety tops were not introduced voluntarily regulations should be made to reduce the number of domestic accidents. In 1981 12,000 children under five were taken to hospitals in England and Wales because they were thought to have swallowed such substances.

Examples of the scope of packaging liabilities are *Hill v Crowe*, 1977, and *Samways v Westgate*, 1963. In *Hill* the manufacturer of a packing case was sued by a lorry driver injured when he stood on the case while loading it. It collapsed because it was badly made, without sufficient nails in the boards, and liability was imposed because the manufacturer should have known it might be used for standing on. *Samways* did not concern manufacturers' duties as such but nonetheless illustrates the need to pack goods with due forethought of those likely to use them. In this case a refuse collector was injured as he picked up a box without noticing a sliver of glass left sticking out through the side. His claim against the company which left the box out for collection was successful.

If packaging is undertaken by a third party such as a distributor and not by the manufacturer, the latter may still be liable for negligence if he fails to take care in selecting a reputable contractor and giving him the information and specifications necessary to enable him to do the job safely. Other aspects of packaging and labelling are considered further under the next heading.

ADVICE AND WARNING

We have emphasised that even the most safety conscious of manufacturers cannot build complete safety into their products. Inherent dangers and possibilities of misuse create irreducible risks. In such cases, where a manufacturer has done all he can realistically be expected to do in terms of design and construction, the only precaution left open to him may be to give advice and warning as to use.

The kind of information he must give varies infinitely with the product. It may be a simple matter of marking 'on' and 'off' in the language of the country to which goods are exported: *Goodchild v Vaclight*, 1965, below. Another salutory reminder of language problems was in *French v Olau Lines*, 1983, where a cleaner suffered chlorine gas injuries because he had mixed two cleaning agents contrary to warning labels printed only in foreign languages. Or it may be necessary to specify in detail the various hazards and precautions, as with warnings against heat and light on aerosol tins. In *Lambert v Lastoplex Chemicals*, 1972 (Can), for example, a general warning of the danger of inflammability was held insufficient to meet the danger of a lacquer sealant which could be ignited even by the spark of an electric light switch. The same conclusion was reached in the hair raising American case of *Martin v Bengue*, 1957, where the plaintiff's chest ointment caught fire while he was smoking in bed. These cases contrast with the decision of the Australian court in *Norton v Streets*, 1968, where it was held that a general warning of the inflammability of an industrial adhesive should have been sufficient to stop the buyer using a burner only 20 feet away from a tray of adhesive in a badly ventilated room.

Different levels of information may be appropriate for different classes of users. So goods used by laymen may need more information on safety than those used by professionals, as eg with regard to drug dosages, but then users such as doctors need a great deal of information on other matters such as adverse reactions to drugs. These particular issues are regulated in part by statute, as noted in chapter 9.

It may be sufficient for a producer to ensure that warning reaches a professional intermediary rather than the ultimate user. So in *Holmes v Ashford*, 1950, the manufacturer knew his hair dye could be dangerous to certain skins. Hairdressers to whom the dye was supplied were told of the danger by notices on the containers. The injured customer's claim that she also should have been warned was rejected.

In other cases again it may be impossible to rely on an intermediary and unsafe to assume that information accompanying but separate from a product will necessarily reach its intended destination, eg an employee. Ideally the danger of safety manuals or warning notices becoming detached or forgotten should be overcome by inscriptions on the products themselves. In some circumstances it might even be possible and desirable to overcome risks of indifference or ignorance by sending out periodic reminders to known users.

Instructions as to use must warn adequately of the dangers of foreseeable misuse. The American case of *Spruill v Boyle-Midway*, 1962, is an instructive example. The product in question was floor polish, known by the manufacturer to

NEGLIGENCE

contain poison. A householder left a tin where a child found it and ate some of the polish. This might seem an extraordinary use for polish, but since the polish was to go on the floor where children might play it was nothing if not predictable. The manufacturer was therefore held to blame for not marking the contents as poison, not so much to deter children as to encourage their parents to keep the tins out of harm's way.

If suitable instructions are duly given then of course the user has only himself to blame if he fails to observe them. The point was clearly made in *Allard v Manahan*, 1974, a Canadian case about an experienced worker killed by the ricochet of a nail he had fired from a nail gun. In his dependants' claim against the manufacturers of the gun the judge observed:

> It is true that a person in the position of the defendant, who deals in firearms, must exercise a high standard of care in the conduct of his business, but that does not mean to say that he is obliged to supply or recommend every safety device which is on the market or can be made available. The manual which is supplied with the tool described these devices and a person renting the tool can avail himself of this additional protection if he so desires.

As indicated in *Allard* and other cases previously mentioned, contributory negligence by a user or conduct which seems to amount to consent to run a risk may well defeat his claim against a manufacturer. But this result of disregarding advice or warning notices must not be confused with the effect of manufacturers' notices expressly excluding liability if anything goes wrong. Exclusion clauses are rigorously controlled by the Unfair Contract Terms Act, as we saw in chapter 4.

WORKMANSHIP

This last category of the causes of accidents includes negligent handling, processing, packaging or distribution of otherwise safely designed products, creating new and unnecessary hazards. The relevant principle of law here is the common law doctrine of vicarious liability, ie liability for someone else's wrongdoing.

VICARIOUS LIABILITY

Employers are held liable under this rule to persons injured by their employees' wrongful acts if committed in the course of their employment. The injured party's task therefore is to prove negligence against an employee, not the employer. Conversely the fact that the employer might have been quite unable to prevent the accident does not in any way reduce his liability. Two main arguments are advanced to justify the rule. First, the employer is in control of the operation and so should take responsibility for the outcome. Second, if the careless employee alone were liable he would not usually have the resources to compensate the injured party, who would thus go without redress. We have noted the effect of the rule already in decisions such as *Hill v Crowe* where the manufacturer had to pay for an accident caused by one of his packing cases which had been badly made.

It might of course be very difficult to prove which particular employee was at fault at any given point on the assembly line. The judges accept therefore that if a plaintiff can show that he was injured by the product and that the nature of the injury is such that there must have been negligence somewhere within the employer's enterprise, he need not 'lay his finger on the exact person in all the chain who was responsible': *Grant v Australian Knitting Mills*, 1936. It follows that vicarious liability claims are almost impossible for an employer to refute and represent a form of strict liability. On the other hand such liability is usually only civil and unlike the employer's personal duty of care it is not reinforced by the criminal sanctions of the Health and Safety at Work Act (see chapter 9).

SUB-CONTRACTORS

As a general rule the doctrine of vicarious liability is confined to the relationship of employer and employee. In other less tightly regulated relationships the law sees less reason for imposing liability on anyone other than the party actually at fault. That in turn means that when an accident is caused by a defective part supplied by a sub-contractor, as distinct from the manufacturer's own employee, the manufacturer who incorporated that part in his own product will not be held vicariously to blame. The manufacturer might still be liable for breach of his own personal duty of care if he failed to select a reputable subcontractor, provide him with all necessary specifications and test or sample the parts supplied: *Rogers v Night Riders*, 1983. Even when all these things are done however a defective part might still slip through, and in that event he could not be liable in tort (though he could of course be liable for breach of contract, if there were in fact a contract between himself and the injured plaintiff). So in *Taylor v Rover*, 1966, a negligence claim against the manufacturer of chisels was rejected when it was proved that the faulty part was supplied by a reputable subcontractor and that it could not have been found by the manufacturer's sample testing system.

While the liability of the sub-contractor himself might not be in doubt the problem from the plaintiff's point of view if suing in tort is first that of finding whether a sub-contractor was involved in the production process and perhaps being time-barred by the time he discovers this, and second the danger of incurring liability for costs for suing the wrong party. At the moment therefore this is a very unsatisfactory area of law. The solutions provided by American product liability rules and those proposed by the Strasbourg Convention and EEC draft Directive (see chapters 7 and 8) might seem much to be preferred.

DISTRIBUTORS' LIABILITIES

In most of the cases considered so far we have seen that if anyone is to blame for a dangerous product it is the manufacturer. This is not necessarily so, however. It is always possible that someone else in the chain of distribution might be guilty of negligence. If the manufacturer also has been negligent then the burden will be shared between them in whatever proportion the court thinks just, or each may be held wholly liable and left to recover what he can from the other. Alternatively the manufacturer may be relieved of all liability and the whole burden imposed upon the retailer, installer, repairer, inspector, certifier, distributor or importer, as the case may be, who has failed to take reasonable care.

The possibilities are illustrated in the following cases. In *Fisher v Harrods*, 1966, a person bought a bottle of jewellery cleaner from Harrods which he sent to Mrs Fisher. When she came to use it the bottle 'exploded' and the liquid went into her eyes, causing pain and temporary blindness. The explosion occurred because of the build-up of pressure of the contents and the way the bottle was sealed. There was no warning of danger on the bottle. From what we have said above it might be thought that liability for the contents and sealing of the bottle, and for the absence of any warning, must be upon the manufacturer. But in this particular case the manufacturer was a 'man of straw', someone not worth suing because he had no money. Mrs Fisher therefore had no choice but to sue Harrods if she was to sue anyone at all. But while Harrods were the sellers Mrs Fisher was not the buyer, and so she had to prove that Harrods were negligent and not merely that the bottle or contents were not reasonably fit for their purpose.

Harrods had tested the product originally to see whether it did what it was supposed to do, ie clean jewellery, and on being satisfied of this they sold it. Evidence was given by Harrods and a buyer from another leading store that it was not their practice to do anything more than test the efficiency of goods they sold, which the judge accepted as normally quite sufficient. To prove negligence Mrs Fisher therefore had to show there was something abnormal about this particular article which demanded exceptional precautions by the retailer, such as inquiries about the safety of the goods or their containers, or the qualifications of the manufacturer. She succeeded because Harrods knew or ought to have known that a solvent strong enough to clean jewellery was inherently dangerous. This should have put them on their guard to inquire about the manufacturer's qualifications, which were in fact virtually non-existent, and the safe packaging of his goods.

The same conclusion would no doubt be reached with regard to electrical or other scientific or mechanical equipment with a range of hazards known to experts but hidden from consumers. So in *Goldsworthy v Cataline Agencies*, 1983, a Canadian court held both a cycle manufacturer and a retailer liable for an accident, the one for making cycles without lock washers to hold the front wheel axle to the fork and the other for assembling the machine without washers and/or failing to warn of their absence. This case and *Burfitt v Kille*, 1939, illustrate in passing the particularly heavy duty of care of retailers supplying potentially dangerous goods – in the latter case, petrol – to children. Conversely if there were no reason to expect any danger there would be no reason for the retailer to make tests or inquiries and so no liability for accidents which might otherwise have been avoided.

Goodchild v Vaclight, 1965, is an interesting case on the duties of distributors – here, importers. The facts were that the plaintiff's husband bought an electric cleaner from a door-to-door salesman. The fan was not properly guarded or isolated and the on/off signs were in German. A couple of weeks later Mrs Goodchild suffered a severe electric shock while using the machine. She could not sue the seller because she could not trace him. Suing the German manufacturer would have been extremely expensive and speculative. The only remaining possibility was the importer. The difficulty here is that a person who is merely a conduit for another's goods is on the face of it unlikely to be responsible for their safety. But in this case, as the judge said,

> ... the defendants were more than mere distributors. They bought about 40,000 machines over five years from the German manufacturers, having at the start stripped and tested one, and they serviced them. The defendants' name was prominently displayed on the machine and they gave a guarantee card and an instruction booklet with their address.

In effect then the importers passed the goods off as their own and were certainly in a position to appreciate the strengths and weaknesses of the product. The judge held them liable as if they were the manufacturers because they should have warned against the inherent dangers of the machine, clearly marked the switch positions and insulated the fan. But the judge also said that Mrs Goodchild as a prudent housewife, uncertain whether the machine was on or off, should have unplugged it or switched it off at the mains before trying to make it work. Her failure to take this precaution cost her half her damages.

Lastly we should note the case of *Devillez v Boots*, 1962. The plaintiff bought a bottle of corn solvent from the defendants. After a bath he put some solvent on his corn. As he was putting the bottle away it tipped over, the cork came out and the contents spilled over his private parts. He wiped himself and looked at the label on the bottle to see what else he should do, but no warning or advice was given. Later he suffered extreme pain and had to undergo plastic surgery. He sued Boots in all their capacities – as sellers, distributors and manufacturers of the product. We have no information about his claim in contract, but he might well have lost under that heading because the corn solvent was undoubtedly reasonably fit for its purpose, whatever harm it might do elsewhere. In alleging negligence Mr Devillez was also in difficulty because Boots established that over the previous 30 years they had sold some 20 million bottles of this preparation under the same label and in the same type of bottle. During that time they had had only a dozen minor complaints. The judge accepted that such a successful and safe commercial record was very much in Boots' favour. He nonetheless held them liable for essentially the same reason we saw in *Fisher*, that they knew the preparation had quite a strong concentration of acid in it and should have anticipated danger to other more tender parts of the body by providing a safer bottle and clearer warning.

SUMMARY

It will be seen that the outcome of years of litigation following injury may in some cases be more or less satisfactory but in all remains speculative and expensive. A person suing a shopkeeper for breach of contract has usually a comparatively simple and straightforward claim against a readily available and responsive defendant. But someone suing in negligence may consider himself lucky if he can find the right party to sue and then overcome the much more difficult burden of proof as to the appropriate standards of design, warning or workmanship. The question of reform is inescapable. We consider the possibilities in chapter 8, after reviewing product liability laws in America and in Common Market countries other than the UK.

7 Product Liability Law in America and the Common Market

This chapter is intended to help manufacturers and their agents exporting goods to North America and Common Market countries by summarising the relevant principles of law they have to contend with there.

AMERICA

We must remember at the outset that there is not one system of law in America but one for every State. While this survey sets out as 'American law' statements of principle accepted in most if not all States, the possibility of local variation should therefore be borne in mind. A model Uniform Product Liability Act is presently under discussion to overcome these difficulties.

American law on this subject is or ought to be of the greatest interest to any British manufacturer, whether or not he exports there. The reasons for its interest and importance are, first, that the system derives directly from the familiar rules of contract and tort liability developed by English judges, as described in our previous chapters. Second, over the past 40 or 50 years American judges have fashioned out of these rules an entirely new form of liability, known simply as product liability law, which in essence if not in detail is what is now proposed for Britain. Their answers are accordingly extremely informative, subject to certain important procedural differences noted in chapter 8, as to what is likely to happen here when the reforms discussed in that chapter finally became law. As we outline their main conclusions we shall mention again one or two points of English law by way of comparison.

The findings of American courts over the previous decades were shortly stated in para 402A of the second *Restatement of Torts*, published in 1965. Headed 'Special Liability of Seller of Product for Physical Harm to User or Consumer', the paragraph declares:

> One who sells any product in a defective condition unreasonably dangerous to the user or consumer or to his property is subject to liability for physical harm thereby caused to the ultimate user or consumer, if (a) the seller is engaged in the business of selling such a product, and (b) it is expected to and does reach the user or consumer without substantial change in the condition in which it is sold. The rule . . . applies *although (a) the seller has exercised all possible care* in the preparation and sale of his product *and (b) the user or consumer has not bought the product from or entered into any contractual relation with the seller.* (author's italics).

This legally implied duty upon the supplier is supplemented by para 402B which effectively holds him to any express warranty he may have given as to the fitness of his goods, whether to his buyer or the world at large.

> One engaged in the business of selling chattels who, by advertising, labels, or otherwise makes to the public a misrepresentation of a material fact concerning the character or quality of a chattel sold by him is subject to liability for physical harm to a consumer of the chattel caused by justifiable reliance upon the misrepresentation, even though (a) it is not made fraudulently or negligently, and (b) the con-

sumer has not bought the chattel from or entered into any contractual relation with the seller . . .

The practical effect of these rules is that strict contractual standards apply in non-contractual contexts, making negligence almost completely irrelevant. This assertion must be qualified in one or two respects, notably as regards drugs (see below), but otherwise the plaintiff in America need prove only that the goods were not reasonably safe, ie that they fell below the normal expectation of their performance. 'The test for determining when a product has an unreasonably dangerous defect is whether a reasonable person would be negligent if he sold the product knowing of the risk involved': *Bacceleri v Hipter*, 1979. Once an unexpected and unnecessary danger is shown the seller or manufacturer is liable because and in so far as he has not taken the precautions necessary to avoid it. What he knew or ought to have known about the likelihood or otherwise of risk 'is of no moment': *Jackson v Coast Paint Co*, 1974.

Thus in *Elmore v American Motors*, 1969, a case involving a car crash thought to have been caused either by loose fastenings on the driving shaft or by metal fatigue, the court made no attempt to find which if either explanation was correct but stated simply that those 'engaged in the business of distributing automobiles to the public (are) strictly liable in tort for personal injuries caused by defects in cars sold by (them)', and so held both manufacturer and retailer liable. English courts in contrast seem firmly to have decided that it is no part of their duty to speculate as to the cause of an injury and that unless the *res ipsa loquitur* rule (see p. 92) applies the plaintiff's claim must be rejected if he cannot prove how his accident happened: *Sumner v Henderson*, 1963. Certainly one might suppose that English judges would have reached a different decision in *Elmore*, where one explanation for the crash, loose fastenings, was consistent with negligence, and the other, metal fatigue, probably not so.

Similarly in *Goodrich v Hammond*, 1959, manufacturers of 'blow-out proof' tyres were held liable without the plaintiff having to prove how or why the tyre burst. The manufacturer was also held responsible in *Henningsen v Bloomfield Motors*, 1960, where a new vehicle suddenly ran off the road and was so badly damaged that it was impossible to discover why it had done so. This kind of difficulty may often arise in serious accidents, but American courts are sometimes willing to say that the explanation must be that 'something was wrong', which in turn could only be the producer's fault: *Scanlon v General Motors*, 1974.

Just as proof of negligence is unnecessary for the purposes of para 402A, so proof of any contractual connection is unnecessary under para 402B in order to give substance to a manufacturer's warranty at least where physical injury is involved. Examples include *Klages v General Ordnance Equipment*, 1976 – manufacturer advertised a mace weapon as causing 'instantaneous incapacitation' of any attacker and was found liable when it failed; and *Crocker v Winthrop Laboratories*, 1974 – manufacturer was found liable for injury caused by drug incorrectly advertised as non-addictive and harmless. From the consumer's point of view this provision compares very favourably with the fundamental uncertainty in English law over the enforceability of manufacturers' guarantees, as discussed in chapter 2 and illustrated in *Lambert v Lewis*, 1980 (p. 30).

But while product liability is strict, it is not absolute. It is not, in other words, and contrary to popular belief, a system imposing liability for any kind of accident however caused. Few if any goods are or could ever be completely safe and the law does not expect them to be. A plaintiff who ordered a meal of fish chowder, for example, could not complain of finding a fishbone there, even though it stuck in her throat: *Webster v Blue Ship*, 1964. In *Scholler v Wilson Certified Foods*, 1977, the American court reached the same conclusion as to the inherent danger of raw pork as in the English case of *Heil v Hedges*, 1951 (p. 59); and *Harris v Northwest Natural Gas*, 1979, a case on gas hazards, was virtually identical with *Pearson v NW Gas Board*, 1968 (p. 104). Innumerable injured users in America have gone and will continue to go uncompensated despite the new system. Claims are often lost because of the user's comparative, or as we would say, contributory negligence – ie because he has voluntarily and unreasonably proceeded to encounter a known danger. It has been argued that since product liability arises independently of negligence it is logically difficult to reduce liability by reference to the user's conduct, but most jurisdictions accept the concept. Generally also American courts have rejected the view that if and insofar as a defect is apparent, a user injured thereby must have only himself to blame, though of course comparative negligence may have a part to play here. Reference was made in chapter 6 to the contrasting approaches of US and English law over the obvious dangers of motor mowers: *Wright v Massey Harris*, 1966; *Crow v Barford*, 1963. A user's failure to seek out or guard against hidden dangers is not an acceptable defence: *Melia v Ford Motors*, 1976.

Misuse as such is a related problem. A car manufacturer will not be blamed because his product, otherwise reasonably safe, is driven at excessive speed, nor if a tyre comes off after an exceptional impact: *Schemel v General Motors*, 1967; *Heaton v Ford Motors*, 1967. Producers of alcohol and tobacco have not yet been held reponsible for the damage their products do when used incautiously: *Lartigue v Reynolds Tobacco*, 1963.

Again, a product might be reasonably safe when made but become less so through wear and tear or through the development of higher safety standards. If the court decides that an accident can be explained on one or other of these grounds the injured user's claim will fail. To the extent that a court accepts a product as safe because manufactured in accordance with the best known standards at the time it clearly accepts also a 'state of the art' defence, contrary to the basic principles of strict liability. This fundamental question remains unresolved. Recent examples include *McCants v Salameh*, 1980, where the issue was decided by reference to standards prevailing at the time of manufacture, and *Beshada v Johns*, 1982, where this same yardstick was rejected.

As regards wear and tear, no blame was attached to the manufacturer in *Stuckey v Young*, 1979, for the condition of an 11-year-old truck which had covered nearly 200,000 miles, been modified by subsequent owners and was overloaded at the time of the accident. But in *Pryor v Lee Moore*, 1958, a drilling rig which collapsed after 15 years' service was found to have done so because of a defect in the original welding, and the suppliers were accordingly held liable. In theory English law should be capable of following the same lines of inquiry, but in practice it has been argued that the passage of time alone was sufficient to preclude any further investigation: *Evans v Triplex*, 1936.

Perhaps the single most vexed issue with regard to product liability is the way it might affect the manufacturers of drugs. As to new drugs in particular, the official commentary on para 402A provides a partial exception to the rule by stating that the seller,

> ... with the qualification that (the drugs) are properly prepared and marketed, and proper warning is given where the situation calls for it, is not to be held to strict liability for unfortunate consequences attending their use merely because he has undertaken to supply the public with an apparently useful and desirable product, attended with a known but apparently reasonable risk.

In practice therefore liability in many American drug cases has turned on the adequacy of testing, warnings, and the probability of injury, much in accordance with current English concepts of negligence.

Upon whom then should the burden of strict liability fall? Para 402A refers to 'seller's' liabilities, but the courts say this expression is 'merely descriptive'. In theory at least anyone engaged in the production or distribution of goods may be held responsible for them. In practice of course most claims are made against manufacturers. The choice of defendant rests with the injured party, and seems to depend largely on questions of his 'reasonable availability', proximity, resources and the like: *Vandermark v Ford*, 1964. The courts may also take account of the relative blameworthiness of manufacturer and retailer, but there is as yet no express rule to that effect. The Uniform Product Liability Act however sees strict liability as essentially a manufacturer's burden and holds that in the absence of contract sellers should be liable only for negligence, as under English law.

American courts are concerned to see that somewhere along the line there should be a defendant to answer an injured party's claim. Present freedom of choice has been justified on the grounds that: 'Strict liability on manufacturer and retailer alike affords maximum protection to the injured plaintiff and works no injustice to the defendants for they can adjust the cost of such protection between them in the course of their continuing relationship': *Vandermark*, above. On the same argument a manufacturer may be held liable for injuries caused by defective parts supplied by his sub-contractor, even though the defects could not have been discovered by any reasonable test or inspection by the manufacturer. This conclusion, as illustrated in *Ford v Mathis*, 1963, has been rejected in the UK: *Taylor v Rover*, 1966. A manufacturer who has taken over another business but continues to trade under its good name may also find that he has inherited its liabilities, unless the period of time between production and injury is such as to absolve him: *Ray v Alad*, 1977 – disapproved in *Bernard v Kee*, 1982.

Another principle of American case law without parallel in England is that of 'market share liability' – devised to meet the hardship of plaintiffs unable to identify the producers responsible for their injuries, eg because they were injured in the womb by drugs taken by their mothers to avoid miscarriages. The Supreme Court of California permitted such a plaintiff in *Sindell v Abbott*, 1980, to sue a group of independent drug manufacturers who between them controlled most of the relevant market. Each producer then had to pay a part of the award equivalent to his market share unless he could prove he had not made the drug which caused the injury. In *Sheffield v Ely Lilley*, 1983, it was held that this doctrine, which perhaps unduly favours those who cannot identify defendants against those who can, applied only to inherently defective drugs and not those negligently manufactured, and only where passage of time made identification impossible.

Strict liability may extend beyond goods to services and land, as in *Schipper v Levitt*, 1965, where a mass developer of houses was held strictly liable for defective workmanship. The court said: 'An entrepreneur in the mass housing business should be subject to the same legal responsibility as a manufacturer or supplier of chattels.' It has subsequently been held that there is no significant difference between a builder developer and a builder contractor: *Moxley v Laramie Builders*, 1980.

But other professional services may be treated differently. There is no mass production of goods nor usually any great difficulty in tracing a defendant: *La Rossa v Scientific Design*, 1968. Medical services in particular have largely escaped strict liability, as for example in *Magrine v Spector*, 1970.

A further most important possibility under the American system is that of ordering compensation for purely economic loss. The references in para 402A to 'personal injury' and 'physical harm', including under para 402A damage to property, suggest of course that economic losses as such are not compensatable in this way. That is certainly the general rule of English law, subject to the recent limited exception recognised by the House of Lords in *Junior Books v Veitchi* (see chapter 5). There are however one or two American cases where 'physical harm' has been interpreted to include loss of use of property, without any prerequisite of harm to the person. On this basis courts have held manufacturers liable for the cost of replacing or repairing defective or useless parts. The most important case is that of *Santor v Karagheusian*, 1965. Here the problem concerned a carpet sold in accordance with the manufacturer's representation as grade 1 but which through the manufacturing process had developed a fault making it worth considerably less. The retailer refused to put the matter right, and eventually went out of business in that State. The buyer then sued the manufacturer. The judge could have reached his decision in the buyer's favour by reference to the warranty rule in para 402B, above, but chose instead to rely on the non-contractual elements of strict liability.

> From the standpoint of principle we perceive no sound reason why the implication of reasonable fitness should be ... actionable against the manufacturer where the defectively made product has caused personal injury, and not actionable when inadequate manufacture has put a worthless article in the hands of an innocent purchaser who has paid the required price for it .... If the article is defective and the defect is chargeable to the manufacturer, his must be the responsibility for the consequent damage or injury.

The damages were assessed at the difference between the retail price and actual value of the carpet, ie the loss of a bargain.

There are many decisions contrary to *Santor* and it still remains to be seen which view will prevail. The proposed Uniform Product Liability Act rejects pure economic loss as a basis for compensation. One might predict nonetheless that the distinctions between economic and physical injuries will be eroded eventually, if only because they depend on the divisions between contract and tort which are themselves undermined by product liability.

Subject to the rules we have outlined, anyone injured by a defect can sue. The plaintiff need not be the owner of the goods. He may be the user, or someone injured by goods in the hands of the user. So for example passers-by injured by vehicles with defective brakes will be protected: *Kuschy v Norris*, 1964. On general duty of care principles English law would presumably give the same extended meaning to 'user' or 'consumer': *Lambert v Lewis* (p. 110).

We observe finally that although producers' liabilities under the new law are partly contractual in origin they cannot be excluded by agreement. The commentary on para 402A prohibits any exclusion or limitation of liability by contract or notice, emphasising that whatever the warranty theories used to justify its development product liability is now essentially tort based.

The combined effect of all these rules and their somewhat unpredictable operation has undoubtedly caused great alarm among American manufacturers. There has been greatly increased expenditure, partly on safety and substantially on insurance and legal fees. The resulting increase in the cost of goods represents a mixed blessing for consumers. The Uniform Product Liability Act put forward in 1983 is an attempt to tackle the difficulties by confining strict liability to cases of non-conformity of goods with manufacturers' own specifications and to breach of express warranty. For other purposes it would reinstate the test of negligence and give a development risk defence. Yet these dramatic changes would not affect at all those aspects of American legal procedure which most clearly and unnecessarily aggravate the complexity and cost of the law, as discussed in chapter 8. We cannot predict the progress of this measure but it must at least be said that if passed it would put the clock back 40 years or more so far as consumer protection is concerned and leave American law well behind certain Continental legal systems, neither of which seem likely events.

In the meantime we must recognise that product liability standards adopted in America pose very real difficulties also for British companies trading there. Insurance cover may be extremely expensive, but is for all practical purposes essential. Its availability and cost depends very largely on proof of technical proficiency and overt concern for consumers' safety. Particular thought should be given to provision of comprehensive instructions for use and warnings against misuse. Advertisements should be factual and not make exaggerated safety claims. Records of research should be kept available.

IRELAND

Turning now to the state of play in Common Market countries other than Britain we begin with Ireland, a country sharing all our own legal traditions but with significantly different rules introduced by the Sale of Goods and Supply of Services Act 1980. The Act's main product liability provisions are as follows. First, in much the same terms as in Britain's Sale of Goods Act 1979 retailers are prevented from excluding liability for defective goods. Second (and unlike the UK Act) s.10 extends the requirement of merchantable quality to include durability. Section 12 seeks to meet the very real grievance that products become worthless if replacement parts are not available or servicing facilities inadequate or non-existent. The new rule provides an implied warranty that spare parts and an adequate after-sales service will be available from the seller for any advertised time or for a reasonable time. The Ministry of Industry, Commerce and Tourism may make orders defining reasonable times for particular classes of goods. Any attempt to exclude the warranty is void.

Next, s.13 declares that in contracts of sale of motor vehicles there is an implied condition that at the time of delivery the vehicle is free from defects endangering the public or anyone in the vehicle. Certain limited exceptions are allowed. Unless the exceptions apply and the implied condition of roadworthiness is excluded, a dealer must give the buyer a certificate stating that the vehicle is free of dangerous defects when delivered. If no certificate is given, it will be presumed that any alleged defect existed at the time of delivery. The section also entitles anyone using the motor vehicle with the owner's consent to sue the seller for breach of the implied condition 'as if he were the buyer' – thus avoiding the anomalies which otherwise arise as between the seller's strict contractual duties to his buyer and his liability only in negligence to anyone else in the car who might be injured through the same defect.

Under s.17 a seller who delivers a manufacturer's guarantee to a buyer is liable for the observance of its terms *as if he were himself the guarantor*, unless he tells the buyer he is not so liable, or gives his own guarantee. Guarantees must not exclude or limit buyers' legal rights and any provisions imposing additional obligations on buyers or making the guarantor or his agent sole judge of the buyer's rights are void. Conversely, s.19 provides that the buyer:

> may maintain an action against a manufacturer or other supplier who fails to observe any of the terms of the guarantee *as if that manufacturer or supplier had sold the goods to the buyer* and had committed a breach of warranty; and the court may order the manufacturer or supplier to take such action as may be necessary to observe the terms of the guarantee or to pay damages to the buyer .... 'Buyer' includes all persons who acquire title to the goods within the duration of the guarantee. (author's italics)

This new rule is particularly valuable in resolving the vexed question of whether or when manufacturers' guarantees are enforceable, which again can only be done by overriding the doctrine of privity of contract. To sum up, therefore, the disparate principles of contract and tort remain the basis of consumers' remedies in Ireland as in the UK, but the 1980 Act makes significant exceptions to these principles.

FRANCE, BELGIUM, LUXEMBOURG

The relevant provisions of French law, adopted also in Belgium and Luxembourg, are particularly noteworthy because they reveal a greater degree of unification of contract and tort principles than has been achieved in other European countries. Considering first the rules of sales law we find in Articles 1625 and 1641 of the Civil Code implied guarantees of the fitness of goods, similar in terms to those of s.14 of the UK Sale of Goods Act. Under Article 1641 the seller is liable for hidden defects in the thing sold which make it unfit for its intended use or which reduce its usefulness to such an extent that the buyer would not have bought it, or would have paid a lower price, had he known of them. The onus is on the buyer to prove that the fault in question existed at the time of sale. Conversely, the seller is not liable for faults which subsequently appear unless it can be argued that they were inherent in the goods. The buyer has only a 'short time' within which to bring his claim, a possibly detrimental restriction. As in Britain sellers' liabilities to buyers cover both economic loss and physical injury resulting from breach of contract.

In theory the seller's strict liability is then offset by the rule that the amount of damages he must pay to the injured buyer varies according to his blameworthiness. If the seller acts in good faith and sells goods unaware of any fault in them, he is liable only to refund the price and reimburse the buyer for any necessary expense he may have incurred: Article 1646. But if he knows of the fault, Article 1645 obliges him to compensate the buyer for all resulting losses. Since 1965, however, French courts have avoided the barren inquiries and arbitrary results which would otherwise arise by deciding that professional sellers are irrefutably deemed to know of the faults in their goods. Bearing in mind also that the use of exclusion clauses is stringently controlled, we can say that in France, much as in Britain, the business seller is subject to an inescapable obligation to provide goods free from faults creating hidden dangers for buyers. In Belgium and Luxembourg, on the other hand, the seller's liability is not quite so strict. He may escape blame if he can show that whatever precautions he might have taken he could not have discovered the defect. All three countries recognise the defence of improper use by the purchaser.

More remarkable from the English point of view, however, is the willingness of the judges in these countries to extend the seller's liability beyond narrow contractual bounds. Courts there have observed the futility and expense of chain actions begun by the ultimate purchaser against the retailer and ending with imposition of liability on the manufacturer. To avoid it they have granted the purchaser at any point in the chain the right to take action directly against either manufacturer or subsequent distributor. The manufacturer has the same duty to the ultimate purchaser as to his immediate purchaser. This so called 'direct action' is obviously useful in giving buyers an alternative claim to overcome problems of sellers becoming insolvent or going out of business.

Beneficial though this type of action may be it still does not completely overcome the contract/tort division. It helps only those who are purchasers, and not their spouses, children, employees or neighbours, nor, it seems, those injured by goods acquired otherwise than under contracts of sale. All these cases must be resolved by reference to liability in tort.

Tort liability in France, Belgium and Luxembourg turns on the application of two very broad principles. Articles 1382 and 1383 of the Civil Code state that every act or omission which causes damage to another must be paid for by the person whose fault it was. Article 1384 states that one is responsible also for the damage caused by persons for whom one is answerable and by things under one's control.

An injured user who has to prove fault against a producer is normally, as we have said, in a more difficult position than an injured buyer suing the seller for breach of warranty. But here again the French courts have done a great deal to help the consumer. Regarding it as irrational to distinguish between contracting and non-contracting parties they have held that the requirement of fault in Article 1382 is fulfilled merely by the *delivery* of a defective, that is, unnecessarily dangerous, product. No other act of negligence need be established. No distinction is drawn between faults inherent in the product, inadequate testing, deceptive packaging or failure to advise of dangers. A presumption of liability thus arises, similar in effect to the English *res ipsa* rule (see p. 92). But whereas in England reversal of the burden of proof, on the rare occasions it is allowed, still does not prevent the producer from proving he has taken reasonable care, the only defences open to him in France are that the defect was caused by a stranger or by Act of God (ie an altogether extraordinary and unpredictable event).

Article 1384 establishes the equally important principle of employers' vicarious liability for defective workmanship by employees. It also imposes strict liability on a 'guardian' for things under his control. This is a complicated area of law, extending somewhat beyond the usual questions of product liability. The owner is usually the 'guardian', but that may mean that the innocent consumer becomes liable when his purchase causes injury. In this event he can of course seek indemnity from the seller. Conversely, the manufacturer ceases to be guardian once he puts goods in circulation, unless it can be argued that in cases of defective design or production he was and remains *guardien de la structure* – responsible for construction. More probably, however, the rule will initially at least impose liability upon the person physically in control at the time of the accident. The same defences of acts of strangers or of God are open to him.

The combined effect of these various rules is that in France the traditional distinction between tortious and contractual responsibilities has lost much of its importance so far as consumers are concerned. There has been an assimilation of remedies which should give the French consumer much the same protection as that contemplated for all Common Market countries by the draft EEC Directive (see chapter 8). In Belgium and Luxembourg the position is similar if not identical. Theoretically at least manufacturers' liability there is still regarded as based on fault, but in practice the results seem indistinguishable.

HOLLAND

The Dutch legal system is largely derived from the French but the day-to-day solutions to consumers' problems given by the courts are markedly different. Article 1540 of the Civil Code lays the usual obligation on the seller to ensure that his goods are free from hidden faults, but since this rule has been held to apply only to specific goods, it is of no importance in product liability issues which essentially involve generic goods. The more general breach of contract rules in Articles 1279 and those following could cover such cases, but sellers can escape liability by proving absence of fault. Contrary to French and British rulings they are not presumed to know of the defects, not even as professional sellers. The courts have not relaxed privity of contract requirements as they have in France, but Articles 7.1.3.7/9 of the draft Consumer Sales Bill would allow a direct action on the French model by the ultimate buyer against the producer. Exclusion clauses are subject to (partial) regulation by the courts, but legislation is proposed.

In Article 1401, the Dutch Civil Code repeats the general principle of liability for unlawful harm caused by fault stated in Article 1382 of the French Code. The Supreme Court explained what was meant by 'unlawful harm' in *Cohen v Lindenbaum*, 1919. Unlawful acts are those (i) in breach of statute; (ii) infringing others' legal rights; (iii) against good morals; or (iv) in breach of the proper standard of care owed to other people or their property. The fourth element expresses the duty of care concept familiar to English lawyers and is effectively the basis of tortious liability in the Netherlands. In a case in 1973 concerning a leaking hot water bottle, the Supreme Court held that a manufacturer was liable for a foreseeable danger created by a hidden defect in his product unless he could prove absence of fault. The Court further decided that he could not discharge this reversed burden of proof merely by showing that practically speaking it was impossible for him to test every single component part. Liability thus becomes almost unavoidable once it is established that injury is a foreseeable result of a certain defect, but there may still be a problem of proving what actually caused the injury. We should also note that under Article 1403 (the equivalent of Article 1384 of the French Code) Dutch law does not impose liability upon 'guardians' of goods, but does hold manufacturers vicariously liable for the negligence of their employees.

ITALY

The Italian legal system, though likewise substantially the same as the French, again provides different answers. Article 1494 of the Italian Code gives the buyer a claim against a seller of defective products if the seller knew or could have known of the defects. As in the Netherlands, knowledge of faults is not imputed to the business seller, so that where, as is commonly the case, the goods are prepacked the buyer's contractual rights are very limited. It seems that Italian law is reluctant to imply general warranties of fitness of goods and that it still acquiesces in the widespread use of exclusion clauses.

With regard to liability in tort the main articles applicable are Articles 2043, 2049, 2050 and 2051. The first holds liable in damages anyone whose fraud, malice or negligence causes unjustified injury to another person. Manufacturers' liability is therefore based firmly on the concept of fault, but subject to the major reservations implicit in the next two provisions.

Article 2049 imposes vicarious liability on employers for their employees' negligence, and Article 2050 states that anyone who injures another in the conduct of an activity dangerous by its nature or because of the means employed is liable unless he can prove he has taken all reasonable care. Following an important decision of the Appeal Court in 1964, Italian courts have tended to apply this reversed burden of proof wherever any kind of product has caused an injury unforeseeable by the consumer. Finally Article 2051 imposes strict liability upon the custodian of goods, as under Article 1384 of the French Code, but this rule does not seem to have much if any impact on product liability in general.

GERMANY

In Germany the rules of contract law play very little part in protecting the consumer against the consequences of product injury. As in other countries the seller is required by law to warrant the absence of hidden defects – Article 459 of the Bürgerliche Gesetzbuch or Civil Code – but in Germany the remedies for breach of warranty are primarily return or reduction of price. Damages can be claimed only if the seller has fraudulently concealed the weakness (Articles 463 and 480) and German courts make no presumptions of fault or knowledge against sellers, professional or otherwise. Claims for damages may also be made under Articles 463 and 480 which are simply for non-performance and so do not require proof of fault. But difficulties then arise in saying what, if any, warranties of fitness there are and whether delivery in breach of warranty constitutes non-performance. It seems overall that these are matters essentially affecting commercial parties' economic losses and not consumers' injuries.

Until relatively recently the scope of German tort law was also somewhat obscure. It was suggested that the same liability should be imposed on manufacturers as on public utilities and railways (and now drug manufacturers) by strict liability statutes, or by quasi-contractual principles like that of the French direct action, or by means of a doctrine of consumer reliance on manufacturers' representations, a theory perhaps derived from American product liability law. These solutions were decisively rejected and rules of tortious liability reasserted in the famous 'fowlpest case' of 1968, where the Federal Supreme Court had to decide upon a vaccine manufacturer's liability for the death of livestock.

The court based its decision on the fundamental rule of tortious liability laid down in Article 823, para 1, of the BGB: 'A person who contrary to law intentionally or negligently injures the life, body, health, freedom, property or other right of another is bound to compensate him for any damage therefrom.' The rule clearly makes fault a prerequisite of liability. The importance of the fowlpest case was in the court's recognition that consumers could not usually prove the precise source of harm and in its holding that accordingly it was for manufacturers to rebut claims by disproving negligence. The burden of disproving liability applies also under Article 823, para 2, which concerns claims for damages arising out of breach of statutory duty. The fact that a product has caused death or injury thus tends to prove some design or organisational failure, which the manufacturer will usually be unable to deny. Indeed subsequent cases have led Hans Micklitz, a German legal writer, to the conclusion that for defective designs and instructions 'the manufacturer is liable without any possibility of exculpation'.

From the consumer's point of view that may seem an eminently satisfactory conclusion, but it is one which overlooks the significance of Article 831. This Article states:

A person who employs another to do any work is bound to compensate for any damage which the other unlawfully causes to a third party in the performance of this work. The duty to compensate does not arise if the employer has exercised ordinary care in the selection of the employee, and, where he has to supply appliances or implements or to superintend work, has also exercised ordinary care as regards such supply or supervision, or if the damage would have arisen notwithstanding the exercise of such care.

It will be seen that in pursuing the idea of personal fault the BGB logically concludes that the rules of vicarious liability as understood in every other EEC country have no application in Germany. This much-criticised provision creates many difficulties both for consumers and for the courts in their attempts to avoid injustice. A new version was proposed in 1967 by the Federal Ministry of Justice to bring German law into line with international practice.

German lawyers have sought to meet these difficulties by devoting much time and effort to the classification of product injuries, as between defective design, defective production, defective instruction and development defect. A 'duty to watch' has also been identified, requiring the manufacturer to keep an eye on the performance of his goods after sale. In English law these are all aspects of the same duty of care, but in German law there is an important practical distinction with regard to defective *production*. When something goes wrong on the production line, so that goods which are otherwise safely designed and normally safely constructed become dangerous in this one case, the fault must normally be that of the worker in charge of the operation. It follows from Article 831 that if blame for a dangerous 'escaper' rests upon an employee the manufacturer himself cannot be liable. In accordance with the ruling in the fowlpest case, however, the onus is on the manufacturer to prove that such was indeed the cause of the accident.

Contrary to French law but in accordance with recent common law developments, German law now allows accident victims with contractual claims to claim alternatively in tort. The French courts' refusal to allow alternative claims is, as we have seen, relatively unimportant because of the breadth of the substantive legal remedies.

GREECE

Greek commercial law is based largely on the German Code. Under Articles 534, 550 and following the Greek Civil Code buyers of generic goods which prove defective may return them to their sellers and recover the purchase price. The same rule applies to goods made to order. A seller is only liable to his buyer in damages if the goods cause injury and he knew or ought to have known of the danger. An injured party suing a manufacturer must likewise prove fault against him, but fault includes liability for employees' negligence on the production line: Article 914 and following.

DENMARK

We turn finally to the law of Denmark, representative of the distinctive Scandinavian systems. While Danish contract law does not seek to compensate for personal injury recent consumer sales legislation is still of considerable interest. Continental systems generally seem much more anxious to give the disappointed buyer what he wanted from his bargain than does the British, which at the moment merely offers repudiation or litigation, that is, a claim for damages. These remedies are of course available in Denmark, but under ss. 78 to 80 of the Danish Sale of Goods Act 1906, as amended by the Consumer Sales Act 1979, a buyer of generic goods may alternatively demand delivery of other goods in conformity with the contract, or require the seller to cure the defect unless this would cause the seller disproportionate cost or significant inconvenience.

The right to have faults corrected is available in all cases unless unreasonable expense or difficulty is involved, which it is for the seller to prove. Defects must be cured without cost to the buyer. If repairs are not done within a reasonable time, the buyer may cancel the contract, even though the fault in question is trivial. Alternatively, a buyer of generic goods may demand their return and have the fault cured by someone else at the seller's expense, again within the bounds of what is reasonable in the circumstances. Where the seller has substantially cured or seems to have cured the faults but further difficulties occur the buyer may have to give the seller another opportunity to repair the goods, but he need not endure 'repeated unsuccessful attempts to repair which cause him significant inconvenience'. These remedies cannot be excluded, but must be exercised promptly and in any event within one year of purchase. It will be recalled from chapter 3 that the Law Commission has suggested that similar rights be provided under the UK Sale of Goods Act.

It seems that Danish contract law also takes a rather more flexible view of contractual relations than the English system. A manufacturer may be under quasi-contractual duties to give accurate or more complete information about his products, or otherwise avoid causing consumers unreasonable risk of loss. Breach of such a 'social contract' may result in liability to the ultimate purchaser.

Liability in tort is firmly based on the fault principle, an area of judge-made law developed and applied much as in Britain. Thus no compensation is given for 'development damage', injury caused by dangers which were unknown when the goods were produced, nor conversely for 'system damage', where the risk is known but is either infinitesimal or unavoidable, as, for example, with cigarettes. There is an interesting contrast with German practice in the Danish treatment of goods made dangerous by bad workmanship. The courts say that goods which are otherwise safely designed could only be flawed in this way if management's quality control procedures had failed. The result is an irrebuttable presumption of negligence.

But perhaps the most important contribution of Danish law in this context is in its application of vicarious liability. This concept is extended well beyond the bounds familiar to English lawyers, as described in chapter 6. Danish courts hold each succeeding party in the chain of production and supply vicariously liable for the acts of those previously involved. A business may even be held liable for faults committed subsequently, as where a manufacturer requires his retail outlets to undertake inspection or testing of his goods, and the job is done badly. A person injured by defectively designed goods may therefore sue seller or manufacturer, or both. This principle overcomes problems arising when manufacturers go out of business or are based abroad. In the words of Professor Dahl, a Danish writer:

> The wish to ensure the consumer compensation calls for a rule on vicarious liability according to which the middleman is jointly and severally liable for the manufacturer's faults. Since the middleman has a claim for indemnity against the manufacturer, the burden of liability will not be too heavy to be borne even by the 'little' middleman.

SUMMARY

As we look across Europe we see unmistakably moves towards the strict liability characteristic of American law, but overall a range of solutions as varied as the countries themselves, some conspicuously more progressive than others. Even omitting the whole vexed question of interstate accidents and resulting conflicts of law it is clear that injured consumers' claims depend essentially on chance combinations of time and place. Was the victim buyer or user of the product? Is the seller subject to strict or qualified liability? Has the buyer a direct action against the manufacturer? Has he the advantage of a reversed burden of proof? Was injury caused by design flaw or production line negligence? Was manufacturer or sub-contractor at fault? Depending on the fortuitous answers to these questions so consumers' rights and manufacturers' liabilities vary dramatically from one country to the next. The variables become still more marked and still less defensible when we observe that injuries in different countries may be caused by one and the same product, internationally distributed. In the next chapter we consider European and domestic proposals for reform.

8 Law Reform

We begin this crucial chapter by briefly restating the basic principles of English law. If the person injured by defective goods is the buyer he can sue the seller. He need only prove the goods were not reasonably fit and that he suffered physical injury or economic loss as a result. In some circumstances the fact of injury may suffice to prove his point. The question of fault or otherwise on the seller's part is irrelevant. As a rule the seller is both accessible and responsive to such claims. But if the seller goes out of business or has not the resources to meet a large claim, or if the injured party is not the buyer, then the legal position changes completely.

In the absence of any contractual relationship an injured party has no redress unless he can prove that someone has been negligent. In the context of prepacked goods that usually means a claim against the manufacturer. Injury alone does not prove negligence. The plaintiff must prove that the manufacturer failed to take the normal or other appropriate precautions. He has immediately no means of knowing what precautions are or are not normal in a particular industry nor whether the manufacturer took the precautions he should have taken. If he did he escapes liability, however serious the accident might be, unless it was his employee's fault the product was defective.

The burden of proof is substantial at the best of times and if goods are manufactured abroad the practical obstacles are all but insuperable. Many people might therefore suffer pain and poverty through no fault of their own and yet have no redress against the manufacturer or supplier whose product caused their injury.

This state of affairs has been tolerated for many years, largely because the injured have no sufficient voice or vote, but within the last decade or so it has become a matter of general public concern. The mainspring was the international Thalidomide tragedy, with all that was suddenly seen to be involved in terms of human suffering on the one hand and legal obstruction on the other. There were other causes also, notably the pressures of American law reform and inequality of trading conditions as between member states in the Common Market.

THE STRASBOURG CONVENTION AND EEC DRAFT DIRECTIVE

In 1970 the Council of Europe, representing the UK and 17 other countries, appointed a committee of experts to propose means of harmonising the product liability laws of member states. At about the same time the Commission of the European Communities began work on a Directive which would have the same effect as between the Common Market countries. In due course the Council produced what is now known as the Strasbourg Convention, while the Commission published a draft Directive, revised in 1979. They are set out in appendices 4 and 5 of this book. Britain signed the Convention in 1977, but is not thereby obliged to give effect to it at any particular time. Conflicting national and commercial interests have deadlocked further discussion of the Directive. Perhaps it will take another major tragedy to bring about progress.

Both Convention and draft Directive are agreed upon the basic direction of reform, while differing on significant points of detail. The reform is fundamental and far-reaching, but can be very shortly stated. It is that *producers of goods which are not reasonably safe shall be strictly liable for personal injury caused thereby*: Article 3(i) of the Convention and Article 1 of the draft Directive. The need to prove negligence in non-contractual claims (see chapters 5 and 6) is ended accordingly. To put the point another way, it is proposed that the liability of manufacturer to user should be the same as that which now applies as between seller and buyer (see chapter 3). What is new therefore is not by any means the concept of strict liability itself, a familiar feature of sales law for many years, but the context in which it will apply.

As we said in chapter 3, strict liability is not absolute liability. It is not proposed that manufacturers should be held to blame for any and every injury directly or indirectly caused by their products. Both Convention and Directive recognise certain defences, notably that the producer did not put the goods into circulation himself, or that they were reasonably safe when he did so, or that they were not produced for business purposes: Article 5 of each agreement. Both agreements exclude primary agricultural produce and the Directive excludes craft and artistic products. But neither agreement provides a 'development risk' defence, ie that there should be no liability because injury was caused in circumstances such that the state of scientific knowledge did not enable the producer either to foresee or guard against it. We return to this vexed issue below.

A particularly important question is whether or to what extent a manufacturer should be liable for harm done by defective component parts supplied by a sub-contractor. Should an aircraft manufacturer be liable if an aeroplane crashes because an altimeter supplied by an independent contractor is faulty? The interests of justice are not easy to reconcile here, but they would not be served at all if the contractor alone were liable since he would not have the resources to meet the huge resulting claims, nor would he be able to insure himself against such calamities. The scale of the aircraft manufacturer's business on the other hand would enable him to effect insurance.

In chapter 6 we noted the inadequacy of English law's answer to this question. The Convention and Directive agree that the just solution is to hold both manufacturer and component supplier liable, each for the whole sum of damages, and each able to recover from the other in accordance with the degree of fault established between them and the availability of funds. We have seen that this is the pattern already adopted in America.

We have used the terms 'manufacturer' and 'producer' interchangeably. In certain cases, however, someone may be held liable under these European proposals as the 'producer' of goods even though he is not the manufacturer of them. If the manufacturer cannot be identified each subsequent supplier of the goods will be liable as producer unless and until he discloses the name of his supplier to the injured party. A person may also be liable as producer if he markets the goods as his own or if he imports them into the Common Market.

Claims must be brought within three years of injury. The right to compensation is lost if the claim is not made within 10 years from the date when the producer put the defective product into circulation. In theory there might still be a claim for negligence after that time if so provided by the relevant local law.

The major distinction then between the Convention and the Directive is that the latter restricts the total liability of a producer for all personal injuries caused by identical articles having the same defect to 25 million European Units of Account (approximately £12m), whereas liability under the Convention is unlimited. On the other hand the Directive allows for damage to property, which the Convention does not.

THE PEARSON REPORT

In 1971 the Government invited the English and Scottish Law Commissions to investigate the effects of our own rules on product liability. The Commissions' inquiries were overtaken by the work of the Royal Commission on Civil Liability and Compensation for Personal Injury appointed in 1973 under the chairmanship of Lord Pearson, but in the event were very largely in agreement with the conclusions of the Commission. We shall confine ourselves accordingly to those conclusions.

So far as product liability was concerned the Pearson Report noted the anomalies and uncertainties in existing law and agreed that reform was necessary. Various solutions were considered and discarded, notably a no-fault insurance scheme, abolishing the rule of privity of contract, and reversing the burden of proof. The Report recommended the introduction of strict liability in tort, basically the principle pioneered in America but in a form which would harmonise with the general approach of the Strasbourg Convention and draft Directive (above).

Detailed recommendations in the Report were that 'defect' and 'product' should be defined as under Article 2 of the Convention; producers of finished products and of component parts should both be strictly liable; distributors should also be liable unless they disclosed the producer's identity, as should producers of 'own brands' and importers. Aircraft manufacturers should be entitled to indemnity from users who ignored service instructions. There should be no financial limits on a producer's liability, since they would inevitably be arbitrary and create further injustice. Insurance should not be compulsory. Claims should be brought within three years of injury. Strict liability should end 10 years after the initial circulation of the product. Damages should be given for pain and suffering and damage to property.

As regards the defences open to the producer the Pearson Report endorsed those in the Convention and Directive and added that it should not be a defence for him to show official certification of his product nor merely to prove he had withdrawn or attempted to withdraw the product. It should not be possible to contract out of liability.

The Report considered at length the controversial question whether there should be a 'development risk' or 'state of the art' defence, for the benefit particularly of industries producing exceptionally dangerous and technologically advanced products such as chemicals, drugs, aircraft and motor vehicles.

> It can be argued that to hold the producer liable in such cases would be to impose on him, and, through him, on the product's consumers as a whole, a responsibility for compensating injuries even when it might have been impossible to prevent the defect occurring. It is further argued that this responsibility, and the cost of insuring against the risks involved, might severely deter the development of new products,

particularly those small developments which might lead cumulatively to a major advance; and that this is sufficiently contrary to the interests of consumers themselves to outweigh the case for tort compensation, at least through the medium of strict liability. On the other hand, to exclude developmental risks from a regime of strict liability would be to leave a gap in the compensation cover, through which, for example the victims of another Thalidomide disaster might easily slip.

The Report accordingly recommended that no such defence should be allowed.

Certain other aspects of the Pearson proposals have been acted on, notably by the introduction of the Vaccine Damage Payments Act, imposing upon the state a limited form of strict liability for vaccine injuries. But nothing whatever has been done to fulfil the Report's general recommendations on product liability, nor, correspondingly, to give effect to the Convention or draft Directive.

There has in fact been a great deal of opposition in Britain in particular to any change in the law. The main objection of British industry to the proposed reform is the absence of a 'development risk' or 'state of the art' defence. Industry's argument here is that if a new product causes entirely unforeseeable injury it is unjust to deprive the manufacturer of the defence that he acted in accordance with the highest known standards of care. And as Pearson noted it is said also to be socially undesirable not to have this defence, on the ground that imposition of liability in these circumstances must inhibit research and thus eventually penalise the society which the law seeks to protect.

These contentions have won strong support in Parliament from both sides of the House, in particular from MPs speaking on behalf of the aeronautical and pharmaceutical industries. Indeed in the last debate on the subject in 1981 Mrs Oppenheim, then Minister for Consumer Affairs, went so far as to say: 'In no way would I wish to see any reform which undermines the law of tort in this country. That law is part of the fabric of society depending as it does on the philosophy of duty and personal responsibility.' This patently absurd remark ignores all the lessons of the last hundred years as to the entirely fortuitous and grotesquely unfair operation of the law and the absolution of personal responsibility by insurance, but be that as it may it reflects the British Government's commitment to a development risk defence, which in turn makes Britain a main obstacle to European product liability reform.

The UK Consumers' Association, among others, has strongly condemned the Government's attitude. A development risk defence would of course nullify the whole point and purpose of the proposed reform. The disastrous side effects of drugs were the mainspring of all the proposed reforms, but with a development risk defence the victims of the next tragedy would be no better off than their predecessors. We may observe in passing also that if the objectors have their way British consumers will be considerably worse off than their counterparts in Germany, where drug manufacturers have been subject to a form of strict liability since 1978.

It is far from clear whether those who oppose law reform and insist on development risk defence actually understand the present state of the law. We have observed that the strict liability of seller to buyer is a fundamental and long-established feature of our sales law. That same liability can as we have said be passed back up the line by each party suing his predecessor in the distributive chain until eventually it is imposed upon the manufacturer. The proposed reform imposes no more or less liability on manufacturers, but makes it independent of contract. It thus enables buyers to sue manufacturers directly without having to go first against sellers (who may be insolvent or no longer in business), and so avoids prolonged, expensive and unnecessary litigation as the seller then sues the distributor and the distributor the manufacturer. The reform also of course enables an injured user other than a buyer to sue directly on the same basis; but what rational justification is there for giving a user an entirely different and inferior set of rights?

Some part of industry's objection to reform may well be based on fears arising from American experience of product liability. There have indeed been many stories, some true and some no doubt apocryphal, of awards of damages of millions of dollars imposed on manufacturers in circumstances which seem unfair, sometimes quite grotesquely so. But we can say with every reasonable confidence that this particular aspect of the American experience has little or no relevance to what will happen here if and when the law is changed.

The basic distinctions between American and British civil trial procedures are first that in America the major cases are still tried by juries. Juries are naturally very sympathetically inclined towards injured or mutilated plaintiffs appearing before them to sue 'big business'. They are anxious to ensure that compensation is provided and so may hold manufacturers liable without any great regard for the judge's detailed directions as to the rules of law. They will have no experience of determining the appropriate sum of damages and make awards which are both excessively generous and wildly variable. Awards may in any case be increased by punitive damages representing degrees of fault. The other major factor is that the jury will be aware in particular of the contingent fee system, under which the plaintiff's lawyer agrees to act without payment if the claim is lost but to receive perhaps a quarter or a third of the damages if successful. Awards are increased again accordingly. None of these factors play any part in the administration of justice in this country. Juries are hardly ever used in civil proceedings. The judges adhere rigorously to the rules, and if they find in a plaintiff's favour will award damages within fairly well-defined limits, incomparably more modest than those apparently normal in America, and excluding any punitive element. Finally, we have no contingent fee system. Lawyers' fees are high by British standards, perhaps £1000 a day in a major High Court case, but they are more or less predictable and unaffected by the outcome of the case. It follows that our response to product liability law reform should not be dictated by fear of the consequences we see in America.

When deciding whether or not we agree with the proposed reforms we should recall once more that no product can be completely safe. Many have inherent and serious risks, but they are risks which can be reduced or eliminated by knowledge and careful use. The law's main concern is with injuries caused by hazards which are both unnecessary and hidden. Ultimately the question is: who is to pay for such injuries? Is there any really convincing reason why manufacturers whose goods injure others dependent upon them should not pay for those injuries, directly or indirectly? Is there any evidence that American, French or German pharmaceutical, aeronautical or automobile industries are less innovative than they once were, or conversely some good reason why they should be less concerned with public safety than they now claim to be?

These questions cannot of course be answered in precise quantitative terms, but on industry's behalf we might fairly suppose that a company which found itself unable to obtain or afford insurance cover would probably hesitate to market an untried high-risk product. If that were so then it is difficult to avoid the conclusion that the principles of product liability might well have achieved a substantial public benefit.

We might observe also, perhaps somewhat surprisingly at this stage, that product liability reform is not necessarily the best or only answer to the problem in hand. As and when the law is changed many injuries will still go without redress. Claims against manufacturers will be easier, but useless if they are 'men of straw'. Compensation may still be halved or quartered by contributory negligence, though the injured parties' needs remain the same. The dividing line between strict and absolute liability will remain, as many consumers will find to their cost. Litigation will not stop; on the contrary it may even marginally increase. For most people legal proceedings are an ordeal. Can we not then find a way of helping the injured, not only consumers but the countless thousands of others injured in the normal course of twentieth century life on the roads and at work, without at the same time subjecting them to this expensive, drawn out, distressing and often quite futile experience? Can we not devise a system which is fair also to the manufacturers upon whom our prosperity depends?

THE NEW ZEALAND ALTERNATIVE

Recent remarkable reforms in New Zealand suggest that there is indeed an alternative. Since 1974, under what is now the Accident Compensation Act 1982, all claims for damages for personal injuries in that country have been abolished. In their place is a state insurance system, for all its limitations essentially rational and comprehensive, which is not concerned with fault (except for deliberate self-injury) and asks only whether the claimant was injured by accident and, if so, what continuing loss of earning capacity he or she suffered thereby. After the first week's loss of earnings, which are made up in part by the employer if the accident happened at work, claimants are entitled to immediate payment of up to 80 per cent of lost capacity, within a statutory ceiling of $NZ600 or some £237 per week. Lump sum payments may also be made for non-economic loss, up to about £15,000. The current annual cost of the scheme, which includes medical and hospital expenses, is some $NZ180,000,000, or $NZ60 per head of the population. Administrative costs represent 10 per cent of the total, whereas in Britain for every £100 paid out in damages a further £85 is paid in insurance and legal costs – nearly all of which serves only to put up the cost of living and is wasted in practical terms.

Such a fundamental reform was rejected by the Pearson Report, for reasons which remain open to argument, but in the present writer's view the certainty of a reasonable and immediate insurance provision must be infinitely preferable to the speculative gains and losses of years of litigation and would undoubtedly serve to lower the overall cost of accidents. It might be objected that the New Zealand system removes the incentive to be careful, but that is not so. Insurance premiums can be loaded by way of deterrent, and the criminal law is still there to punish the worst offenders. The crucial point is that in New Zealand guilt or innocence is no longer worked out at the expense of the injured party, as it is in this country. While product liability reform is thus generally to be welcomed for its own sake, we may hope that its greatest significance will be as a step on the way to a much better solution.

INSURANCE

When the Strasbourg Convention or some variant of it is finally adopted there will inevitably be questions of the availability and cost of insurance cover, which would ultimately be borne by the consumer. The Pearson Report found that claims concerning products and services accounted for only about 1 per cent of all insurance claims, but acknowledged that the problem was growing. The Report noted also that while insurance was compulsory for employers and motor vehicle users it was not required by law for product liability purposes. There is, as the Report observed, a significant difference between the comparatively limited nature of the risk facing employers and vehicle owners, and the more unpredictable and occasionally very much greater liability which might arise out of defective products. For this reason insurance companies are willing to provide policies without financial limit for employment and driving purposes, but not for product liability accidents. But if product liability is to become more stringent, will it not then be necessary to compel manufacturers to insure themselves and, correspondingly, to compel insurance companies to accept liabilities thus far found unacceptable?

Although as we have seen the Pearson Commission rejected financial limits upon manufacturers' liabilities it also rejected the idea of compulsory insurance. It was for producer and insurer to agree on their own requirements. The Commission thought that only a small minority of producers would be unable to meet claims, whether through their own resources or by insurance (though even one such would be too many), even under a strict liability regime. But on the other hand the Commission anticipated great problems in enforcing compulsory insurance rules at any reasonable cost in money and manpower. It would be necessary in each individual case to agree on the amount of cover which could reasonably be required.

What then would be the cost of an additional insurance burden which industry would wish to undertake in its own interest as and when product liability principles are adopted? The Confederation of British Industry has put the figure as high as £200 million, but the Pearson Report believed it would be very much lower.

We can do no better than to cite the conclusions of the Report in this respect.

> It is not possible to estimate accurately the costs of our proposals. On the basis of data supplied to us by the British Insurance Association, the number and

current value of tort payments stand at about 1700 and £1.6 m a year, respectively. Much would depend on the extent to which victims and their legal advisers would be encouraged by strict liability to pursue more claims. The experience of other countries, for example France and the USA, does not provide us with a consistent model. A further unknown is whether there might be future disasters of the dimensions of the Thalidomide tragedy. The cost of insurance cover is the more difficult to assess because insurance companies would themselves need to make such predictions, on little evidence at first, producer by producer. Nevertheless, we have *no reason to believe that the total effect of introducing strict liability would be more than a small proportion of product costs as a whole.* We think this a justifiable price for consumers and producers to pay for the benefits which the victims stand to gain by it. (author's italics)

SUMMARY

The call for reform of manufacturers' liabilities was prompted as much as anything by the Thalidomide drug tragedies. The motive was to ensure compensation. Continental European reform proposals are embodied in two documents, the Strasbourg Convention and the EEC draft Directive. British support was given by the Pearson Report and recommendations of the English and Scottish Law Commissions. All agree that the next step must be to make manufacturers liable without proof of fault if their goods are not reasonably safe. This form of liability, strict liability, is the same as that already imposed on business sellers. It is nonetheless rejected by Parliament and industry in this country because it makes no allowance for 'development risks'. A defence of this kind would nullify the reform and defeat in particular the original purpose of ensuring compensation for those injured by new drugs. Fears of unreasonable liability and excessive damages which derive from American practice are unfounded. But in any case a preferable answer would probably be an insurance system like that adopted in New Zealand.

9 Suppliers' Criminal Liabilities

The liabilities of producers of goods and others in the distributive chain examined in previous chapters have all been those of civil law, whose purpose is to compensate the victim rather than punish the wrongdoer. It remains for us now to describe the more specific and often serious areas of wrongdoing punishable by the criminal law.

Criminal law seeks to prevent injury or loss occurring in the first place. A person may therefore be held liable for failing to take precautions even though no one is actually injured. If someone is injured there may also be liability in damages. But what the injured party has to prove in such cases depends on the purpose and wording of the Act of Parliament creating the crime. When unfit food is sold in the course of business, for example, the seller commits a crime under the Food and Drugs Act but that fact alone does not entitle the consumer to compensation. He has to prove a separate civil wrong – breach of contract or negligence — before he can succeed: *Buckley v La Reserve*, 1959. Yet when a worker is injured by his employer's breach of the Factories Act, another criminal statute, the breach is at the same time a civil wrong, entitling him to compensation. There seems no rhyme or reason behind this particular distinction, though the underlying problem is clear enough. Many crimes are of a minor or administrative nature and it might well be very unfair to make someone liable for say £100,000 damages just because he has broken a technical rule punishable by no more than a £50 fine.

Criminal liability is usually strict, which makes a person who commits a crime guilty even though he did not mean to commit it or indeed did everything he could to avoid doing so. This rule is qualified in the more serious crimes by the requirement of a 'guilty mind' or *mens rea*, and in many less serious crimes by defences of accident or exercise of all due diligence, etc. But the position is different again under the Health and Safety at Work Act to which we now turn.

THE HEALTH AND SAFETY AT WORK ACT

This Act is of paramount importance to all industrial suppliers, whether designers, manufacturers, distributors or installers. Section 6, reproduced in appendix 6, obliges suppliers of articles and substances *for use at work* to ensure *so far as is reasonably practicable* that they can be used in safety. This phrase will have a familiar ring for readers of our earlier chapters. Taking precautions 'so far as reasonably practicable' under s.6 involves essentially the same standard of care, 'reasonable care', as that long since laid down by the common law and enforceable by claims for damages.

It follows that s.6 does not create any new duties. Its effect is only to make punishable by the criminal law that which was already a civil wrong. To see what is meant by 'reasonably practicable' therefore we need only turn back to our discussions of likelihood and seriousness of risk, cost of precautions and the like in chapters 5 and 6 and to the day-to-day illustrations given there of the working of the law.

There are nonetheless two significant differences between the criminal and civil versions of the duty of care, apart from the penalties imposed for breach. The Act reverses the burden of proof, so that suppliers must disprove negligence in the event of accident. Secondly the precautions required by s.6 relate to the proper use of products and not, as at common law, to likely misuse as well.

There is then nothing really new about s.6 apart, again, from the possibility of unlimited fines and imprisonment up to two years, but the practical results of expressing the longstanding civil duty in criminal terms are very considerable. The object of the criminal law is as we have said to prevent injury. Section 6 seeks to do that in the industrial context by stopping dangerous machinery and other products getting onto the market in the first place. Health and Safety inspectors are empowered thereby to visit the places where articles and substances for use at work are made and if they do not seem reasonably safe to issue prohibition or improvement notices to stop them being made or to require further precautions. Appeals against such orders are made to industrial tribunals, but breach is punishable in magistrates' courts or in Scotland in the Sheriff Court.

Looking now at the details of s.6 we see it is concerned with the safe design and manufacture of articles and components for use at work in this country, whether new or secondhand. It does not apply to articles used exclusively for consumer purposes, though this is of course a difficult line to draw. Articles intended primarily for consumer use may also be used at work, and in that case s.6 applies. It affects also the liabilities of manufacturers, importers and suppliers of substances to be used at work, exclusively or otherwise. 'Substances' may be natural or artificial, solid or liquid or in gas or vapour form.

The duty of care in relation to these products is explained by reference in particular to their testing and examination, provision of information as to the results of tests and safe use, research to eliminate or reduce risks and safe installation. Responsibility falls equally on designers, manufacturers, importers, suppliers, erectors and installers, on companies and their employees and on individuals in business in so far as the matter is one within the control of the company or person concerned. This proviso limits the liability of those who repair goods or deal in used goods. Employees as such are unlikely to be prosecuted unless they act with wilful disregard for others' safety. If articles or substances are supplied on credit responsibility falls upon the supplier and not the finance house, and if leased, upon the lessor.

Guidance Note GS8 issued by the Health and Safety

Commission in 1977 indicates the appropriate level of precautions.

> Consideration should be given to ensuring, so far as is reasonably practicable, that the best known health and safety practices, techniques and knowledge have been incorporated in the design and manufacture, etc. and that there are adequate margins of safety. This would include such factors as design strength, guarding of dangerous parts, construction of enclosures, provision of safety devices, construction of electrical apparatus for use in potentially explosive atmospheres, double insulation techniques, extraction of dust and fume, etc.

So far as testing and research is concerned there is no need to duplicate that which has already been well established by others, but the decision whether to rely on information provided by someone else remains a matter of personal responsibility. If further testing or research is desirable but beyond a particular manufacturer's resources he might be advised to combine with others to provide appropriate facilities or use those of existing commercial or governmental test centres or laboratories.

The HSC Guidance Note tells us:

> Research might be necessary to discover safe working loads, the safety and reliability of the article in relation to externally applied forces and internal stresses created, for example, during fabrication; the need for built-in safeguards, whether the equipment is adequately earthed, methods for further noise reduction, whether fume given off as the result of a process is adequately dealt with, what the safe maximum cutting/grinding/operating rate is and whether the user should take any specific precautions, etc.

As regards provision of information we may refer again to the Guidance Note for a convenient summary of the issues.

> In deciding how much information should be available designers, manufacturers, importers and

SUPPLIERS' CRIMINAL LIABILITIES

suppliers should aim to strike a balance between the provision of excessive and of inadequate information. Some hazards are common to all articles and need not be spelt out, eg any article may be hazardous if dropped from a sufficient height. On the other hand, it is not sufficient merely to draw the attention of a user to the dangerous nature of the article. Reference should also be made to the specific nature of the hazards, including any noise hazards, and the best means of reducing or removing them. Information should also be available in order that the user may use the supplied article safely. If the information is not sufficient, the health or safety of those using the article may be endangered. Manufacturers, etc, should attempt to present the information clearly and precisely and avoid the provision of excessive information which may lead to the essential facts becoming obscured.

As we said in chapter 6, there is also the possibility that research may reveal new precautions or new hazards, in which case consumers may need to be informed of these facts.

The various references to noise in the Guidance Note reflect ever-growing recognition of this particular hazard. Many claims for damages for deafness caused at work are now being made, and although usually made against employers might equally be made against manufacturers of unnecessarily noisy equipment. Noise limits are specified by law for woodworking machines and agricultural tractors. Otherwise the problem is dealt with only by the general terms of the Health and Safety at Work Act, ie as one to be overcome 'so far as practicable'. The HSE has produced a code of practice envisaging a limit of eight hours' exposure to a noise level not exceeding 90 decibels on average. Use of ear protection should be disregarded in determining a machine's noise level. If machinery inevitably exceeds these limits the manufacturer or supplier must give all requisite information about noise levels and appropriate precautions. Further legislation is contemplated and a new average limit of 85 decibels has been proposed.

Sub-section 8 of s.6 raises an important point of detail. On the face of it it relieves the supplier of liability if his customer promises in writing to take all necessary steps to ensure that the article or substance provided will be safe for use at work. This provision recognises the limits on the supplier's liability to make his products equally safe for all the many different uses to which they may be put. It is doubtful however whether the scope of this defence is as wide as it appears. One might assume that it will not apply unless the supplier has already made the article or substance as safe as he can, otherwise he would be able to opt out of his duty simply by securing his customer's written permission to do so, which would seem to defeat the whole purpose of the Act.

Conversely a customer might make it a condition of purchase that the supplier gives a written undertaking of his own compliance with the Act. That of itself would not affect the supplier's liability (since the question is whether he took the precautions, not whether he said he did), and if and in so far as he has fulfilled his promise that might indicate that any subsequent accident is actually the customer's fault.

The purpose and effect of s.6 and corresponding civil law is to impose personal liability upon anyone taking part in the distribution of articles and substances for use at work without doing whatever is practicable to ensure they are reasonably safe. We have seen above and in chapters 5 and 6 that certain main facets of this duty can be examined and explained. But undeniably its general terms may not provide a ready answer to any particular query as to the safety of a specific product. Manufacturers might well prefer a system under which they could submit their products for prior approval or licensing by some central safety organisation. For better or worse no such system exists in this country, except with regard to drugs (see below). Ultimately only a court or tribunal can say whether a person has fulfilled his duty.

Both manufacturer and court, however, will be helped by Health and Safety Executive guidelines on product safety. As their name indicates the guidelines are not rules or requirements. They are intended only as advice as to the best working practices. In the event of accident a manufacturer or supplier who has followed HSE advice will probably escape liability for that very reason, unless he knew or should have known of some particular reason why the advice was inadequate. And even if he has ignored the guidelines he may still escape liability if he can show the precautions he did in fact take were as good as or better than those recommended.

Guidelines have been issued on the safe construction or use of the following articles or substances: hand and foot operated presses; platen machines; drop forging hammers; mechanical power presses; drilling machines; nitrate salt baths; lighting; horizontal milling machines; seats; polyurethane foam; poisonous chemicals on farms; highly flammable materials on building sites; highly flammable liquids in the paint industry; lift trucks; fabric production; cotton and allied fibres; storage of liquified petroleum gas; evaporating and other ovens; abrasive wheels; portable power operated grinding machines; power operated mobile work platforms; packaging and labelling of dangerous substances.

DANGEROUS SUBSTANCES

The Packaging and Labelling of Dangerous Substances Regulations 1978 are enforced in the same way as rules made under the Health and Safety at Work Act. They apply to the classification, packing and labelling of over 1000 prescribed dangerous substances. Exceptions are substances supplied for use as motor fuel, munitions, pesticides or as medical products, or where delivered by means of a pipe or into a storage tank or for export. Compressed, liquified or dissolved gas is also excluded as is paraffin supplied into a container provided for the person to whom it is supplied. No prescribed dangerous substance may be supplied unless in a container designed, constructed and secured so as to prevent escape of its contents in 'normal handling'. The container and fastening must be made of materials which would not be affected by the contents. Suitable warnings in both words and symbols must be attached.[1]

THE CONSUMER SAFETY ACT

Criminal liability for dangerous *domestic* goods other than motor vehicles is most likely to arise under the Consumer Safety Act 1978. This Act replaced the Consumer Protection Act of 1961. Section 1 of the new Act enables the Secretary of State for Trade to make safety regulations on the composition, contents, design, construction, finish or packing of goods, or 'other matters relating to goods'. The Secretary can require goods to conform to particular standards and information to be given in appropriate ways to show conformity. He can regulate the testing or inspection of goods and require warnings or instructions to be marked on or to accompany goods. He can also exclude 'inappropriate information' which might mislead. The Secretary can prohibit anyone from supplying or possessing for supply goods he has found unsafe.

A person supplying goods in the course of business (excluding sales for export or for scrap or reconditioning) in breach of regulations under the Act may be fined up to £2,000 and/or imprisoned for up to three months. Prosecutions are undertaken by local authority trading standards departments. No liability arises if the defendant can prove the offence was committed because of the act or default of some other person. Usually this 'other person' will be an independent third party but may possibly be an employee of the defendant, if and in so far as what he does is both contrary to orders and beyond the defendant's immediate control: *Tesco v Nattrass*, 1971. Another defence is that the defendant took all reasonable steps and exercised all due diligence to avoid committing the offence. That defence does not of itself enable a seller to rely without question on a manufacturer's advertisements or assurances: *Taylor v Fraser*, 1977. Breach of the regulations also gives rise to strict civil liability to anyone injured thereby, an unusual provision in our criminal law.

Regulations made under the Consumer Safety Act and similar provisions in the Consumer Protection Act are:

Nightdresses (Safety) Regulations 1967. These require that children's nightdresses (although not other night attire) be made of flame resistant material and that appropriate washing instructions be given. Other nightdresses may have fire warning labels instead, together with washing instructions.

Stands for Carrycots (Safety) Regulations 1966. Capacity, strength and stability rules are laid down.

Toys (Safety) Regulations 1974. The rules here concern flammability, toxic finishes, electrical hazards, sharp or detachable components, plastic bags, etc. There have been many successful prosecutions under these regulations.

Electrical Appliances (Colour Code) Regulations 1969, amended in 1977. The regulations apply to electrical appliances for domestic use, indoor or out, requiring a voltage of at least 100 volts and having a mains lead with three electricity conductors. Earth wires must be green and yellow, neutral blue and live brown.

Electric Blankets (Safety) Regulations 1977. Blankets must meet the requirements of the British Electrotechnical Approval Board Standards Institution. Safety devices are necessary and warnings against misuse must be attached.

Cooking Utensils (Safety) Regulations 1972, Glazed Ceramic Ware (Safety) Regulations 1975, and Vitreous Enamel Ware (Safety) Regulations 1976. The rules limit the amount of lead which may be used in manufacture.

Heating Appliances (Fireguards) Regulations 1973. Fireguards must be fitted to most domestic heating appliances, complying with BSI requirements.

Pencils and Graphic Instruments (Safety) Regulations 1974. The toxic content and finish of pencils, pens, crayons etc, is stringently controlled.

Electrical Equipment (Safety) Regulations 1975 and 1976. As regards all domestic electrical equipment, for indoor or outdoor use, comprehensive provision is made here for insulation, earthing, accessibility of live or dangerous parts, and radiation. These rules give effect to a European Community Directive on low voltage electrical equipment.

Children's Clothing (Hood Cords) Regulations 1976. Hood cords are forbidden.

Oil Heaters (Safety) Regulations 1977. These provisions are

intended to prevent emission of smoke or fumes from domestic paraffin heaters and to guard against risks of fire or explosion. There are general requirements as to construction, materials and strength and more specific provisions regarding stability and self extinction, and warnings against misuse.

Babies' Dummies (Safety) Regulations 1978. BSI requirements as to design, construction and dimensions must be complied with. Dummies must be sold in a clean condition in a closed container and instructions provided for safe use.

Cosmetic Products Regulations 1978, amended in 1983. The regulations give effect to EEC Directives. They require safety in normal use and list numerous substances which cosmetics must not contain and others which may be used only within limits. Cosmetic products must bear the name and address of the manufacturer and the batch number.

Perambulators and Pushchairs (Safety) Regulations 1978. BSI standards are used to determine stability, braking, locking, etc requirements.

Nightwear (Safety) Order 1978. Children's nightwear must not be treated with trisphosphate. This order was extended by the Dangerous Substances Regulations (see p. 171).

Oil Lamps (Safety) Regulations 1980, amended in 1983. Specifications ensure the safety and stability of domestic paraffin lamps. Warnings and instructions on use are required. Continuous burning and draught resistance tests are laid down.

Upholstered Furniture (Safety) Regulations 1980, amended in 1983. The regulations apply to most domestic upholstered furniture and certain children's furniture. They lay down the 'smouldering cigarette', 'failed match' and 'crib' tests, defined by reference to BSI standards, to establish fire resistant qualities of upholstered seating, etc. New furniture must pass the cigarette and crib tests and if it fails the match test can only be sold if it carries both display and permanent labels to that effect.

Novelties (Safety) Regulations 1980. It is illegal to supply any substance containing benzene for the manufacture of balloons. Injurious tear gas capsules and articles 'designed to afford amusement . . . . by causing discomfort' are also prohibited.

Toy Water Snakes (Safety) Order 1983. Supply of these commodities containing E. coli bacterium is forbidden.

Pedal Bicycles (Safety) Regulations 1984. Supply of two-wheeled pedal cycles adapted or constructed for propulsion by mechanical power is illegal unless specified British Standards are complied with.

Scented Erasers (Safety) Order 1984. The order prohibits supply of erasers smelling of food or flowers with any two dimensions less than 45 mm.

It is convenient to note here also the Aerosol Dispensers (EEC Requirements) Regulations 1977, amended in 1981, made under the European Communities Act 1972. These implement EEC Directive 72/324 on the construction of aerosol dispensers and provision of warnings as to safe use. In 1980 the rules were supplemented by the Dangerous Substances and Preparations (Safety) Regulations which banned the use of chlorethylene as an aerosol propellant and certain liquids producing light or colour effects in ornamental objects.

Apart from the safety regulation aspect the Consumer Safety Act gives other important powers to the Secretary of State. Under s.3 he may issue prohibition orders forbidding supply of any type of goods he specifies as unsafe. The orders are of immediate and general effect, subject only to the requirement in Schedule 1 of advance warning and discussion with interested parties if practicable and to a 12-month limit on duration. He may serve prohibition notices on individuals, forbidding them to supply prescribed goods or permitting supply only on prescribed terms. The Secretary may also serve a 'notice to warn' on individual traders requiring them to publish at their own expense whatever warning he thinks necessary about unsafe goods they have already supplied. Again there must be prior notification and consultation if practicable. Goods apparently supplied in breach of the Act may be seized, but compensation is payable if no conviction follows. There is no general power to seize dangerous goods, and partly for that reason the Act has proved inadequate to deal immediately with dangerous goods already on the market.

Section 9 is the definition section. It excludes food, drugs, licensed medicinal products apart from cosmetic and toilet preparations, animal feeding stuffs and fertilisers from the scope of the Act. All these are controlled by other legislation. Dealers and not finance houses are held answerable by this section for dangerous goods supplied on credit. Goods are 'safe' if risk of death or injury in the circumstances in which they may be kept or used is 'prevented' or 'adequately reduced'. It will be seen therefore that the Act is concerned with protection against foreseeable misuse as well as normal or proper use – a problem discussed in chapters 5 and 6.

In 1984 a government report on Safety of Goods, Cmnd. 9302, observed that every year some 7000 people were killed and 3 million injured in home accidents in Great Britain — even more than on our roads. Relatively few of these accidents were caused by defective products, but the law's part in accident prevention was nonetheless crucial. The report noted Consumer Safety Act shortcomings and proposed stronger and wider powers of enforcement. Its most controversial proposal was a general safety duty to be enforced by the criminal law on all suppliers of goods unless for export or used or otherwise exempted. Compliance with 'sound modern safety standards', which might be specifically approved, would be a defence, as would 'due diligence'. Retailers would be entitled to prior warning. Suppliers in breach of duty would become strictly liable to anyone injured thereby. These proposals, while undeniably important, do not of themselves resolve the product liability problem. 'Safe' goods may still cause injury, still without redress.

THE FOOD AND DRUGS ACT

The Food and Drugs Act 1955 lays down the basic rules as to the safety and quality of these products. Under s.1 it is an offence to add anything to or subtract anything from foodstuffs or drugs which renders them injurious to health, with the intention that they be sold in that state. It is likewise forbidden to sell or offer or advertise for sale for human consumption food or drugs so treated. Section 2 prohibits sale to the prejudice of the purchaser of any food or drugs for human consumption which is not of the nature or substance or quality demanded. Liability may be avoided by proof that the addition to or subtraction from the food or drug was not carried out fraudulently and that the article is sold with a conspicuously visible notice or wrapper or container stating the nature of the operation. If food contains extraneous matter it is a defence to prove that its presence was an unavoidable consequence of the process of collection or preparation (s.3).

Another major offence is that defined by s.8: the sale or offering or exposing for sale or having in one's possession for the purposes of sale or preparation for the sale of or depositing with or consigning to any person for such purpose any food which is intended for human consumption but unfit for that purpose. A person charged may prove that he gave notice that the food was not intended for human consumption or that when delivered or despatched it was fit and he did not know and could not with reasonable diligence have known that it was unfit. The same rules apply to foodstuffs offered as prizes or rewards. The normal penalty under the Act is a fine of up to £2,000 or imprisonment for up to three months, or both.

By way of comment on these rules we may observe first that the 'nature or substance' of food may be determined by prescribed minimum standards such as those listed below, or in the case of drugs by reference to the British Pharmacopoeia. Where extraneous matter is present the question of liability will only arise where it would cause an ordinary reasonable purchaser to regard the whole article as unfit, whether or not it is actually harmful: *Barber v CWS*, 1983 – plastic straw in milk – not necessarily harmful but reasonable ground for objection.

Smedleys v Breed, 1974, was a House of Lords decision on this issue of general interest and importance. The prosecution was based on the presence of caterpillar larvae found in a tin of peas despite the very elaborate precautions which were proved to have been taken to avoid any foreign matter. The defendants had produced some 3,500,000 tins of peas that season and had had only four complaints. 'The chances of it happening again were . . . 3,499,999 to 1'. As Lord Hailsham said after the consumer reported her discovery,

> the caterpillar achieved a sort of posthumous apotheosis. From local authority to the Dorchester magistrates, from the Dorchester magistrates to a Divisional Court presided over by the Lord Chief Justice of England, from the Lord Chief Justice to the House of Lords the immolated insect has at length plodded its methodical way to the highest tribunal in the land.

Their Lordships held that in order to establish a defence under s.3 the defendants would have to show that the presence of the extraneous matter could not have been avoided by any human agency — which they were of course unable to do. At the same time the court emphasised that local authorities were not bound to prosecute in cases such as this where only very strictly speaking could it be said that an offence had been committed. They should keep a sense of proportion and consider whether prosecution was really necessary to protect the interests of consumers. Magistrates who thought prosecutions unnecessary were advised by their Lordships that they might find liability but nonetheless grant an absolute discharge.

Regulations and Orders have also been made under the Food and Drugs Act prescribing the composition of numerous foodstuffs and forbidding the sale or labelling or advertisement of these products except in accordance with the regulations. The items in question include baking powder, bread, butter, canned meats, cheese, cocoa and chocolate products, coffee and coffee products, condensed milk cream, curry powder, dried milk, fish cakes, fish and meat spreads, flour, fruit juices, gelatine, ice cream, margarine, meat pies and sausage rolls, preserves, salad cream, sausages and other meat products, soft drinks, suet, sugar products and tomato ketchup. Restrictions are imposed on the sale and advertisement of goods with certain added antioxidants, colouring matter, stabilisers or emulsifiers, or other miscellaneous additives, preservatives and solvents.

Regulations forbid the sale or importation of food containing arsenic, fluorine, lead or mineral hydrocarbons beyond the prescribed amounts or other than in the natural forms specifically exempted. A recent measure is an EEC Directive imposing strict controls on any material or article intended to come into contact with food and containing vinyl chloride. More general regulations made in 1978 require that packaging materials must not contaminate foodstuffs.

DRUGS

So far as drugs are concerned the matter is in the hands of the Committee on Safety of Medicines, an independent and expert licensing body created by the Medicines Act 1968. Issue of a licence now depends on proof of adequate staff and equipment and quality control facilities, the Committee's certificate that the drug in question has been appropriately tested on animals, and a product licence certifying the Committee's belief in the safety and quality of the drug. The Committee will refuse a licence unless satisfied of the positive value and safety and quality of the drug. For this purpose it relies on information supplied by the manufacturers and does not conduct its own trials or research. The Committee urges doctors to report adverse reactions, and manufacturers are required to keep a record of such information. The success of these requirements remains open to question.

The Medicines Act divides drugs into those which can only be obtained on prescription and those safe enough to be bought without prescription. Regulations require that the latter should be named, carry particulars of their ingredients, quantity, use, warnings as to side effects, expiry date, product licence, batch reference and manufacturer's licence. Not all of these particulars are necessary for prescribed drugs. Aspirin and paracetamol among others must be sold in 'childproof' containers.

MOTOR VEHICLES

One specific product whose safety and quality is outstandingly important to the consumer is the motor vehicle. This has been the subject of a great deal of highly specialised legislation. The main Act at present in force is the Road Traffic Act 1972. Various very detailed regulations have been made under it by the

Ministry of Transport, notably the Motor Vehicles (Construction and Use) Regulations 1973, as subsequently amended. The regulations specify what equipment must be fitted and the standards of fitness for numerous parts and accessories including tyres, brakes, mirrors, speedometers, seat belts, lights, etc. They also list the numerous EEC Directives on vehicle design, construction and equipment to which vehicles must conform. Regulations have also been made on the design of motor cycle helmets.

MISCELLANEOUS PROVISIONS

Miscellaneous other provisions affecting the safety and suitability of different kinds of goods include the Explosives (Age of Purchase etc) Act 1976, which raised the minimum age of children to whom fireworks could be sold from 13 to 16 (and at the same time the Government secured an agreement with manufacturers and retailers of fireworks reducing both the production of more dangerous types of fireworks and the time during which fireworks are on sale). Among Acts protecting agricultural standards are the Seeds Act 1920, and Plant Varieties and Seeds Act 1964, which require most kinds of agricultural, vegetable, grass and flower seeds to be tested and the result to be disclosed by the seller. Warranties of fitness are implied. The Fabrics (Misdescription) Act 1913 prohibits the sale of textile fabrics or products described as non-flammable or flame resistant unless they comply with the prescribed standards (now specified in regulations passed in 1980), which invoke the tests laid down by the Upholstered Furniture Regulations (see p. 174) The Rag, Flock and Other Filling Materials Act 1954 regulates the purity of fillings used in mattresses, cushions, toys and other goods.

THE TRADE DESCRIPTIONS ACT

Despite its commercial importance we have left the law against deceptive advertising to the end, since it does not relate directly to questions of fitness or safety of goods. But there is still a connection. If advertised goods are unsuitable or dangerous they may thereby prove the advertisement untrue and the advertiser guilty. The criminal court can make a compensation order as well as imposing a fine or imprisonment.

It may be helpful therefore to conclude with a brief review of the main provisions of the Trade Descriptions Act 1968, our most comprehensive attempt to control advertising standards. The Act concentrates on three problem areas: advertisements about goods, prices and services.

The basic rules on goods are laid down in ss.1 to 3. Section 1 creates the offence of 'applying a false trade description' to goods. Section 2 explains the meaning of trade description, and s.3 that of falsehood. Their short effect is as follows. The Act only applies to statements made in the course of trade or business, a phrase we discussed in chapter 3. It is immaterial whether or not the false statement was made with the intention to deceive. The statement itself may be written or spoken, or appear in or on the goods, as eg on a car's odometer. The seller can only avoid making a statement of this kind by making another statement equally as 'bold, precise and compelling' – *R v Hammerton*, 1976 – disclaiming all responsibility for the accuracy of the reading. The disclaimer must be brought to the buyer's attention before sale. It should preferably be in the car and the odometer itself taped over.

Section 2 defines a trade description as 'an indication, direct or indirect, and by whatever means given' relating to any of the following aspects of goods: their quantity, size or gauge; manufacture, production, processing or reconditioning; composition; fitness for purpose; strength, performance, behaviour or accuracy; other physical characteristics; testing and results; approval or type conformity; other history including previous ownership or use. A straightforward example of breach of this part of the Act was in the salesman's statement in *Robertson v Diciccio*, 1972, that the car was 'beautiful' when in fact it was in urgent need of repair. Statements affecting any other aspects of goods are not within the Act and so even if made with intent to deceive attract no liability. An example is a false statement as to value or worth: *Cadbury v Halliday*, 1975.

Under s.3 the test is whether a trade description is 'false to a material degree', whether or not anyone is deceived by it. Small discrepancies might sometimes be both unavoidable and unimportant. So in *R v Ford*, 1974, it was held that whether a car could properly be sold as 'new' after the dealer had repaired it depended on the extent of the damage and quality of the repairs. No offence was committed in *Simmons v Ravenhill*, 1983, where a car was sold with a De Luxe badge though actually only a standard model car with certain De Luxe refinements. A trade description might also be illegal if simply 'misleading' as to one of the matters specified in s.2, without actually being false. Similarly a statement which though not within s.2 could be taken as such will result in liability if materially false.

The interesting and important problem of 'slackfill' should be noted in this context. Many goods are supplied in containers whose size bears little or no relation to their contents, and which seem designed to deceive the consumer. Sometimes containers have to state the weight of their contents, but even so it could surely be argued that the size of a container is 'an indication, direct or indirect and by whatever means given' as to the 'quantity, size or gauge' of the goods inside, and if unnecessarily large must be 'misleading'. Strangely enough, however, there appears to be no agreed policy on this matter, and there has been only one successful reported prosecution.

The next major issue in the Act is that of false statements of price; section 11. Only three forms of deception are provided for. First it is an offence for a supplier to suggest falsely that his price is equal to or less than the recommended price. This means a price recommended by the manufacturer or producer and applicable in the area where the goods are offered, unless the contrary is stated. Secondly, the supplier must not indicate that he is offering goods at a price lower than their actual price. To charge more than a stated price is an infringement of the section. It must be clear whether the price includes VAT: *Richards v Westminster Motors*, 1975. Thirdly the seller must not falsely claim reductions in his own previous prices. But how can it be shown whether a purported reduction is genuine? The Act says that unless the price label states otherwise, the reduction is presumed to be from the price the seller has charged for those goods for at least 28 consecutive days in the preceding six months; section 11(3)(a)(ii). The onus of proving the seller has not sold at that price for that length of time is upon the prosecution – in practice an impossible task: *House of Holland v Brent LBC*, 1971.

As regards advertisements for services, s.14 makes it an offence for anyone in the course of business knowingly or recklessly to make a false statement about any of the following, or any statement likely to be taken as such: the provision in the course of business of any services, accommodation or facilities; the nature of such services, etc, or the time at which or manner in which or person by whom they will be provided; their examination or approval; the location or amenities of any accommodation so provided. According to *MFI v Nattrass*, 1971, a false statement is made 'knowingly or recklessly' if made without certainty in its truth. If every effort is made to correct a false statement liability may be avoided: *Wings v Ellis*, 1983.

By listing different offences rather than creating one general offence the Act again leaves loopholes. It seems that 'services, accommodation or facilities' exclude sales of land, so many optimistic statements in builders' and estate agents' advertisements are beyond the reach of the Act. A sale is not a 'facility', so no offence is committed when a dealer falsely advertises a 'closing down sale': *Westminster CC v Alan*, 1981. Various other statements which have slipped through the net include the promise of a free gift with every purchase, when the promise is fulfilled by increasing the purchase price: *Newell v Hicks*, 1983.

Perhaps the most difficult question regarding services is that posed by cases such as *Beckett v Cohen* and *R v Sunair Holidays*, both in 1973. In *Beckett* a builder promised to build a garage to a particular design and within an agreed time, knowing that he might be unable to finish the job and in the event failing to do so. On the face of it this was a promise within the terms of section 14 (i) and (iii), but the court expressed reluctance to turn what was essentially a breach of contract into a crime. Accordingly in this and the *Sunair* case, where various hotel amenities were promised but not provided, it was held that a promise of future services could only be criminal if it could be *proved untrue at the time it was made*; a considerable reduction in the apparent scope of the Act. A travel agency could therefore be criminally liable for booking rooms in a hotel which had not been built, for example, but not for promising services which could have been provided but were not. A trader who tries to repudiate a promise, eg by denying his liability under a guarantee, might thereby indicate that the promise was false at the time he made it: *Banbury v Hounslow LBC*, 1971.

DEFENCES

The last main area of interest in the Trade Descriptions Act is in section 24(i). This says that a person charged with breach of the rules discussed above can escape liability if he can prove:

> (a) that the commission of the offence was due to a mistake or to reliance on information supplied to him or to the act or default of another person, an accident or some other cause beyond his control; and (b) that he took all reasonable precautions and exercised all due diligence to avoid the commission of such an offence by himself or any person under his control [or] . . . that he did not know, and could not with reasonable diligence have ascertained, that the goods did not conform to the description or that the description had been applied to the goods.

Under paragraphs (a) and (b) the defendant must show that the wrong was someone else's fault and not his own fault. In *Tesco Supermarkets v Nattrass*, 1972, the House of Lords held that 'another person' could include the defendant's own employee, though the decision turned on the precautions which head office proved it had in fact taken and on the very substantial size of the organisation. In smaller enterprises where personal supervision is possible, the *Tesco* ruling should not provide any defence.

Section 24(1)(b) above shows that it is not sufficient for the defendant just to accept another's word: he must make enquiries himself where practicable to test or confirm the truth of the matter. So where a trader advertised watches as 'waterproof' in reliance on the manufacturer's erroneous assurance to that effect the court held that he could and should have tested one himself: *Sherratt v Gerald*, 1970. Similarly a used car dealer may need to contact the previous owner of a trade-in vehicle or have it examined by experts if the mileage is in doubt: *Naish v Gore*, 1971.

REFORMS

The Office of Fair Trading has suggested ways of making the Trade Descriptions Act more effective. It proposes for example that the items listed in s.2 should include the identity, standing or commercial importance of the supplier, the contents and authorship of books, records and the like, and the veracity of any alleged tests of the goods. (On the other hand, a proposed EEC Directive would simplify matters by a general prohibition of misleading advertising, which might be preferable.) As regards prices the OFT suggests that when 'recommended prices' are quoted the manufacturer and retailer should be independent parties unless otherwise stated, and that claimed reductions should be tested by reference to prices charged over the previous 28 days. Another answer might be to compel the trader to state in writing what his own previous price was and how long it had been effective. The OFT has also said that the rules as to services should specifically include land, and that the difficulty posed by *Beckett v Cohen*, above, should be resolved by making it illegal to promise services which the promisor has no intention or reasonable expectation of providing.

Certain changes were effected by the Price Marking (Bargain Offers) Order 1979. With limited exceptions the Order forbids a retailer of consumer goods or services to claim reductions from his own previous prices (whether specified or not, eg '10p off'), or reduction from someone else's prices for or valuation of the same goods or services (eg 'Worth £100; our price £75'). But the Order does not apply if the retailer or another identified person has actually charged or from a given date proposes to charge the higher price in the course of business. Reductions from manufacturers' recommended prices may also be claimed except in sales of beds, carpets, furniture and various domestic electrical products.

SUMMARY

'Product liability' usually refers only to the liabilities of manufacturers to compensate injured users of their goods. There are however circumstances in which the supply of dangerous goods may be a crime, whether or not anyone is injured thereby. Probably the most far reaching of these criminal provisions is the Health and Safety at Work Act. Section 6 requires everyone involved in the supply of articles or substances for use at work to ensure their safety so far as is reasonably practicable. The standard of care here is the same as that imposed in civil cases by the common law, as discussed in chapters 5 and 6, except that there is no criminal liability for injuries caused by misuse of equipment.

Regulations on consumer goods made under the Consumer Safety Act lay down detailed standards of design, construction and instructions to users, breach of which is again a criminal offence. Anyone injured as a result of such breach is entitled to damages. The Act is to be amended so as to impose a general safety duty on suppliers. Miscellaneous other important rules concern food and drugs, packaging of dangerous substances, motor vehicle safety, etc.

Anyone who supplies unfit or dangerous goods in the course of business may commit a crime also under the Trade Descriptions Act if by word or conduct he has advertised them as safe or suitable for a particular purpose.

NOTE

1) These regulations are to be replaced by the Classification, Packaging and Labelling of Dangerous Substances Regulations 1984. The new rules and accompanying codes of practice cover all substances classified by the Health and Safety Executive as dangerous for supply and conveyance by road. These substances must be packaged to prevent leakage in all normal circumstances and labelled with words and symbols as under the 1978 regulations to indicate hazards and appropriate precautions. The products concerned are largely industrial but consumer goods such as paints, strippers, bleaches and wood preservatives are included. The regulations take effect from 1 January 1986, with a further year's grace for certain packages under 25 litres.

Appendix 1 Sale of Goods Act 1979

[Schedules omitted]

CHAPTER 54

ARRANGEMENT OF SECTIONS

PART I
CONTRACTS TO WHICH ACT APPLIES

Section
1. Contracts to which Act applies.

PART II
FORMATION OF THE CONTRACT

Contract of sale

2. Contract of sale.
3. Capacity to buy and sell.

Formalities of contract

4. How contract of sale is made.

Subject matter of contract

5. Existing or future goods.
6. Goods which have perished.
7. Goods perishing before sale but after agreement to sell.

The price

8. Ascertainment of price.
9. Agreement to sell at valuation.

Conditions and warranties

10. Stipulations about time.
11. When condition to be treated as warranty.
12. Implied terms about title, etc.
13. Sale by description.
14. Implied terms about quality or fitness.

Sale by sample

15. Sale by sample.

PART III

EFFECTS OF THE CONTRACT

Transfer of property as between seller and buyer

16. Goods must be ascertained.
17. Property passes when intended to pass.
18. Rules for ascertaining intention.
19. Reservation of right of disposal.
20. Risk prima facie passes with property.

Transfer of title

21. Sale by person not the owner.
22. Market overt.
23. Sale under voidable title.
24. Seller in possession after sale.
25. Buyer in possession after sale.
26. Supplementary to sections 24 and 25.

PART IV

PERFORMANCE OF THE CONTRACT

27. Duties of seller and buyer.
28. Payment and delivery are concurrent conditions.
29. Rules about delivery.
30. Delivery of wrong quantity.
31. Instalment deliveries.
32. Delivery to carrier.
33. Risk where goods are delivered at distant place.
34. Buyer's right of examining the goods.
35. Acceptance.
36. Buyer not bound to return rejected goods.
37. Buyer's liability for not taking delivery of goods.

PART V

RIGHTS OF UNPAID SELLER AGAINST THE GOODS

Preliminary

38. Unpaid seller defined.
39. Unpaid seller's rights.
40. Attachment by seller in Scotland.

Unpaid seller's lien

41. Seller's lien.
42. Part delivery.
43. Termination of lien.

Stoppage in transit

44. Right of stoppage in transit.
45. Duration of transit.
46. How stoppage in transit is effected.

Re-sale etc. by buyer

47. Effect of sub-sale etc. by buyer.

Rescission : and re-sale by seller

48. Rescission : and re-sale by seller.

PART VI

ACTIONS FOR BREACH OF THE CONTRACT

Seller's remedies

49. Action for price.
50. Damages for non-acceptance.

Buyer's remedies

51. Damages for non-delivery.
52. Specific performance.
53. Remedy for breach of warranty.

Interest, etc.

54 Interest, etc.

PART VII
SUPPLEMENTARY

55. Exclusion of implied terms.
56. Conflict of laws.
57. Auction sales.
58. Payment into court in Scotland.
59. Reasonable time a question of fact.
60. Rights etc. enforceable by action.
61. Interpretation.
62. Savings: rules of law etc.
63. Consequential amendments, repeals and savings.
64. Short title and commencement.

An Act to consolidate the law relating to the sale of goods. [6th December 1979]

Be it enacted by the Queen's most Excellent Majesty, by and with the advice and consent of the Lords Spiritual and Temporal, and Commons, in this present Parliament assembled, and by the authority of the same, as follows:—

Part I

Contracts to Which Act Applies

1.—(1) This Act applies to contracts of sale of goods made on or after (but not to those made before) 1 January 1894. Contracts to which Act applies.

(2) In relation to contracts made on certain dates, this Act applies subject to the modification of certain of its sections as mentioned in Schedule 1 below.

(3) Any such modification is indicated in the section concerned by a reference to Schedule 1 below.

(4) Accordingly, where a section does not contain such a reference, this Act applies in relation to the contract concerned without such modification of the section.

Part II

Formation of the Contract

Contract of sale

2.—(1) A contract of sale of goods is a contract by which the seller transfers or agrees to transfer the property in goods to the buyer for a money consideration, called the price. Contract of sale.

PART II

(2) There may be a contract of sale between one part owner and another.

(3) A contract of sale may be absolute or conditional.

(4) Where under a contract of sale the property in the goods is transferred from the seller to the buyer the contract is called a sale.

(5) Where under a contract of sale the transfer of the property in the goods is to take place at a future time or subject to some condition later to be fulfilled the contract is called an agreement to sell.

(6) An agreement to sell becomes a sale when the time elapses or the conditions are fulfilled subject to which the property in the goods is to be transferred.

Capacity to buy and sell.

3.—(1) Capacity to buy and sell is regulated by the general law concerning capacity to contract and to transfer and acquire property.

(2) Where necessaries are sold and delivered to a minor or to a person who by reason of mental incapacity or drunkenness is incompetent to contract, he must pay a reasonable price for them.

(3) In subsection (2) above " necessaries " means goods suitable to the condition in life of the minor or other person concerned and to his actual requirements at the time of the sale and delivery.

Formalities of contract

How contract of sale is made.

4.—(1) Subject to this and any other Act, a contract of sale may be made in writing (either with or without seal), or by word of mouth, or partly in writing and partly by word of mouth, or may be implied from the conduct of the parties.

(2) Nothing in this section affects the law relating to corporations.

Subject matter of contract

Existing or future goods.

5.—(1) The goods which form the subject of a contract of sale may be either existing goods, owned or possessed by the seller, or goods to be manufactured or acquired by him after the making of the contract of sale, in this Act called future goods.

(2) There may be a contract for the sale of goods the acquisition of which by the seller depends on a contingency which may or may not happen.

APPENDIX 1 SALE OF GOODS ACT 1979

(3) Where by a contract of sale the seller purports to effect a present sale of future goods, the contract operates as an agreement to sell the goods.

PART II

6. Where there is a contract for the sale of specific goods, and the goods without the knowledge of the seller have perished at the time when the contract is made, the contract is void.

Goods which have perished.

7. Where there is an agreement to sell specific goods and subsequently the goods, without any fault on the part of the seller or buyer, perish before the risk passes to the buyer, the agreement is avoided.

Goods perishing before sale but after agreement to sell.

The price

8.—(1) The price in a contract of sale may be fixed by the contract, or may be left to be fixed in a manner agreed by the contract, or may be determined by the course of dealing between the parties.

Ascertainment of price.

(2) Where the price is not determined as mentioned in subsection (1) above the buyer must pay a reasonable price.

(3) What is a reasonable price is a question of fact dependent on the circumstances of each particular case.

9.—(1) Where there is an agreement to sell goods on the terms that the price is to be fixed by the valuation of a third party, and he cannot or does not make the valuation, the agreement is avoided; but if the goods or any part of them have been delivered to and appropriated by the buyer he must pay a reasonable price for them.

Agreement to sell at valuation.

(2) Where the third party is prevented from making the valuation by the fault of the seller or buyer, the party not at fault may maintain an action for damages against the party at fault.

Conditions and warranties

10.—(1) Unless a different intention appears from the terms of the contract, stipulations as to time of payment are not of the essence of a contract of sale.

Stipulations about time.

(2) Whether any other stipulation as to time is or is not of the essence of the contract depends on the terms of the contract.

(3) In a contract of sale " month " prima facie means calendar month.

PART II
When condition to be treated as warranty.

11.—(1) Subsections (2) to (4) and (7) below do not apply to Scotland and subsection (5) below applies only to Scotland.

(2) Where a contract of sale is subject to a condition to be fulfilled by the seller, the buyer may waive the condition, or may elect to treat the breach of the condition as a breach of warranty and not as a ground for treating the contract as repudiated.

(3) Whether a stipulation in a contract of sale is a condition, the breach of which may give rise to a right to treat the contract as repudiated, or a warranty, the breach of which may give rise to a claim for damages but not to a right to reject the goods and treat the contract as repudiated, depends in each case on the construction of the contract; and a stipulation may be a condition, though called a warranty in the contract.

(4) Where a contract of sale is not severable and the buyer has accepted the goods or part of them, the breach of a condition to be fulfilled by the seller can only be treated as a breach of warranty, and not as a ground for rejecting the goods and treating the contract as repudiated, unless there is an express or implied term of the contract to that effect.

(5) In Scotland, failure by the seller to perform any material part of a contract of sale is a breach of contract, which entitles the buyer either within a reasonable time after delivery to reject the goods and treat the contract as repudiated, or to retain the goods and treat the failure to perform such material part as a breach which may give rise to a claim for compensation or damages.

(6) Nothing in this section affects a condition or warranty whose fulfilment is excused by law by reason of impossibility or otherwise.

(7) Paragraph 2 of Schedule 1 below applies in relation to a contract made before 22 April 1967 or (in the application of this Act to Northern Ireland) 28 July 1967.

Implied terms about title, etc.

12.—(1) In a contract of sale, other than one to which subsection (3) below applies, there is an implied condition on the part of the seller that in the case of a sale he has a right to sell the goods, and in the case of an agreement to sell he will have such a right at the time when the property is to pass.

(2) In a contract of sale, other than one to which subsection (3) below applies, there is also an implied warranty that—

(a) the goods are free, and will remain free until the time when the property is to pass, from any charge or encumbrance not disclosed or known to the buyer before the contract is made, and

APPENDIX 1 SALE OF GOODS ACT 1979

(b) the buyer will enjoy quiet possession of the goods except so far as it may be disturbed by the owner or other person entitled to the benefit of any charge or encumbrance so disclosed or known.

PART II

(3) This subsection applies to a contract of sale in the case of which there appears from the contract or is to be inferred from its circumstances an intention that the seller should transfer only such title as he or a third person may have.

(4) In a contract to which subsection (3) above applies there is an implied warranty that all charges or encumbrances known to the seller and not known to the buyer have been disclosed to the buyer before the contract is made.

(5) In a contract to which subsection (3) above applies there is also an implied warranty that none of the following will disturb the buyer's quiet possession of the goods, namely—

(a) the seller;
(b) in a case where the parties to the contract intend that the seller should transfer only such title as a third person may have, that person;
(c) anyone claiming through or under the seller or that third person otherwise than under a charge or encumbrance disclosed or known to the buyer before the contract is made.

(6) Paragraph 3 of Schedule 1 below applies in relation to a contract made before 18 May 1973.

13.—(1) Where there is a contract for the sale of goods by description, there is an implied condition that the goods will correspond with the description.

Sale-by description.

(2) If the sale is by sample as well as by description it is not sufficient that the bulk of the goods corresponds with the sample if the goods do not also correspond with the description.

(3) A sale of goods is not prevented from being a sale by description by reason only that, being exposed for sale or hire, they are selected by the buyer.

(4) Paragraph 4 of Schedule 1 below applies in relation to a contract made before 18 May 1973.

14.—(1) Except as provided by this section and section 15 below and subject to any other enactment, there is no implied condition or warranty about the quality or fitness for any particular purpose of goods supplied under a contract of sale.

Implied terms about quality or fitness.

(2) Where the seller sells goods in the course of a business, there is an implied condition that the goods supplied under the

PART II   contract are of merchantable quality, except that there is no such condition—
  (a) as regards defects specifically drawn to the buyer's attention before the contract is made ; or
  (b) if the buyer examines the goods before the contract is made, as regards defects which that examination ought to reveal.

(3) Where the seller sells goods in the course of a business and the buyer, expressly or by implication, makes known—
  (a) to the seller, or
  (b) where the purchase price or part of it is payable by instalments and the goods were previously sold by a credit-broker to the seller, to that credit-broker,
any particular purpose for which the goods are being bought, there is an implied condition that the goods supplied under the contract are reasonably fit for that purpose, whether or not that is a purpose for which such goods are commonly supplied, except where the circumstances show that the buyer does not rely, or that it is unreasonable for him to rely, on the skill or judgment of the seller or credit-broker.

(4) An implied condition or warranty about quality or fitness for a particular purpose may be annexed to a contract of sale by usage.

(5) The preceding provisions of this section apply to a sale by a person who in the course of a business is acting as agent for another as they apply to a sale by a principal in the course of a business, except where that other is not selling in the course of a business and either the buyer knows that fact or reasonable steps are taken to bring it to the notice of the buyer before the contract is made.

(6) Goods of any kind are of merchantable quality within the meaning of subsection (2) above if they are as fit for the purpose or purposes for which goods of that kind are commonly bought as it is reasonable to expect having regard to any description applied to them, the price (if relevant) and all the other relevant circumstances.

(7) Paragraph 5 of Schedule 1 below applies in relation to a contract made on or after 18 May 1973 and before the appointed day, and paragraph 6 in relation to one made before 18 May 1973.

(8) In subsection (7) above and paragraph 5 of Schedule 1 below references to the appointed day are to the day appointed for the purposes of those provisions by an order of the Secretary of State made by statutory instrument.

APPENDIX 1 SALE OF GOODS ACT 1979

Sale by sample — PART II

15.—(1) A contract of sale is a contract for sale by sample where there is an express or implied term to that effect in the contract. — Sale by sample.

(2) In the case of a contract for sale by sample there is an implied condition—
- (*a*) that the bulk will correspond with the sample in quality;
- (*b*) that the buyer will have a reasonable opportunity of comparing the bulk with the sample;
- (*c*) that the goods will be free from any defect, rendering them unmerchantable, which would not be apparent on reasonable examination of the sample.

(3) In subsection (2)(*c*) above " unmerchantable " is to be construed in accordance with section 14(6) above.

(4) Paragraph 7 of Schedule 1 below applies in relation to a contract made before 18 May 1973.

PART III
EFFECTS OF THE CONTRACT
Transfer of property as between seller and buyer

16. Where there is a contract for the sale of unascertained goods no property in the goods is transferred to the buyer unless and until the goods are ascertained. — Goods must be ascertained.

17.—(1) Where there is a contract for the sale of specific or ascertained goods the property in them is transferred to the buyer at such time as the parties to the contract intend it to be transferred. — Property passes when intended to pass.

(2) For the purpose of ascertaining the intention of the parties regard shall be had to the terms of the contract, the conduct of the parties and the circumstances of the case.

18. Unless a different intention appears, the following are rules for ascertaining the intention of the parties as to the time at which the property in the goods is to pass to the buyer. — Rules for ascertaining intention.

Rule 1.—Where there is an unconditional contract for the sale of specific goods in a deliverable state the property in the goods passes to the buyer when the contract is made, and it is immaterial whether the time of payment or the time of delivery, or both, be postponed.

Rule 2.—Where there is a contract for the sale of specific goods and the seller is bound to do something to the goods for the purpose of putting them into a deliverable state, the property does not pass until the thing is done and the buyer has notice that it has been done.

PART III

Rule 3.—Where there is a contract for the sale of specific goods in a deliverable state but the seller is bound to weigh, measure, test, or do some other act or thing with reference to the goods for the purpose of ascertaining the price, the property does not pass until the act or thing is done and the buyer has notice that it has been done.

Rule 4.—When goods are delivered to the buyer on approval or on sale or return or other similar terms the property in the goods passes to the buyer:—

(*a*) when he signifies his approval or acceptance to the seller or does any other act adopting the transaction ;

(*b*) if he does not signify his approval or acceptance to the seller but retains the goods without giving notice of rejection, then, if a time has been fixed for the return of the goods, on the expiration of that time, and, if no time has been fixed, on the expiration of a reasonable time.

Rule 5.—(1) Where there is a contract for the sale of unascertained or future goods by description, and goods of that description and in a deliverable state are unconditionally appropriated to the contract, either by the seller with the assent of the buyer or by the buyer with the assent of the seller, the property in the goods then passes to the buyer ; and the assent may be express or implied, and may be given either before or after the appropriation is made.

(2) Where, in pursuance of the contract, the seller delivers the goods to the buyer or to a carrier or other bailee or custodier (whether named by the buyer or not) for the purpose of transmission to the buyer, and does not reserve the right of disposal, he is to be taken to have unconditionally appropriated the goods to the contract.

Reservation of right of disposal.

19.—(1) Where there is a contract for the sale of specific goods or where goods are subsequently appropriated to the contract, the seller may, by the terms of the contract or appropriation, reserve the right of disposal of the goods until certain conditions are fulfilled ; and in such a case, notwithstanding the delivery of the goods to the buyer, or to a carrier or other bailee or custodier for the purpose of transmission to the buyer, the property in the goods does not pass to the buyer until the conditions imposed by the seller are fulfilled.

(2) Where goods are shipped, and by the bill of lading the goods are deliverable to the order of the seller or his agent, the seller is prima facie to be taken to reserve the right of disposal.

APPENDIX 1 SALE OF GOODS ACT 1979

(3) Where the seller of goods draws on the buyer for the price, and transmits the bill of exchange and bill of lading to the buyer together to secure acceptance or payment of the bill of exchange, the buyer is bound to return the bill of lading if he does not honour the bill of exchange, and if he wrongfully retains the bill of lading the property in the goods does not pass to him.

PART III

20.—(1) Unless otherwise agreed, the goods remain at the seller's risk until the property in them is transferred to the buyer, but when the property in them is transferred to the buyer the goods are at the buyer's risk whether delivery has been made or not.

Risk prima facie passes with property.

(2) But where delivery has been delayed through the fault of either buyer or seller the goods are at the risk of the party at fault as regards any loss which might not have occurred but for such fault.

(3) Nothing in this section affects the duties or liabilities of either seller or buyer as a bailee or custodier of the goods of the other party.

Transfer of title

21.—(1) Subject to this Act, where goods are sold by a person who is not their owner, and who does not sell them under the authority or with the consent of the owner, the buyer acquires no better title to the goods than the seller had, unless the owner of the goods is by his conduct precluded from denying the seller's authority to sell.

Sale by person not the owner.

(2) Nothing in this Act affects—
  (a) the provisions of the Factors Acts or any enactment enabling the apparent owner of goods to dispose of them as if he were their true owner;
  (b) the validity of any contract of sale under any special common law or statutory power of sale or under the order of a court of competent jurisdiction.

22.—(1) Where goods are sold in market overt, according to the usage of the market, the buyer acquires a good title to the goods, provided he buys them in good faith and without notice of any defect or want of title on the part of the seller.

Market overt.

(2) This section does not apply to Scotland.

(3) Paragraph 8 of Schedule 1 below applies in relation to a contract under which goods were sold before 1 January 1968 or (in the application of this Act to Northern Ireland) 29 August 1967.

PART III
Sale under voidable title.

23. When the seller of goods has a voidable title to them, but his title has not been avoided at the time of the sale, the buyer acquires a good title to the goods, provided he buys them in good faith and without notice of the seller's defect of title.

Seller in possession after sale.

24. Where a person having sold goods continues or is in possession of the goods, or of the documents of title to the goods, the delivery or transfer by that person, or by a mercantile agent acting for him, of the goods or documents of title under any sale, pledge, or other disposition thereof, to any person receiving the same in good faith and without notice of the previous sale, has the same effect as if the person making the delivery or transfer were expressly authorised by the owner of the goods to make the same.

Buyer in possession after sale.

25.—(1) Where a person having bought or agreed to buy goods obtains, with the consent of the seller, possession of the goods or the documents of title to the goods, the delivery or transfer by that person, or by a mercantile agent acting for him, of the goods or documents of title, under any sale, pledge, or other disposition thereof, to any person receiving the same in good faith and without notice of any lien or other right of the original seller in respect of the goods, has the same effect as if the person making the delivery or transfer were a mercantile agent in possession of the goods or documents of title with the consent of the owner.

(2) For the purposes of subsection (1) above—

(*a*) the buyer under a conditional sale agreement is to be taken not to be a person who has bought or agreed to buy goods, and

(*b*) " conditional sale agreement " means an agreement for the sale of goods which is a consumer credit agreement within the meaning of the Consumer Credit Act 1974 under which the purchase price or part of it is payable by instalments, and the property in the goods is to remain in the seller (notwithstanding that the buyer is to be in possession of the goods) until such conditions as to the payment of instalments or otherwise as may be specified in the agreement are fulfilled.

1974 c. 39.

(3) Paragraph 9 of Schedule 1 below applies in relation to a contract under which a person buys or agrees to buy goods and which is made before the appointed day.

(4) In subsection (3) above and paragraph 9 of Schedule 1 below references to the appointed day are to the day appointed for the purposes of those provisions by an order of the Secretary of State made by statutory instrument.

26. In sections 24 and 25 above "mercantile agent" means a mercantile agent having in the customary course of his business as such agent authority either—

    (a) to sell goods, or
    (b) to consign goods for the purpose of sale, or
    (c) to buy goods, or
    (d) to raise money on the security of goods.

Part III Supplementary to sections 24 and 25.

Part IV

Performance of the Contract

27. It is the duty of the seller to deliver the goods, and of the buyer to accept and pay for them, in accordance with the terms of the contract of sale.

Duties of seller and buyer.

28. Unless otherwise agreed, delivery of the goods and payment of the price are concurrent conditions, that is to say, the seller must be ready and willing to give possession of the goods to the buyer in exchange for the price and the buyer must be ready and willing to pay the price in exchange for possession of the goods.

Payment and delivery are concurrent conditions.

29.—(1) Whether it is for the buyer to take possession of the goods or for the seller to send them to the buyer is a question depending in each case on the contract, express or implied, between the parties.

Rules about delivery.

(2) Apart from any such contract, express or implied, the place of delivery is the seller's place of business if he has one, and if not, his residence; except that, if the contract is for the sale of specific goods, which to the knowledge of the parties when the contract is made are in some other place, then that place is the place of delivery.

(3) Where under the contract of sale the seller is bound to send the goods to the buyer, but no time for sending them is fixed, the seller is bound to send them within a reasonable time.

(4) Where the goods at the time of sale are in the possession of a third person, there is no delivery by seller to buyer unless and until the third person acknowledges to the buyer that he holds the goods on his behalf; but nothing in this section affects the operation of the issue or transfer of any document of title to goods.

(5) Demand or tender of delivery may be treated as ineffectual unless made at a reasonable hour; and what is a reasonable hour is a question of fact.

(6) Unless otherwise agreed, the expenses of and incidental to putting the goods into a deliverable state must be borne by the seller.

Delivery of wrong quantity.

30.—(1) Where the seller delivers to the buyer a quantity of goods less than he contracted to sell, the buyer may reject them, but if the buyer accepts the goods so delivered he must pay for them at the contract rate.

(2) Where the seller delivers to the buyer a quantity of goods larger than he contracted to sell, the buyer may accept the goods included in the contract and reject the rest, or he may reject the whole.

(3) Where the seller delivers to the buyer a quantity of goods larger than he contracted to sell and the buyer accepts the whole of the goods so delivered he must pay for them at the contract rate.

(4) Where the seller delivers to the buyer the goods he contracted to sell mixed with goods of a different description not included in the contract, the buyer may accept the goods which are in accordance with the contract and reject the rest, or he may reject the whole.

(5) This section is subject to any usage of trade, special agreement, or course of dealing between the parties.

Instalment deliveries.

31.—(1) Unless otherwise agreed, the buyer of goods is not bound to accept delivery of them by instalments.

(2) Where there is a contract for the sale of goods to be delivered by stated instalments, which are to be separately paid for, and the seller makes defective deliveries in respect of one or more instalments, or the buyer neglects or refuses to take delivery of or pay for one or more instalments, it is a question in each case depending on the terms of the contract and the circumstances of the case whether the breach of contract is a repudiation of the whole contract or whether it is a severable breach giving rise to a claim for compensation but not to a right to treat the whole contract as repudiated.

Delivery to carrier.

32.—(1) Where, in pursuance of a contract of sale, the seller is authorised or required to send the goods to the buyer, delivery of the goods to a carrier (whether named by the buyer or not) for the purpose of transmission to the buyer is prima facie deemed to be a delivery of the goods to the buyer.

(2) Unless otherwise authorised by the buyer, the seller must make such contract with the carrier on behalf of the buyer as may be reasonable having regard to the nature of the goods and the other circumstances of the case ; and if the seller omits to do

APPENDIX 1 SALE OF GOODS ACT 1979

so, and the goods are lost or damaged in course of transit, the buyer may decline to treat the delivery to the carrier as a delivery to himself or may hold the seller responsible in damages.

(3) Unless otherwise agreed, where goods are sent by the seller to the buyer by a route involving sea transit, under circumstances in which it is usual to insure, the seller must give such notice to the buyer as may enable him to insure them during their sea transit; and if the seller fails to do so, the goods are at his risk during such sea transit.

33. Where the seller of goods agrees to deliver them at his own risk at a place other than that where they are when sold, the buyer must nevertheless (unless otherwise agreed) take any risk of deterioration in the goods necessarily incident to the course of transit. *Risk where goods are delivered at distant place.*

34.—(1) Where goods are delivered to the buyer, and he has not previously examined them, he is not deemed to have accepted them until he has had a reasonable opportunity of examining them for the purpose of ascertaining whether they are in conformity with the contract. *Buyer's right of examining the goods.*

(2) Unless otherwise agreed, when the seller tenders delivery of goods to the buyer, he is bound on request to afford the buyer a reasonable opportunity of examining the goods for the purpose of ascertaining whether they are in conformity with the contract.

35.—(1) The buyer is deemed to have accepted the goods when he intimates to the seller that he has accepted them, or (except where section 34 above otherwise provides) when the goods have been delivered to him and he does any act in relation to them which is inconsistent with the ownership of the seller, or when after the lapse of a reasonable time he retains the goods without intimating to the seller that he has rejected them. *Acceptance.*

(2) Paragraph 10 of Schedule 1 below applies in relation to a contract made before 22 April 1967 or (in the application of this Act to Northern Ireland) 28 July 1967.

36. Unless otherwise agreed, where goods are delivered to the buyer, and he refuses to accept them, having the right to do so, he is not bound to return them to the seller, but it is sufficient if he intimates to the seller that he refuses to accept them. *Buyer not bound to return rejected goods.*

37.—(1) When the seller is ready and willing to deliver the goods, and requests the buyer to take delivery, and the buyer does not within a reasonable time after such request take delivery of the goods, he is liable to the seller for any loss occasioned by his neglect or refusal to take delivery, and also for a reasonable charge for the care and custody of the goods. *Buyer's liability for not taking delivery of goods.*

PART IV

(2) Nothing in this section affects the rights of the seller where the neglect or refusal of the buyer to take delivery amounts to a repudiation of the contract.

PART V

RIGHTS OF UNPAID SELLER AGAINST THE GOODS

Preliminary

Unpaid seller defined.

38.—(1) The seller of goods is an unpaid seller within the meaning of this Act—

(*a*) when the whole of the price has not been paid or tendered;

(*b*) when a bill of exchange or other negotiable instrument has been received as conditional payment, and the condition on which it was received has not been fulfilled by reason of the dishonour of the instrument or otherwise.

(2) In this Part of this Act " seller " includes any person who is in the position of a seller, as, for instance, an agent of the seller to whom the bill of lading has been indorsed, or a consignor or agent who has himself paid (or is directly responsible for) the price.

Unpaid seller's rights.

39.—(1) Subject to this and any other Act, notwithstanding that the property in the goods may have passed to the buyer, the unpaid seller of goods, as such, has by implication of law—

(*a*) a lien on the goods or right to retain them for the price while he is in possession of them;

(*b*) in case of the insolvency of the buyer, a right of stopping the goods in transit after he has parted with the possession of them;

(*c*) a right of re-sale as limited by this Act.

(2) Where the property in goods has not passed to the buyer, the unpaid seller has (in addition to his other remedies) a right of withholding delivery similar to and co-extensive with his rights of lien or retention and stoppage in transit where the property has passed to the buyer.

Attachment by seller in Scotland.

40. In Scotland a seller of goods may attach them while in his own hands or possession by arrestment or poinding; and such arrestment or poinding shall have the same operation and effect in a competition or otherwise as an arrestment or poinding by a third party.

APPENDIX 1 SALE OF GOODS ACT 1979

Unpaid seller's lien
PART V

41.—(1) Subject to this Act, the unpaid seller of goods who is in possession of them is entitled to retain possession of them until payment or tender of the price in the following cases:— [Seller's lien.]
  (a) where the goods have been sold without any stipulation as to credit;
  (b) where the goods have been sold on credit but the term of credit has expired;
  (c) where the buyer becomes insolvent.

(2) The seller may exercise his lien or right of retention notwithstanding that he is in possession of the goods as agent or bailee or custodier for the buyer.

42. Where an unpaid seller has made part delivery of the goods, he may exercise his lien or right of retention on the remainder, unless such part delivery has been made under such circumstances as to show an agreement to waive the lien or right of retention. [Part delivery.]

43.—(1) The unpaid seller of goods loses his lien or right of retention in respect of them— [Termination of lien.]
  (a) when he delivers the goods to a carrier or other bailee or custodier for the purpose of transmission to the buyer without reserving the right of disposal of the goods;
  (b) when the buyer or his agent lawfully obtains possession of the goods;
  (c) by waiver of the lien or right of retention.

(2) An unpaid seller of goods who has a lien or right of retention in respect of them does not lose his lien or right of retention by reason only that he has obtained judgment or decree for the price of the goods.

Stoppage in transit

44. Subject to this Act, when the buyer of goods becomes insolvent the unpaid seller who has parted with the possession of the goods has the right of stopping them in transit, that is to say, he may resume possession of the goods as long as they are in course of transit, and may retain them until payment or tender of the price. [Right of stoppage in transit.]

45.—(1) Goods are deemed to be in course of transit from the time when they are delivered to a carrier or other bailee or custodier for the purpose of transmission to the buyer, until the buyer or his agent in that behalf takes delivery of them from the carrier or other bailee or custodier. [Duration of transit.]

(2) If the buyer or his agent in that behalf obtains delivery of the goods before their arrival at the appointed destination, the transit is at an end.

(3) If, after the arrival of the goods at the appointed destination, the carrier or other bailee or custodier acknowledges to the buyer or his agent that he holds the goods on his behalf and continues in possession of them as bailee or custodier for the buyer or his agent, the transit is at an end, and it is immaterial that a further destination for the goods may have been indicated by the buyer.

(4) If the goods are rejected by the buyer, and the carrier or other bailee or custodier continues in possession of them, the transit is not deemed to be at an end, even if the seller has refused to receive them back.

(5) When goods are delivered to a ship chartered by the buyer it is a question depending on the circumstances of the particular case whether they are in the possession of the master as a carrier or as agent to the buyer.

(6) Where the carrier or other bailee or custodier wrongfully refuses to deliver the goods to the buyer or his agent in that behalf, the transit is deemed to be at an end.

(7) Where part delivery of the goods has been made to the buyer or his agent in that behalf, the remainder of the goods may be stopped in transit, unless such part delivery has been made under such circumstances as to show an agreement to give up possession of the whole of the goods.

How stoppage in transit is effected.

46.—(1) The unpaid seller may exercise his right of stoppage in transit either by taking actual possession of the goods or by giving notice of his claim to the carrier or other bailee or custodier in whose possession the goods are.

(2) The notice may be given either to the person in actual possession of the goods or to his principal.

(3) If given to the principal, the notice is ineffective unless given at such time and under such circumstances that the principal, by the exercise of reasonable diligence, may communicate it to his servant or agent in time to prevent a delivery to the buyer.

(4) When notice of stoppage in transit is given by the seller to the carrier or other bailee or custodier in possession of the goods, he must re-deliver the goods to, or according to the directions of, the seller; and the expenses of the re-delivery must be borne by the seller.

Re-sale etc. by buyer

47.—(1) Subject to this Act, the unpaid seller's right of lien or retention or stoppage in transit is not affected by any sale or other disposition of the goods which the buyer may have made, unless the seller has assented to it. [*Effect of sub-sale etc. by buyer.*]

(2) Where a document of title to goods has been lawfully transferred to any person as buyer or owner of the goods, and that person transfers the document to a person who takes it in good faith and for valuable consideration, then—

(a) if the last-mentioned transfer was by way of sale the unpaid seller's right of lien or retention or stoppage in transit is defeated; and

(b) if the last-mentioned transfer was made by way of pledge or other disposition for value, the unpaid seller's right of lien or retention or stoppage in transit can only be exercised subject to the rights of the transferee.

Rescission: and re-sale by seller

48.—(1) Subject to this section, a contract of sale is not rescinded by the mere exercise by an unpaid seller of his right of lien or retention or stoppage in transit. [*Rescission: and re-sale by seller.*]

(2) Where an unpaid seller who has exercised his right of lien or retention or stoppage in transit re-sells the goods, the buyer acquires a good title to them as against the original buyer.

(3) Where the goods are of a perishable nature, or where the unpaid seller gives notice to the buyer of his intention to re-sell, and the buyer does not within a reasonable time pay or tender the price, the unpaid seller may re-sell the goods and recover from the original buyer damages for any loss occasioned by his breach of contract.

(4) Where the seller expressly reserves the right of re-sale in case the buyer should make default, and on the buyer making default re-sells the goods, the original contract of sale is rescinded but without prejudice to any claim the seller may have for damages.

Part VI

Actions for Breach of the Contract

Seller's remedies

49.—(1) Where, under a contract of sale, the property in the goods has passed to the buyer and he wrongfully neglects or refuses to pay for the goods according to the terms of the contract, the seller may maintain an action against him for the price of the goods. [*Action for price.*]

PART VI

(2) Where, under a contract of sale, the price is payable on a day certain irrespective of delivery and the buyer wrongfully neglects or refuses to pay such price, the seller may maintain an action for the price, although the property in the goods has not passed and the goods have not been appropriated to the contract.

(3) Nothing in this section prejudices the right of the seller in Scotland to recover interest on the price from the date of tender of the goods, or from the date on which the price was payable, as the case may be.

Damages for non-acceptance.

50.—(1) Where the buyer wrongfully neglects or refuses to accept and pay for the goods, the seller may maintain an action against him for damages for non-acceptance.

(2) The measure of damages is the estimated loss directly and naturally resulting, in the ordinary course of events, from the buyer's breach of contract.

(3) Where there is an available market for the goods in question the measure of damages is prima facie to be ascertained by the difference between the contract price and the market or current price at the time or times when the goods ought to have been accepted or (if no time was fixed for acceptance) at the time of the refusal to accept.

Buyer's remedies

Damages for non-delivery.

51.—(1) Where the seller wrongfully neglects or refuses to deliver the goods to the buyer, the buyer may maintain an action against the seller for damages for non-delivery.

(2) The measure of damages is the estimated loss directly and naturally resulting, in the ordinary course of events, from the seller's breach of contract.

(3) Where there is an available market for the goods in question the measure of damages is prima facie to be ascertained by the difference between the contract price and the market or current price of the goods at the time or times when they ought to have been delivered or (if no time was fixed) at the time of the refusal to deliver.

Specific performance.

52.—(1) In any action for breach of contract to deliver specific or ascertained goods the court may, if it thinks fit, on the plaintiff's application, by its judgment or decree direct that the contract shall be performed specifically, without giving the defendant the option of retaining the goods on payment of damages.

(2) The plaintiff's application may be made at any time before judgment or decree.

(3) The judgment or decree may be unconditional, or on such terms and conditions as to damages, payment of the price and otherwise as seem just to the court.

(4) The provisions of this section shall be deemed to be supplementary to, and not in derogation of, the right of specific implement in Scotland.

53.—(1) Where there is a breach of warranty by the seller, or where the buyer elects (or is compelled) to treat any breach of a condition on the part of the seller as a breach of warranty, the buyer is not by reason only of such breach of warranty entitled to reject the goods ; but he may—

    (a) set up against the seller the breach of warranty in diminution or extinction of the price, or

    (b) maintain an action against the seller for damages for the breach of warranty.

(2) The measure of damages for breach of warranty is the estimated loss directly and naturally resulting, in the ordinary course of events, from the breach of warranty.

(3) In the case of breach of warranty of quality such loss is prima facie the difference between the value of the goods at the time of delivery to the buyer and the value they would have had if they had fulfilled the warranty.

(4) The fact that the buyer has set up the breach of warranty in diminution or extinction of the price does not prevent him from maintaining an action for the same breach of warranty if he has suffered further damage.

(5) Nothing in this section prejudices or affects the buyer's right of rejection in Scotland as declared by this Act.

Interest, etc.

54. Nothing in this Act affects the right of the buyer or the seller to recover interest or special damages in any case where by law interest or special damages may be recoverable, or to recover money paid where the consideration for the payment of it has failed.

PART VII

SUPPLEMENTARY

55.—(1) Where a right, duty or liability would arise under a contract of sale of goods by implication of law, it may (subject to the Unfair Contract Terms Act 1977) be negatived or varied by express agreement, or by the course of dealing between the parties, or by such usage as binds both parties to the contract.

PART VII

(2) An express condition or warranty does not negative a condition or warranty implied by this Act unless inconsistent with it.

(3) Paragraph 11 of Schedule 1 below applies in relation to a contract made on or after 18 May 1973 and before 1 February 1978, and paragraph 12 in relation to one made before 18 May 1973.

Conflict of laws.

56. Paragraph 13 of Schedule 1 below applies in relation to a contract made on or after 18 May 1973 and before 1 February 1978, so as to make provision about conflict of laws in relation to such a contract.

Auction sales.

57.—(1) Where goods are put up for sale by auction in lots, each lot is prima facie deemed to be the subject of a separate contract of sale.

(2) A sale by auction is complete when the auctioneer announces its completion by the fall of the hammer, or in other customary manner ; and until the announcement is made any bidder may retract his bid.

(3) A sale by auction may be notified to be subject to a reserve or upset price, and a right to bid may also be reserved expressly by or on behalf of the seller.

(4) Where a sale by auction is not notified to be subject to a right to bid by or on behalf of the seller, it is not lawful for the seller to bid himself or to employ any person to bid at the sale, or for the auctioneer knowingly to take any bid from the seller or any such person.

(5) A sale contravening subsection (4) above may be treated as fraudulent by the buyer.

(6) Where, in respect of a sale by auction, a right to bid is expressly reserved (but not otherwise) the seller or any one person on his behalf may bid at the auction.

Payment into court in Scotland.

58. In Scotland where a buyer has elected to accept goods which he might have rejected, and to treat a breach of contract as only giving rise to a claim for damages, he may, in an action by the seller for the price, be required, in the discretion of the court before which the action depends, to consign or pay into court the price of the goods, or part of the price, or to give other reasonable security for its due payment.

Reasonable time a question of fact.

59. Where a reference is made in this Act to a reasonable time the question what is a reasonable time is a question of fact.

APPENDIX 1 SALE OF GOODS ACT 1979 211

60. Where a right, duty or liability is declared by this Act, it may (unless otherwise provided by this Act) be enforced by action.

PART VII
Rights etc. enforceable by action.

61.—(1) In this Act, unless the context or subject matter otherwise requires,—

Interpretation.

"action" includes counterclaim and set-off, and in Scotland condescendence and claim and compensation;

"business" includes a profession and the activities of any government department (including a Northern Ireland department) or local or public authority;

"buyer" means a person who buys or agrees to buy goods;

"contract of sale" includes an agreement to sell as well as a sale;

"credit-broker" means a person acting in the course of a business of credit brokerage carried on by him, that is a business of effecting introductions of individuals desiring to obtain credit—

(a) to persons carrying on any business so far as it relates to the provision of credit, or

(b) to other persons engaged in credit brokerage;

"defendant" includes in Scotland defender, respondent, and claimant in a multiplepoinding;

"delivery" means voluntary transfer of possession from one person to another;

"document of title to goods" has the same meaning as it has in the Factors Acts;

"Factors Acts" means the Factors Act 1889, the Factors (Scotland) Act 1890, and any enactment amending or substituted for the same;

1889 c. 45
1890 c. 40

"fault" means wrongful act or default;

"future goods" means goods to be manufactured or acquired by the seller after the making of the contract of sale;

"goods" includes all personal chattels other than things in action and money, and in Scotland all corporeal moveables except money; and in particular "goods" includes emblements, industrial growing crops, and things attached to or forming part of the land which are agreed to be severed before sale or under the contract of sale;

"plaintiff" includes pursuer, complainer, claimant in a multiplepoinding and defendant or defender counter-claiming;

PART VII

"property" means the general property in goods, and not merely a special property;

"quality", in relation to goods, includes their state or condition;

"sale" includes a bargain and sale as well as a sale and delivery;

"seller" means a person who sells or agrees to sell goods;

"specific goods" means goods identified and agreed on at the time a contract of sale is made;

"warranty" (as regards England and Wales and Northern Ireland) means an agreeement with reference to goods which are the subject of a contract of sale, but collateral to the main purpose of such contract, the breach of which gives rise to a claim for damages, but not to a right to reject the goods and treat the contract as repudiated.

(2) As regards Scotland a breach of warranty shall be deemed to be a failure to perform a material part of the contract.

(3) A thing is deemed to be done in good faith within the meaning of this Act when it is in fact done honestly, whether it is done negligently or not.

(4) A person is deemed to be insolvent within the meaning of this Act if he has either ceased to pay his debts in the ordinary course of business or he cannot pay his debts as they become due, whether he has committed an act of bankruptcy or not, and whether he has become a notour bankrupt or not.

(5) Goods are in a deliverable state within the meaning of this Act when they are in such a state that the buyer would under the contract be bound to take delivery of them.

(6) As regards the definition of "business" in subsection (1) above, paragraph 14 of Schedule 1 below applies in relation to a contract made on or after 18 May 1973 and before 1 February 1978, and paragraph 15 in relation to one made before 18 May 1973.

Savings: rules of law etc.

62.—(1) The rules in bankruptcy relating to contracts of sale apply to those contracts, notwithstanding anything in this Act.

(2) The rules of the common law, including the law merchant, except in so far as they are inconsistent with the provisions of this Act, and in particular the rules relating to the law of principal and agent and the effect of fraud, misrepresentation, duress or coercion, mistake, or other invalidating cause, apply to contracts for the sale of goods.

(3) Nothing in this Act or the Sale of Goods Act 1893 affects the enactments relating to bills of sale, or any enactment relating to the sale of goods which is not expressly repealed or amended by this Act or that.

PART VII
1893 c. 71.

(4) The provisions of this Act about contracts of sale do not apply to a transaction in the form of a contract of sale which is intended to operate by way of mortgage, pledge, charge, or other security.

(5) Nothing in this Act prejudices or affects the landlord's right of hypothec or sequestration for rent in Scotland.

63.—(1) Without prejudice to section 17 of the Interpretation Act 1978 (repeal and re-enactment), the enactments mentioned in Schedule 2 below have effect subject to the amendments there specified (being amendments consequential on this Act).

Consequential amendments, repeals and savings.
1978 c. 30.

(2) The enactments mentioned in Schedule 3 below are repealed to the extent specified in column 3, but subject to the savings in Schedule 4 below.

(3) The savings in Schedule 4 below have effect.

64.—(1) This Act may be cited as the Sale of Goods Act 1979.

Short title and commencement.

(2) This Act comes into force on 1 January 1980.

[Schedules omitted]

Appendix 2 Supply of Goods and Services Act 1982

[Schedules omitted]

CHAPTER 29

ARRANGEMENT OF SECTIONS

PART I
SUPPLY OF GOODS

Contracts for the transfer of property in goods

Section
1. The contracts concerned.
2. Implied terms about title, etc.
3. Implied terms where transfer is by description.
4. Implied terms about quality or fitness.
5. Implied terms where transfer is by sample.

Contracts for the hire of goods

6. The contracts concerned.
7. Implied terms about right to transfer possession, etc.
8. Implied terms where hire is by description.
9. Implied terms about quality or fitness.
10. Implied terms where hire is by sample.

Exclusion of implied terms, etc.

11. Exclusion of implied terms, etc.

PART II
SUPPLY OF SERVICES

12. The contracts concerned.
13. Implied term about care and skill.
14. Implied term about time for performance.
15. Implied term about consideration.
16. Exclusion of implied terms, etc.

PART III
SUPPLEMENTARY

17. Minor and consequential amendments.
18. Interpretation: general.
19. Interpretation: references to Acts.
20. Citation, transitional provisions, commencement and extent.

An Act to amend the law with respect to the terms to be implied in certain contracts for the transfer of the property in goods, in certain contracts for the hire of goods and in certain contracts for the supply of a service; and for connected purposes. [13th July 1982]

BE IT ENACTED by the Queen's most Excellent Majesty, by and with the advice and consent of the Lords Spiritual and Temporal, and Commons, in this present Parliament assembled, and by the authority of the same, as follows:—

PART I

SUPPLY OF GOODS

Contracts for the transfer of property in goods

1.—(1) In this Act a "contract for the transfer of goods" means a contract under which one person transfers or agrees to transfer to another the property in goods, other than an excepted contract. _{The contracts concerned.}

(2) For the purposes of this section an excepted contract means any of the following:—

(a) a contract of sale of goods;

(b) a hire-purchase agreement;

(c) a contract under which the property in goods is (or is to be) transferred in exchange for trading stamps on their redemption;

PART I

(d) a transfer or agreement to transfer which is made by deed and for which there is no consideration other than the presumed consideration imported by the deed;

(e) a contract intended to operate by way of mortgage, pledge, charge or other security.

(3) For the purposes of this Act a contract is a contract for the transfer of goods whether or not services are also provided or to be provided under the contract, and (subject to subsection (2) above) whatever is the nature of the consideration for the transfer or agreement to transfer.

Implied terms about title, etc.

2.—(1) In a contract for the transfer of goods, other than one to which subsection (3) below applies, there is an implied condition on the part of the transferor that in the case of a transfer of the property in the goods he has a right to transfer the property and in the case of an agreement to transfer the property in the goods he will have such a right at the time when the property is to be transferred.

(2) In a contract for the transfer of goods, other than one to which subsection (3) below applies, there is also an implied warranty that—

(a) the goods are free, and will remain free until the time when the property is to be transferred, from any charge or encumbrance not disclosed or known to the transferee before the contract is made, and

(b) the transferee will enjoy quiet possession of the goods except so far as it may be disturbed by the owner or other person entitled to the benefit of any charge or encumbrance so disclosed or known.

(3) This subsection applies to a contract for the transfer of goods in the case of which there appears from the contract or is to be inferred from its circumstances an intention that the transferor should transfer only such title as he or a third person may have.

(4) In a contract to which subsection (3) above applies there is an implied warranty that all charges or encumbrances known to the transferor and not known to the transferee have been disclosed to the transferee before the contract is made.

(5) In a contract to which subsection (3) above applies there is also an implied warranty that none of the following will disturb the transferee's quiet possession of the goods, namely—

(a) the transferor;

(b) in a case where the parties to the contract intend that the transferor should transfer only such title as a third person may have, that person;

(c) anyone claiming through or under the transferor or that third person otherwise than under a charge or encumbrance disclosed or known to the transferee before the contract is made.

3.—(1) This section applies where, under a contract for the transfer of goods, the transferor transfers or agrees to transfer the property in the goods by description. Implied terms where transfer is by description.

(2) In such a case there is an implied condition that the goods will correspond with the description.

(3) If the transferor transfers or agrees to transfer the property in the goods by sample as well as by description it is not sufficient that the bulk of the goods corresponds with the sample if the goods do not also correspond with the description.

(4) A contract is not prevented from falling within subsection (1) above by reason only that, being exposed for supply, the goods are selected by the transferee.

4.—(1) Except as provided by this section and section 5 below and subject to the provisions of any other enactment, there is no implied condition or warranty about the quality or fitness for any particular purpose of goods supplied under a contract for the transfer of goods. Implied terms about quality or fitness.

(2) Where, under such a contract, the transferor transfers the property in goods in the course of a business, there is (subject to subsection (3) below) an implied condition that the goods supplied under the contract are of merchantable quality.

(3) There is no such condition as is mentioned in subsection (2) above—
 (a) as regards defects specifically drawn to the transferee's attention before the contract is made; or
 (b) if the transferee examines the goods before the contract is made, as regards defects which that examination ought to reveal.

(4) Subsection (5) below applies where, under a contract for the transfer of goods, the transferor transfers the property in goods in the course of a business and the transferee, expressly or by implication, makes known—
 (a) to the transferor, or
 (b) where the consideration or part of the consideration for the transfer is a sum payable by instalments and the goods were previously sold by a credit-broker to the transferor, to that credit-broker,
any particular purpose for which the goods are being acquired.

APPENDIX 2 SUPPLY OF GOODS AND SERVICES ACT 1982

PART I

(5) In that case there is (subject to subsection (6) below) an implied condition that the goods supplied under the contract are reasonably fit for that purpose, whether or not that is a purpose for which such goods are commonly supplied.

(6) Subsection (5) above does not apply where the circumstances show that the transferee does not rely, or that it is unreasonable for him to rely, on the skill or judgment of the transferor or credit-broker.

(7) An implied condition or warranty about quality or fitness for a particular purpose may be annexed by usage to a contract for the transfer of goods.

(8) The preceding provisions of this section apply to a transfer by a person who in the course of a business is acting as agent for another as they apply to a transfer by a principal in the course of a business, except where that other is not transferring in the course of a business and either the transferee knows that fact or reasonable steps are taken to bring it to the transferee's notice before the contract concerned is made.

(9) Goods of any kind are of merchantable quality within the meaning of subsection (2) above if they are as fit for the purpose or purposes for which goods of that kind are commonly supplied as it is reasonable to expect having regard to any description applied to them, the price (if relevant) and all the other relevant circumstances.

Implied terms where transfer is by sample.

5.—(1) This section applies where, under a contract for the transfer of goods, the transferor transfers or agrees to transfer the property in the goods by reference to a sample.

(2) In such a case there is an implied condition—

   (a) that the bulk will correspond with the sample in quality; and

   (b) that the transferee will have a reasonable opportunity of comparing the bulk with the sample; and

   (c) that the goods will be free from any defect, rendering them unmerchantable, which would not be apparent on reasonable examination of the sample.

(3) In subsection (2)(c) above " unmerchantable " is to be construed in accordance with section 4(9) above.

(4) For the purposes of this section a transferor transfers or agrees to transfer the property in goods by reference to a sample where there is an express or implied term to that effect in the contract concerned.

Contracts for the hire of goods

6.—(1) In this Act a "contract for the hire of goods" means a contract under which one person bails or agrees to bail goods to another by way of hire, other than an excepted contract. *[The contracts concerned.]*

(2) For the purposes of this section an excepted contract means any of the following:—

(a) a hire-purchase agreement;

(b) a contract under which goods are (or are to be) bailed in exchange for trading stamps on their redemption.

(3) For the purposes of this Act a contract is a contract for the hire of goods whether or not services are also provided or to be provided under the contract, and (subject to subsection (2) above) whatever is the nature of the consideration for the bailment or agreement to bail by way of hire.

7.—(1) In a contract for the hire of goods there is an implied condition on the part of the bailor that in the case of a bailment he has a right to transfer possession of the goods by way of hire for the period of the bailment and in the case of an agreement to bail he will have such a right at the time of the bailment. *[Implied terms about right to transfer possession, etc.]*

(2) In a contract for the hire of goods there is also an implied warranty that the bailee will enjoy quiet possession of the goods for the period of the bailment except so far as the possession may be disturbed by the owner or other person entitled to the benefit of any charge or encumbrance disclosed or known to the bailee before the contract is made.

(3) The preceding provisions of this section do not affect the right of the bailor to repossess the goods under an express or implied term of the contract.

8.—(1) This section applies where, under a contract for the hire of goods, the bailor bails or agrees to bail the goods by description. *[Implied terms where hire is by description.]*

(2) In such a case there is an implied condition that the goods will correspond with the description.

(3) If under the contract the bailor bails or agrees to bail the goods by reference to a sample as well as a description it is not sufficient that the bulk of the goods corresponds with the sample if the goods do not also correspond with the description.

(4) A contract is not prevented from falling within subsection (1) above by reason only that, being exposed for supply, the goods are selected by the bailee.

APPENDIX 2 SUPPLY OF GOODS AND SERVICES ACT 1982   221

PART I
Implied terms
about quality
or fitness.

9.—(1) Except as provided by this section and section 10 below and subject to the provisions of any other enactment, there is no implied condition or warranty about the quality or fitness for any particular purpose of goods bailed under a contract for the hire of goods.

(2) Where, under such a contract, the bailor bails goods in the course of a business, there is (subject to subsection (3) below) an implied condition that the goods supplied under the contract are of merchantable quality.

(3) There is no such condition as is mentioned in subsection (2) above—

    (*a*) as regards defects specifically drawn to the bailee's attention before the contract is made ; or

    (*b*) if the bailee examines the goods before the contract is made, as regards defects which that examination ought to reveal.

(4) Subsection (5) below applies where, under a contract for the hire of goods, the bailor bails goods in the course of a business and the bailee, expressly or by implication, makes known—

    (*a*) to the bailor in the course of negotiations conducted by him in relation to the making of the contract, or

    (*b*) to a credit-broker in the course of negotiations conducted by that broker in relation to goods sold by him to the bailor before forming the subject matter of the contract,

any particular purpose for which the goods are being bailed.

(5) In that case there is (subject to subsection (6) below) an implied condition that the goods supplied under the contract are reasonably fit for that purpose, whether or not that is a purpose for which such goods are commonly supplied.

(6) Subsection (5) above does not apply where the circumstances show that the bailee does not rely, or that it is unreasonable for him to rely, on the skill or judgment of the bailor or credit-broker.

(7) An implied condition or warranty about quality or fitness for a particular purpose may be annexed by usage to a contract for the hire of goods.

(8) The preceding provisions of this section apply to a bailment by a person who in the course of a business is acting as agent for another as they apply to a bailment by a principal in the course of a business, except where that other is not bailing in the course of a business and either the bailee knows that fact or reasonable steps are taken to bring it to the bailee's notice before the contract concerned is made.

(9) Goods of any kind are of merchantable quality within the meaning of subsection (2) above if they are as fit for the purpose or purposes for which goods of that kind are commonly supplied as it is reasonable to expect having regard to any description applied to them, the consideration for the bailment (if relevant) and all the other relevant circumstances.

10.—(1) This section applies where, under a contract for the hire of goods, the bailor bails or agrees to bail the goods by reference to a sample. *Implied terms where hire is by sample.*

(2) In such a case there is an implied condition—

  (a) that the bulk will correspond with the sample in quality; and

  (b) that the bailee will have a reasonable opportunity of comparing the bulk with the sample; and

  (c) that the goods will be free from any defect, rendering them unmerchantable, which would not be apparent on reasonable examination of the sample.

(3) In subsection (2)(c) above "unmerchantable" is to be construed in accordance with section 9(9) above.

(4) For the purposes of this section a bailor bails or agrees to bail goods by reference to a sample where there is an express or implied term to that effect in the contract concerned.

Exclusion of implied terms, etc.

11.—(1) Where a right, duty or liability would arise under a contract for the transfer of goods or a contract for the hire of goods by implication of law, it may (subject to subsection (2) below and the 1977 Act) be negatived or varied by express agreement, or by the course of dealing between the parties, or by such usage as binds both parties to the contract. *Exclusion of implied terms, etc.*

(2) An express condition or warranty does not negative a condition or warranty implied by the preceding provisions of this Act unless inconsistent with it.

(3) Nothing in the preceding provisions of this Act prejudices the operation of any other enactment or any rule of law whereby any condition or warranty (other than one relating to quality or fitness) is to be implied in a contract for the transfer of goods or a contract for the hire of goods.

Part II

Supply of Services

The contracts concerned.
12.—(1) In this Act a "contract for the supply of a service" means, subject to subsection (2) below, a contract under which a person ("the supplier") agrees to carry out a service.

(2) For the purposes of this Act, a contract of service or apprenticeship is not a contract for the supply of a service.

(3) Subject to subsection (2) above, a contract is a contract for the supply of a service for the purposes of this Act whether or not goods are also—

(a) transferred or to be transferred, or

(b) bailed or to be bailed by way of hire,

under the contract, and whatever is the nature of the consideration for which the service is to be carried out.

(4) The Secretary of State may by order provide that one or more of sections 13 to 15 below shall not apply to services of a description specified in the order, and such an order may make different provision for different circumstances.

(5) The power to make an order under subsection (4) above shall be exercisable by statutory instrument subject to annulment in pursuance of a resolution of either House of Parliament.

Implied term about care and skill.
13. In a contract for the supply of a service where the supplier is acting in the course of a business, there is an implied term that the supplier will carry out the service with reasonable care and skill.

Implied term about time for performance.
14.—(1) Where, under a contract for the supply of a service by a supplier acting in the course of a business, the time for the service to be carried out is not fixed by the contract, left to be fixed in a manner agreed by the contract or determined by the course of dealing between the parties, there is an implied term that the supplier will carry out the service within a reasonable time.

(2) What is a reasonable time is a question of fact.

Implied term about consideration.
15.—(1) Where, under a contract for the supply of a service, the consideration for the service is not determined by the contract, left to be determined in a manner agreed by the contract or determined by the course of dealing between the parties, there is an implied term that the party contracting with the supplier will pay a reasonable charge.

(2) What is a reasonable charge is a question of fact.

16.—(1) Where a right, duty or liability would arise under a contract for the supply of a service by virtue of this Part of this Act, it may (subject to subsection (2) below and the 1977 Act) be negatived or varied by express agreement, or by the course of dealing between the parties, or by such usage as binds both parties to the contract.

PART II
Exclusion of implied terms, etc.

(2) An express term does not negative a term implied by this Part of this Act unless inconsistent with it.

(3) Nothing in this Part of this Act prejudices—

  (a) any rule of law which imposes on the supplier a duty stricter than that imposed by section 13 or 14 above; or

  (b) subject to paragraph (a) above, any rule of law whereby any term not inconsistent with this Part of this Act is to be implied in a contract for the supply of a service.

(4) This Part of this Act has effect subject to any other enactment which defines or restricts the rights, duties or liabilities arising in connection with a service of any description.

PART III

SUPPLEMENTARY

17.—(1) In section 10(2) of the 1973 Act, as originally enacted and as prospectively substituted by paragraph 35 of Schedule 4 to the 1974 Act (implied condition in hire-purchase agreement that goods are of merchantable quality), after " implied condition that the goods " there shall be inserted " supplied under the agreement ".

Minor and consequential amendments.

(2) The following subsection shall be inserted after section 7(3) of the 1977 Act:—

  " (3A) Liability for breach of the obligations arising under section 2 of the Supply of Goods and Services Act 1982 (implied terms about title etc. in certain contracts for the transfer of the property in goods) cannot be excluded or restricted by reference to any such term."

(3) In consequence of subsection (2) above, in section 7(4) of the 1977 Act, after " cannot " there shall be inserted " (in a case to which subsection (3A) above does not apply) ".

18.—(1) In the preceding provisions of this Act and this section—

Interpretation: general.

  " bailee ", in relation to a contract for the hire of goods means (depending on the context) a person to whom the goods are bailed under the contract, or a person to whom they are to be so bailed, or a person to whom the rights under the contract of either of those persons have passed;

"bailor", in relation to a contract for the hire of goods, means (depending on the context) a person who bails the goods under the contract, or a person who agrees to do so, or a person to whom the duties under the contract of either of those persons have passed;

"business" includes a profession and the activities of any government department or local or public authority;

"credit-broker" means a person acting in the course of a business of credit brokerage carried on by him;

"credit brokerage" means the effecting of introductions—
 (a) of individuals desiring to obtain credit to persons carrying on any business so far as it relates to the provision of credit; or
 (b) of individuals desiring to obtain goods on hire to persons carrying on a business which comprises or relates to the bailment of goods under a contract for the hire of goods; or
 (c) of individuals desiring to obtain credit, or to obtain goods on hire, to other credit-brokers;

"enactment" means any legislation (including subordinate legislation) of the United Kingdom or Northern Ireland;

"goods" include all personal chattels (including emblements, industrial growing crops, and things attached to or forming part of the land which are agreed to be severed before the transfer or bailment concerned or under the contract concerned), other than things in action and money;

"hire-purchase agreement" has the same meaning as in the 1974 Act;

"property", in relation to goods, means the general property in them and not merely a special property;

"quality", in relation to goods, includes their state or condition;

"redemption", in relation to trading stamps, has the same meaning as in the Trading Stamps Act 1964 or, as respects Northern Ireland, the Trading Stamps Act (Northern Ireland) 1965;

"trading stamps" has the same meaning as in the said Act of 1964 or, as respects Northern Ireland, the said Act of 1965;

"transferee", in relation to a contract for the transfer of goods, means (depending on the context) a person to whom the property in the goods is transferred under the contract, or a person to whom the property is to be so transferred, or a person to whom the rights under the contract of either of those persons have passed;

"transferor", in relation to a contract for the transfer of goods, means (depending on the context) a person who transfers the property in the goods under the contract, or a person who agrees to do so, or a person to whom the duties under the contract of either of those persons have passed.

(2) In subsection (1) above, in the definitions of bailee, bailor, transferee and transferor, a reference to rights or duties passing is to their passing by assignment, operation of law or otherwise.

19. In this Act—
"the 1973 Act" means the Supply of Goods (Implied Terms) Act 1973;
"the 1974 Act" means the Consumer Credit Act 1974;
"the 1977 Act" means the Unfair Contract Terms Act 1977; and
"the 1979 Act" means the Sale of Goods Act 1979.

20.—(1) This Act may be cited as the Supply of Goods and Services Act 1982.

(2) The transitional provisions in the Schedule to this Act shall have effect.

(3) Part I of this Act together with section 17 and so much of sections 18 and 19 above as relates to that Part shall not come into operation until 4th January 1983; and Part II of this Act together with so much of sections 18 and 19 above as relates to that Part shall not come into operation until such day as may be appointed by an order made by the Secretary of State.

(4) The power to make an order under subsection (3) above shall be exercisable by statutory instrument.

(5) No provision of this Act applies to a contract made before the provision comes into operation.

(6) This Act extends to Northern Ireland but not to Scotland.

[Schedule omitted]

Appendix 3 Unfair Contract Terms Act 1977

1977 CHAPTER 50

ARRANGEMENT OF SECTIONS

PART I
AMENDMENT OF LAW FOR ENGLAND AND WALES AND NORTHERN IRELAND

Introductory

Section
1. Scope of Part I.

Avoidance of liability for negligence, breach of contract, etc.
2. Negligence liability.
3. Liability arising in contract.
4. Unreasonable indemnity clauses.

Liability arising from sale or supply of goods
5. "Guarantee" of consumer goods.
6. Sale and hire-purchase.
7. Miscellaneous contracts under which goods pass.

Other provisions about contracts
8. Misrepresentation.
9. Effect of breach.
10. Evasion by means of secondary contract.

Explanatory provisions
11. The "reasonableness" test.
12. "Dealing as consumer".
13. Varieties of exemption clause.
14. Interpretation of Part I.

PART II

AMENDMENT OF LAW FOR SCOTLAND

15. Scope of Part II.
16. Liability for breach of duty.
17. Control of unreasonable exemptions in consumer or standard form contracts.
18. Unreasonable indemnity clauses in consumer contracts.
19. "Guarantee" of consumer goods.
20. Obligations implied by law in sale and hire-purchase contracts.
21. Obligations implied by law in other contracts for the supply of goods.
22. Consequence of breach.
23. Evasion by means of secondary contract.
24. The "reasonableness" test.
25. Interpretation of Part II.

PART II

PROVISIONS APPLYING TO WHOLE OF UNITED KINGDOM

Miscellaneous
26. International supply contracts.
27. Choice of law clauses.
28. Temporary provision for sea carriage of passengers.
29. Saving for other relevant legislation.
30. Obligations under Consumer Protection Acts.

General
31. Commencement; amendment; repeals.
32. Citation and extent.

SCHEDULES:

Schedule 1—Scope of ss. 2 to 4 and 7.
Schedule 2—"Guidelines" for application of reasonableness test.
Schedule 3—Amendment of enactments.
Schedule 4—Repeals.

APPENDIX 3 UNFAIR CONTRACT TERMS ACT 1977

An Act to impose further limits on the extent to which under the law of England and Wales and Northern Ireland civil liability for breach of contract, or for negligence or other breach of duty, can be avoided by means of contract terms and otherwise, and under the law of Scotland civil liability can be avoided by means of contract terms. [26th October 1977]

BE IT ENACTED by the Queen's most Excellent Majesty, by and with the advice and consent of the Lords Spiritual and Temporal, and Commons, in this present Parliament assembled, and by the authority of the same, as follows:—

PART I

AMENDMENT OF LAW FOR ENGLAND AND WALES AND NORTHERN IRELAND

Introductory

1.—(1) For the purposes of this Part of this Act, " negligence " means the breach— *Scope of Part I.*

    (*a*) of any obligation, arising from the express or implied terms of a contract, to take reasonable care or exercise reasonable skill in the performance of the contract;

    (*b*) of any common law duty to take reasonable care or exercise reasonable skill (but not any stricter duty);

PART I
1957 c. 31.
1957 c. 25
(N.I.).

(c) of the common duty of care imposed by the Occupiers' Liability Act 1957 or the Occupiers' Liability Act (Northern Ireland) 1957.

(2) This Part of this Act is subject to Part III; and in relation to contracts, the operation of sections 2 to 4 and 7 is subject to the exceptions made by Schedule 1.

(3) In the case of both contract and tort, sections 2 to 7 apply (except where the contrary is stated in section 6(4)) only to business liability, that is liability for breach of obligations or duties arising—
 (a) from things done or to be done by a person in the course of a business (whether his own business or another's); or
 (b) from the occupation of premises used for business purposes of the occupier;
and references to liability are to be read accordingly.

(4) In relation to any breach of duty or obligation, it is immaterial for any purpose of this Part of this Act whether the breach was inadvertent or intentional, or whether liability for it arises directly or vicariously.

Avoidance of liability for negligence, breach of contract, etc.

Negligence liability.

2.—(1) A person cannot by reference to any contract term or to a notice given to persons generally or to particular persons exclude or restrict his liability for death or personal injury resulting from negligence.

(2) In the case of other loss or damage, a person cannot so exclude or restrict his liability for negligence except in so far as the term or notice satisfies the requirement of reasonableness.

(3) Where a contract term or notice purports to exclude or restrict liability for negligence a person's agreement to or awareness of it is not of itself to be taken as indicating his voluntary acceptance of any risk.

Liability arising in contract.

3.—(1) This section applies as between contracting parties where one of them deals as consumer or on the other's written standard terms of business.

(2) As against that party, the other cannot by reference to any contract term—
 (a) when himself in breach of contract, exclude or restrict any liability of his in respect of the breach; or
 (b) claim to be entitled—
  (i) to render a contractual performance substantially different from that which was reasonably expected of him, or

APPENDIX 3 UNFAIR CONTRACT TERMS ACT 1977

(ii) in respect of the whole or any part of his contractual obligation, to render no performance at all,

except in so far as (in any of the cases mentioned above in this subsection) the contract term satisfies the requirement of reasonableness.

4.—(1) A person dealing as consumer cannot by reference to any contract term be made to indemnify another person (whether a party to the contract or not) in respect of liability that may be incurred by the other for negligence or breach of contract, except in so far as the contract term satisfies the requirement of reasonableness.

Unreasonable indemnity clauses.

(2) This section applies whether the liability in question—
   (a) is directly that of the person to be indemnified or is incurred by him vicariously;
   (b) is to the person dealing as consumer or to someone else.

Liability arising from sale or supply of goods

5.—(1) In the case of goods of a type ordinarily supplied for private use or consumption, where loss or damage—
   (a) arises from the goods proving defective while in consumer use; and
   (b) results from the negligence of a person concerned in the manufacture or distribution of the goods,

liability for the loss or damage cannot be excluded or restricted by reference to any contract term or notice contained in or operating by reference to a guarantee of the goods.

" Guarantee " of consumer goods.

(2) For these purposes—
   (a) goods are to be regarded as " in consumer use " when a person is using them, or has them in his possession for use, otherwise than exclusively for the purposes of a business; and
   (b) anything in writing is a guarantee if it contains or purports to contain some promise or assurance (however worded or presented) that defects will be made good by complete or partial replacement, or by repair, monetary compensation or otherwise.

(3) This section does not apply as between the parties to a contract under or in pursuance of which possession or ownership of the goods passed.

6.—(1) Liability for breach of the obligations arising from—
   (a) section 12 of the Sale of Goods Act 1893 (seller's implied undertakings as to title, etc.);

Sale and hire-purchase.
56 & 57 Vict.
c. 71.

PART I
1973 c. 13.

(b) section 8 of the Supply of Goods (Implied Terms) Act 1973 (the corresponding thing in relation to hire-purchase),

cannot be excluded or restricted by reference to any contract term.

(2) As against a person dealing as consumer, liability for breach of the obligations arising from—

(a) section 13, 14 or 15 of the 1893 Act (seller's implied undertakings as to conformity of goods with description or sample, or as to their quality or fitness for a particular purpose);

(b) section 9, 10 or 11 of the 1973 Act (the corresponding things in relation to hire-purchase),

cannot be excluded or restricted by reference to any contract term.

(3) As against a person dealing otherwise than as consumer, the liability specified in subsection (2) above can be excluded or restricted by reference to a contract term, but only in so far as the term satisfies the requirement of reasonableness.

(4) The liabilities referred to in this section are not only the business liabilities defined by section 1(3), but include those arising under any contract of sale of goods or hire-purchase agreement.

Miscellaneous contracts under which goods pass.

7.—(1) Where the possession or ownership of goods passes under or in pursuance of a contract not governed by the law of sale of goods or hire-purchase, subsections (2) to (4) below apply as regards the effect (if any) to be given to contract terms excluding or restricting liability for breach of obligation arising by implication of law from the nature of the contract.

(2) As against a person dealing as consumer, liability in respect of the goods' correspondence with description or sample, or their quality or fitness for any particular purpose, cannot be excluded or restricted by reference to any such term.

(3) As against a person dealing otherwise than as consumer, that liability can be excluded or restricted by reference to such a term, but only in so far as the term satisfies the requirement of reasonableness.

(4) Liability in respect of—

(a) the right to transfer ownership of the goods, or give possession; or

(b) the assurance of quiet possession to a person taking goods in pursuance of the contract, cannot be excluded or restricted by reference to any such term except in so far as the term satisfies the requirement of reasonableness.

PART I

(5) This section does not apply in the case of goods passing on a redemption of trading stamps within the Trading Stamps Act 1964 or the Trading Stamps Act (Northern Ireland) 1965.

1964 c. 71.
1965 c. 6.
(N.I.).

Other provisions about contracts

8.—(1) In the Misrepresentation Act 1967, the following is substituted for section 3—

Misrepresentation.

"Avoidance of provision excluding liability for misrepresentation.

3. If a contract contains a term which would exclude or restrict—

1967 c. 7.

(a) any liability to which a party to a contract may be subject by reason of any misrepresentation made by him before the contract was made ; or

(b) any remedy available to another party to the contract by reason of such a misrepresentation,

that term shall be of no effect except in so far as it satisfies the requirement of reasonableness as stated in section 11(1) of the Unfair Contract Terms Act 1977 ; and it is for those claiming that the term satisfies that requirement to show that it does.".

(2) The same section is substituted for section 3 of the Misrepresentation Act (Northern Ireland) 1967.

1967 c. 14
(N.I.).

9.—(1) Where for reliance upon it a contract term has to satisfy the requirement of reasonableness, it may be found to do so and be given effect accordingly notwithstanding that the contract has been terminated either by breach or by a party electing to treat it as repudiated.

Effect of breach.

(2) Where on a breach the contract is nevertheless affirmed by a party entitled to treat it as repudiated, this does not of itself exclude the requirement of reasonableness in relation to any contract term.

10. A person is not bound by any contract term prejudicing or taking away rights of his which arise under, or in connection with the performance of, another contract, so far as those rights extend to the enforcement of another's liability which this Part of this Act prevents that other from excluding or restricting.

Evasion by means of secondary contract.

PART I

Explanatory provisions

The "reasonableness" test.
1967 c. 7.
1967 c. 14. (N.I.).

11.—(1) In relation to a contract term, the requirement of reasonableness for the purposes of this Part of this Act, section 3 of the Misrepresentation Act 1967 and section 3 of the Misrepresentation Act (Northern Ireland) 1967 is that the term shall have been a fair and reasonable one to be included having regard to the circumstances which were, or ought reasonably to have been, known to or in the contemplation of the parties when the contract was made.

(2) In determining for the purposes of section 6 or 7 above whether a contract term satisfies the requirement of reasonableness, regard shall be had in particular to the matters specified in Schedule 2 to this Act; but this subsection does not prevent the court or arbitrator from holding, in accordance with any rule of law, that a term which purports to exclude or restrict any relevant liability is not a term of the contract.

(3) In relation to a notice (not being a notice having contractual effect), the requirement of reasonableness under this Act is that it should be fair and reasonable to allow reliance on it, having regard to all the circumstances obtaining when the liability arose or (but for the notice) would have arisen.

(4) Where by reference to a contract term or notice a person seeks to restrict liability to a specified sum of money, and the question arises (under this or any other Act) whether the term or notice satisfies the requirement of reasonableness, regard shall be had in particular (but without prejudice to subsection (2) above in the case of contract terms) to—

(*a*) the resources which he could expect to be available to him for the purpose of meeting the liability should it arise; and

(*b*) how far it was open to him to cover himself by insurance.

(5) It is for those claiming that a contract term or notice satisfies the requirement of reasonableness to show that it does.

"Dealing as consumer".

12.—(1) A party to a contract "deals as consumer" in relation to another party if—

(*a*) he neither makes the contract in the course of a business nor holds himself out as doing so; and

(*b*) the other party does make the contract in the course of a business; and

(c) in the case of a contract governed by the law of sale of goods or hire-purchase, or by section 7 of this Act, the goods passing under or in pursuance of the contract are of a type ordinarily supplied for private use or consumption.

(2) But on a sale by auction or by competitive tender the buyer is not in any circumstances to be regarded as dealing as consumer.

(3) Subject to this, it is for those claiming that a party does not deal as consumer to show that he does not.

13.—(1) To the extent that this Part of this Act prevents the exclusion or restriction of any liability it also prevents— *Varieties of exemption clause.*

   (a) making the liability or its enforcement subject to restrictive or onerous conditions ;

   (b) excluding or restricting any right or remedy in respect of the liability, or subjecting a person to any prejudice in consequence of his pursuing any such right or remedy ;

   (c) excluding or restricting rules of evidence or procedure ;

and (to that extent) sections 2 and 5 to 7 also prevent excluding or restricting liability by reference to terms and notices which exclude or restrict the relevant obligation or duty.

(2) But an agreement in writing to submit present or future differences to arbitration is not to be treated under this Part of this Act as excluding or restricting any liability.

14. In this Part of this Act— *Interpretation of Part I.*

   " business " includes a profession and the activities of any government department or local or public authority ;

   " goods " has the same meaning as in the Sale of Goods Act 1893 ; *56 & 57 Vict. c. 71.*

   " hire-purchase agreement " has the same meaning as in the Consumer Credit Act 1974 ; *1974 c. 39.*

   " negligence " has the meaning given by section 1(1) ;

   " notice " includes an announcement, whether or not in writing, and any other communication or pretended communication ; and

   " personal injury " includes any disease and any impairment of physical or mental condition.

Part II

Amendment of Law for Scotland

Scope of Part II.

15.—(1) This Part of this Act applies only to contracts, is subject to Part III of this Act and does not affect the validity of any discharge or indemnity given by a person in consideration of the receipt by him of compensation in settlement of any claim which he has.

(2) Subject to subsection (3) below, sections 16 to 18 of this Act apply to any contract only to the extent that the contract—

(*a*) relates to the transfer of the ownership or possession of goods from one person to another (with or without work having been done on them);

(*b*) constitutes a contract of service or apprenticeship;

(*c*) relates to services of whatever kind, including (without prejudice to the foregoing generality) carriage, deposit and pledge, care and custody, mandate, agency, loan and services relating to the use of land;

(*d*) relates to the liability of an occupier of land to persons entering upon or using that land;

(*e*) relates to a grant of any right or permission to enter upon or use land not amounting to an estate or interest in the land.

(3) Notwithstanding anything in subsection (2) above, sections 16 to 18—

(*a*) do not apply to any contract to the extent that the contract—

(i) is a contract of insurance (including a contract to pay an annuity on human life);

(ii) relates to the formation, constitution or dissolution of any body corporate or unincorporated association or partnership;

(*b*) apply to—

a contract of marine salvage or towage;

a charter party of a ship or hovercraft;

a contract for the carriage of goods by ship or hovercraft; or,

a contract to which subsection (4) below relates,

only to the extent that—

(i) both parties deal or hold themselves out as dealing in the course of a business (and then only in so far as the contract purports to exclude or restrict liability for breach of duty in respect of death or personal injury); or

(ii) the contract is a consumer contract (and then only in favour of the consumer).

APPENDIX 3 UNFAIR CONTRACT TERMS ACT 1977

(4) This subsection relates to a contract in pursuance of which goods are carried by ship or hovercraft and which either—
- (a) specifies ship or hovercraft as the means of carriage over part of the journey to be covered; or
- (b) makes no provision as to the means of carriage and does not exclude ship or hovercraft as that means,

in so far as the contract operates for and in relation to the carriage of the goods by that means.

16.—(1) Where a term of a contract purports to exclude or restrict liability for breach of duty arising in the course of any business or from the occupation of any premises used for business purposes of the occupier, that term— *Liability for breach of duty.*
- (a) shall be void in any case where such exclusion or restriction is in respect of death or personal injury;
- (b) shall, in any other case, have no effect if it was not fair and reasonable to incorporate the term in the contract.

(2) Subsection (1)(a) above does not affect the validity of any discharge and indemnity given by a person, on or in connection with an award to him of compensation for pneumoconiosis attributable to employment in the coal industry, in respect of any further claim arising from his contracting that disease.

(3) Where under subsection (1) above a term of a contract is void or has no effect, the fact that a person agreed to, or was aware of, the term shall not of itself be sufficient evidence that he knowingly and voluntarily assumed any risk.

17.—(1) Any term of a contract which is a consumer contract or a standard form contract shall have no effect for the purpose of enabling a party to the contract— *Control of unreasonable exemptions in consumer or standard form contracts.*
- (a) who is in breach of a contractual obligation, to exclude or restrict any liability of his to the consumer or customer in respect of the breach;
- (b) in respect of a contractual obligation, to render no performance, or to render a performance substantially different from that which the consumer or customer reasonably expected from the contract;

if it was not fair and reasonable to incorporate the term in the contract.

(2) In this section " customer " means a party to a standard form contract who deals on the basis of written standard terms of business of the other party to the contract who himself deals in the course of a business.

PART II
Unreasonable indemnity clauses in consumer contracts.

18.—(1) Any term of a contract which is a consumer contract shall have no effect for the purpose of making the consumer indemnify another person (whether a party to the contract or not) in respect of liability which that other person may incur as a result of breach of duty or breach of contract, if it was not fair and reasonable to incorporate the term in the contract.

(2) In this section " liability " means liability arising in the course of any business or from the occupation of any premises used for business purposes of the occupier.

" Guarantee " of consumer goods.

19.—(1) This section applies to a guarantee—

(a) in relation to goods which are of a type ordinarily supplied for private use or consumption ; and

(b) which is not a guarantee given by one party to the other party to a contract under or in pursuance of which the ownership or possession of the goods to which the guarantee relates is transferred.

(2) A term of a guarantee to which this section applies shall be void in so far as it purports to exclude or restrict liability for loss or damage (including death or personal injury)—

(a) arising from the goods proving defective while—

(i) in use otherwise than exclusively for the purposes of a business ; or

(ii) in the possession of a person for such use ; and

(b) resulting from the breach of duty of a person concerned in the manufacture or distribution of the goods.

(3) For the purposes of this section, any document is a guarantee if it contains or purports to contain some promise or assurance (however worded or presented) that defects will be made good by complete or partial replacement, or by repair, monetary compensation or otherwise.

Obligations implied by law in sale and hire-purchase contracts.
56 & 57
Vict. c. 71.
1973 c. 13.

20.—(1) Any term of a contract which purports to exclude or restrict liability for breach of the obligations arising from—

(a) section 12 of the Sale of Goods Act 1893 (seller's implied undertakings as to title etc.) ;

(b) section 8 of the Supply of Goods (Implied Terms) Act 1973 (implied terms as to title in hire-purchase agreements),

shall be void.

APPENDIX 3 UNFAIR CONTRACT TERMS ACT 1977

PART II

(2) Any term of a contract which purports to exclude or restrict liability for breach of the obligations arising from—
  (a) section 13, 14 or 15 of the said Act of 1893 (seller's implied undertakings as to conformity of goods with description or sample, or as to their quality or fitness for a particular purpose);
  (b) section 9, 10 or 11 of the said Act of 1973 (the corresponding provisions in relation to hire-purchase),

shall—
  (i) in the case of a consumer contract, be void against the consumer;
  (ii) in any other case, have no effect if it was not fair and reasonable to incorporate the term in the contract.

Obligations implied by law in other contracts for the supply of goods.

21.—(1) Any term of a contract to which this section applies purporting to exclude or restrict liability for breach of an obligation—
  (a) such as is referred to in subsection (3)(a) below—
    (i) in the case of a consumer contract, shall be void against the consumer, and
    (ii) in any other case, shall have no effect if it was not fair and reasonable to incorporate the term in the contract;
  (b) such as is referred to in subsection (3)(b) below, shall have no effect if it was not fair and reasonable to incorporate the term in the contract.

(2) This section applies to any contract to the extent that it relates to any such matter as is referred to in section 15(2)(a) of this Act, but does not apply to—
  (a) a contract of sale of goods or a hire-purchase agreement; or
  (b) a charterparty of a ship or hovercraft unless it is a consumer contract (and then only in favour of the consumer).

(3) An obligation referred to in this subsection is an obligation incurred under a contract in the course of a business and arising by implication of law from the nature of the contract which relates—
  (a) to the correspondence of goods with description or sample, or to the quality or fitness of goods for any particular purpose; or
  (b) to any right to transfer ownership or possession of goods, or to the enjoyment of quiet possession of goods.

(4) Nothing in this section applies to the supply of goods on a redemption of trading stamps within the Trading Stamps Act 1964. 1964 c. 71.

PART II
Consequence of breach.

22. For the avoidance of doubt, where any provision of this Part of this Act requires that the incorporation of a term in a contract must be fair and reasonable for that term to have effect—

  (a) if that requirement is satisfied, the term may be given effect to notwithstanding that the contract has been terminated in consequence of breach of that contract;

  (b) for the term to be given effect to, that requirement must be satisfied even where a party who is entitled to rescind the contract elects not to rescind it.

Evasion by means of secondary contract.

23. Any term of any contract shall be void which purports to exclude or restrict, or has the effect of excluding or restricting—

  (a) the exercise, by a party to any other contract, of any right or remedy which arises in respect of that other contract in consequence of breach of duty, or of obligation, liability for which could not by virtue of the provisions of this Part of this Act be excluded or restricted by a term of that other contract;

  (b) the application of the provisions of this Part of this Act in respect of that or any other contract.

The "reasonableness" test.

24.—(1) In determining for the purposes of this Part of this Act whether it was fair and reasonable to incorporate a term in a contract, regard shall be had only to the circumstances which were, or ought reasonably to have been, known to or in the contemplation of the parties to the contract at the time the contract was made.

(2) In determining for the purposes of section 20 or 21 of this Act whether it was fair and reasonable to incorporate a term in a contract, regard shall be had in particular to the matters specified in Schedule 2 to this Act; but this subsection shall not prevent a court or arbiter from holding, in accordance with any rule of law, that a term which purports to exclude or restrict any relevant liability is not a term of the contract.

(3) Where a term in a contract purports to restrict liability to a specified sum of money, and the question arises for the purposes of this Part of this Act whether it was fair and reasonable to incorporate the term in the contract, then, without prejudice to subsection (2) above, regard shall be had in particular to—

  (a) the resources which the party seeking to rely on that term could expect to be available to him for the purpose of meeting the liability should it arise;

APPENDIX 3 UNFAIR CONTRACT TERMS ACT 1977   241

   (b) how far it was open to that party to cover himself by insurance.   PART II

(4) The onus of proving that it was fair and reasonable to incorporate a term in a contract shall lie on the party so contending.

25.—(1) In this Part of this Act—   Interpretation of Part II.
    " breach of duty " means the breach—

       (a) of any obligation, arising from the express or implied terms of a contract, to take reasonable care or exercise reasonable skill in the performance of the contract ;

       (b) of any common law duty to take reasonable care or exercise reasonable skill ;

       (c) of the duty of reasonable care imposed by section 2(1) of the Occupiers' Liability (Scotland) Act 1960 ;   1960 c. 30.

" business " includes a profession and the activities of any government department or local or public authority ;

" consumer " has the meaning assigned to that expression in the definition in this section of " consumer contract " ;

" consumer contract " means a contract (not being a contract of sale by auction or competitive tender) in which—

       (a) one party to the contract deals, and the other party to the contract (" the consumer ") does not deal or hold himself out as dealing, in the course of a business, and

       (b) in the case of a contract such as is mentioned in section 15(2)(a) of this Act, the goods are of a type ordinarily supplied for private use or consumption ;

and for the purposes of this Part of this Act the onus of proving that a contract is not to be regarded as a consumer contract shall lie on the party so contending ;

" goods " has the same meaning as in the Sale of Goods Act 1893 ;   56 & 57 Vict. c. 71.

" hire-purchase agreement " has the same meaning as in section 189(1) of the Consumer Credit Act 1974 ;   1974 c. 39.

" personal injury " includes any disease and any impairment of physical or mental condition.

(2) In relation to any breach of duty or obligation, it is immaterial for any purpose of this Part of this Act whether the act or omission giving rise to that breach was inadvertent or

intentional, or whether liability for it arises directly or vicariously.

(3) In this Part of this Act, any reference to excluding or restricting any liability includes—

(a) making the liability or its enforcement subject to any restrictive or onerous conditions ;

(b) excluding or restricting any right or remedy in respect of the liability, or subjecting a person to any prejudice in consequence of his pursuing any such right or remedy ;

(c) excluding or restricting any rule of evidence or procedure ;

(d) excluding or restricting any liability by reference to a notice having contractual effect,

but does not include an agreement to submit any question to arbitration.

(4) In subsection (3)(d) above " notice " includes an announcement, whether or not in writing, and any other communication or pretended communication.

(5) In sections 15 and 16 and 19 to 21 of this Act, any reference to excluding or restricting liability for breach of an obligation or duty shall include a reference to excluding or restricting the obligation or duty itself.

PART III

PROVISIONS APPLYING TO WHOLE OF UNITED KINGDOM

Miscellaneous

International supply contracts.

26.—(1) The limits imposed by this Act on the extent to which a person may exclude or restrict liability by reference to a contract term do not apply to liability arising under such a contract as is described in subsection (3) below.

(2) The terms of such a contract are not subject to any requirement of reasonableness under section 3 or 4: and nothing in Part II of this Act shall require the incorporation of the terms of such a contract to be fair and reasonable for them to have effect.

(3) Subject to subsection (4), that description of contract is one whose characteristics are the following—

(a) either it is a contract of sale of goods or it is one under or in pursuance of which the possession or ownership of goods passes ; and

APPENDIX 3 UNFAIR CONTRACT TERMS ACT 1977   243

(b) it is made by parties whose places of business (or, if PART III they have none, habitual residences) are in the territories of different States (the Channel Islands and the Isle of Man being treated for this purpose as different States from the United Kingdom).

(4) A contract falls within subsection (3) above only if either—
   (a) the goods in question are, at the time of the conclusion of the contract, in the course of carriage, or will be carried, from the territory of one State to the territory of another ; or
   (b) the acts constituting the offer and acceptance have been done in the territories of different States ; or
   (c) the contract provides for the goods to be delivered to the territory of a State other than that within whose territory those acts were done.

27.—(1) Where the proper law of a contract is the law of any Choice of part of the United Kingdom only by choice of the parties (and law clauses. apart from that choice would be the law of some country outside the United Kingdom) sections 2 to 7 and 16 to 21 of this Act do not operate as part of the proper law.

(2) This Act has effect notwithstanding any contract term which applies or purports to apply the law of some country outside the United Kingdom, where (either or both)—
   (a) the term appears to the court, or arbitrator or arbiter to have been imposed wholly or mainly for the purpose of enabling the party imposing it to evade the operation of this Act ; or
   (b) in the making of the contract one of the parties dealt as consumer, and he was then habitually resident in the United Kingdom, and the essential steps necessary for the making of the contract were taken there, whether by him or by others on his behalf.

(3) In the application of subsection (2) above to Scotland, for paragraph (b) there shall be substituted—
   " (b) the contract is a consumer contract as defined in Part II of this Act, and the consumer at the date when the contract was made was habitually resident in the United Kingdom, and the essential steps necessary for the making of the contract were taken there, whether by him or by others on his behalf.".

28.—(1) This section applies to a contract for carriage by Temporary sea of a passenger or of a passenger and his luggage where provision the provisions of the Athens Convention (with or without modi- for sea fication) do not have, in relation to the contract, the force of passengers. law in the United Kingdom.

(2) In a case where—

(a) the contract is not made in the United Kingdom, and

(b) neither the place of departure nor the place of destination under it is in the United Kingdom,

a person is not precluded by this Act from excluding or restricting liability for loss or damage, being loss or damage for which the provisions of the Convention would, if they had the force of law in relation to the contract, impose liability on him.

(3) In any other case, a person is not precluded by this Act from excluding or restricting liability for that loss or damage—

(a) in so far as the exclusion or restriction would have been effective in that case had the provisions of the Convention had the force of law in relation to the contract ; or

(b) in such circumstances and to such extent as may be prescribed, by reference to a prescribed term of the contract.

(4) For the purposes of subsection (3)(a), the values which shall be taken to be the official values in the United Kingdom of the amounts (expressed in gold francs) by reference to which liability under the provisions of the Convention is limited shall be such amounts in sterling as the Secretary of State may from time to time by order made by statutory instrument specify.

(5) In this section,—

(a) the references to excluding or restricting liability include doing any of those things in relation to the liability which are mentioned in section 13 or section 25(3) and (5) ; and

(b) " the Athens Convention " means the Athens Convention relating to the Carriage of Passengers and their Luggage by Sea, 1974 ; and

(c) " prescribed " means prescribed by the Secretary of State by regulations made by statutory instrument ;

and a statutory instrument containing the regulations shall be subject to annulment in pursuance of a resolution of either House of Parliament.

Saving for other relevant legislation.

29.—(1) Nothing in this Act removes or restricts the effect of, or prevents reliance upon, any contractual provision which—

(a) is authorised or required by the express terms or necessary implication of an enactment ; or

APPENDIX 3 UNFAIR CONTRACT TERMS ACT 1977

(b) being made with a view to compliance with an international agreement to which the United Kingdom is a party, does not operate more restrictively than is contemplated by the agreement.

(2) A contract term is to be taken—

(a) for the purposes of Part I of this Act, as satisfying the requirement of reasonableness; and

(b) for those of Part II, to have been fair and reasonable to incorporate,

if it is incorporated or approved by, or incorporated pursuant to a decision or ruling of, a competent authority acting in the exercise of any statutory jurisdiction or function and is not a term in a contract to which the competent authority is itself a party.

(3) In this section—

"competent authority" means any court, arbitrator or arbiter, government department or public authority;

"enactment" means any legislation (including subordinate legislation) of the United Kingdom or Northern Ireland and any instrument having effect by virtue of such legislation; and

"statutory" means conferred by an enactment.

30.—(1) In section 3 of the Consumer Protection Act 1961 (provisions against marketing goods which do not comply with safety requirements), after subsection (1) there is inserted— *Obligations under Consumer Protection Acts. 1961 c. 40.*

"(1A) Any term of an agreement which purports to exclude or restrict, or has the effect of excluding or restricting, any obligation imposed by or by virtue of that section, or any liability for breach of such an obligation, shall be void.".

(2) The same amendment is made in section 3 of the Consumer Protection Act (Northern Ireland) 1965. *1965 c. 14 (N.I.).*

General

31.—(1) This Act comes into force on 1st February 1978. *Commencement; amendments; repeals.*

(2) Nothing in this Act applies to contracts made before the date on which it comes into force; but subject to this, it applies to liability for any loss or damage which is suffered on or after that date.

(3) The enactments specified in Schedule 3 to this Act are amended as there shown.

(4) The enactments specified in Schedule 4 to this Act are repealed to the extent specified in column 3 of that Schedule.

PART III
Citation and extent.

32.—(1) This Act may be cited as the Unfair Contract Terms Act 1977.

(2) Part I of this Act extends to England and Wales and to Northern Ireland; but it does not extend to Scotland.

(3) Part II of this Act extends to Scotland only.

(4) This Part of this Act extends to the whole of the United Kingdom.

SCHEDULES
SCHEDULE 1
Section 1(2).

SCOPE OF SECTIONS 2 TO 4 AND 7

1. Sections 2 to 4 of this Act do not extend to—
   (a) any contract of insurance (including a contract to pay an annuity on human life);
   (b) any contract so far as it relates to the creation or transfer of an interest in land, or to the termination of such an interest, whether by extinction, merger, surrender, forfeiture or otherwise;
   (c) any contract so far as it relates to the creation or transfer of a right or interest in any patent, trade mark, copyright, registered design, technical or commercial information or other intellectual property, or relates to the termination of any such right or interest;
   (d) any contract so far as it relates—
      (i) to the formation or dissolution of a company (which means any body corporate or unincorporated association and includes a partnership), or
      (ii) to its constitution or the rights or obligations of its corporators or members;
   (e) any contract so far as it relates to the creation or transfer of securities or of any right or interest in securities.

2. Section 2(1) extends to—
   (a) any contract of marine salvage or towage;
   (b) any charterparty of a ship or hovercraft; and
   (c) any contract for the carriage of goods by ship or hovercraft;
but subject to this sections 2 to 4 and 7 do not extend to any such contract except in favour of a person dealing as consumer.

3. Where goods are carried by ship or hovercraft in pursuance of a contract which either—
   (a) specifies that as the means of carriage over part of the journey to be covered, or
   (b) makes no provision as to the means of carriage and does not exclude that means,
then sections 2(2), 3 and 4 do not, except in favour of a person dealing as consumer, extend to the contract as it operates for and in relation to the carriage of the goods by that means.

4. Section 2(1) and (2) do not extend to a contract of employment, except in favour of the employee.

5. Section 2(1) does not affect the validity of any discharge and indemnity given by a person, on or in connection with an award to him of compensation for pneumoconiosis attributable to employment in the coal industry, in respect of any further claim arising from his contracting that disease.

Sections 11(2) and 24(2).

SCHEDULE 2

"Guidelines" for Application of Reasonableness Test

The matters to which regard is to be had in particular for the purposes of sections 6(3), 7(3) and (4), 20 and 21 are any of the following which appear to be relevant—

(a) the strength of the bargaining positions of the parties relative to each other, taking into account (among other things) alternative means by which the customer's requirements could have been met;

(b) whether the customer received an inducement to agree to the term, or in accepting it had an opportunity of entering into a similar contract with other persons, but without having to accept a similar term;

(c) whether the customer knew or ought reasonably to have known of the existence and extent of the term (having regard, among other things, to any custom of the trade and any previous course of dealing between the parties);

(d) where the term excludes or restricts any relevant liability if some condition is not complied with, whether it was reasonable at the time of the contract to expect that compliance with that condition would be practicable;

(e) whether the goods were manufactured, processed or adapted to the special order of the customer.

Section 31(3).

SCHEDULE 3

Amendment of Enactments

56 & 57 Vict. c. 71.

In the Sale of Goods Act 1893—

(a) in section 55(1), for the words "the following provisions of this section" substitute "the provisions of the Unfair Contract Terms Act 1977";

(b) in section 62(1), in the definition of "business", for "local authority or statutory undertaker" substitute "or local or public authority".

1973 c. 13. 1974 c. 39.

In the Supply of Goods (Implied Terms) Act 1973 (as originally enacted and as substituted by the Consumer Credit Act 1974)—

(a) in section 14(1) for the words from "conditional sale" to the end substitute "a conditional sale agreement where the buyer deals as consumer within Part I of the Unfair Contract Terms Act 1977 or, in Scotland, the agreement is a consumer contract within Part II of that Act";

(b) in section 15(1), in the definition of "business", for "local authority or statutory undertaker" substitute "or local or public authority".

SCHEDULE 4

Section 31(4).

REPEALS

Chapter	Short title	Extent of repeal
56 & 57 Vict. c. 71.	Sale of Goods Act 1893.	In section 55, subsections (3) to (11). Section 55A. Section 61(6). In section 62(1) the definition of "contract for the international sale of goods".
1962 c. 46.	Transport Act 1962.	Section 43(7).
1967 c. 45.	Uniform Laws on International Sales Act 1967.	In section 1(4), the words "55 and 55A".
1972 c. 33.	Carriage by Railway Act 1972.	In section 1(1), the words from " and shall have " onwards.
1973 c. 13.	Supply of Goods (Implied Terms) Act 1973.	Section 5(1). Section 6. In section 7(1), the words from "contract for the international sale of goods" onwards. In section 12, subsections (2) to (9). Section 13. In section 15(1), the definition of "consumer sale".

The repeals in sections 12 and 15 of the Supply of Goods (Implied Terms) Act 1973 shall have effect in relation to those sections as originally enacted and as substituted by the Consumer Credit Act 1974. 1974 c. 39.

Appendix 4 Council of Europe: Convention on Products Liability in regard to Personal Injury and Death, 27.1.77

Preamble

The member States of the Council of Europe, signatory hereto.

Considering that the aim of the Council of Europe is to achieve a greater unity between its Members;

Considering the development of case law in the majority of member States extending liability of producers prompted by a desire to protect consumers taking into account the new production techniques and marketing and sales methods;

Desiring to ensure better protection of the public and, at the same time, to take producers' legitimate interests into account;

Considering that priority should be given to compensation for personal injury and death;

Aware of the importance of introducing special rules on the liability of producers at European level,

Have agreed as follows:

Article 1

1 Each Contracting State shall make its national law conform with the provisions of this Convention not later than the date of the entry into force of the Convention in respect of that State.

2 Each Contracting State shall communicate to the Secretary General of the Council of Europe, not later than the date of the entry into force of the Convention in respect of that State, any text adopted or a statement of the contents of the existing law which it relies on to implement the Convention.

Article 2

For the purpose of this Convention:
a the term 'product' indicates all movables, natural or industrial, whether raw or manufactured, even though incorporated into another movable or into an immovable;
b the term 'producer' indicates the manufacturers of finished products or of component parts and the producers of natural products;
c a product has a 'defect' when it does not provide the safety which a person is entitled to expect, having regard to all the circumstances including the presentation of the product;
d a product has been 'put into circulation' when the producer has delivered it to another person.

Article 3

1 The producer shall be liable to pay compensation for death or personal injuries caused by a defect in his product.

2 Any person who has imported a product for putting it into circulation in the course of a business and any person who has presented a product as his product by causing his name, trademark or other distinguishing feature to appear on the product, shall be deemed to be producers for the purpose of this Convention and shall be liable as such.

3 When the product does not indicate the identity of any of the persons liable under paragraphs 1 and 2 of this Article, each supplier shall be deemed to be a producer for the purpose of this Convention and liable as such, unless he discloses, within a reasonable time, at the request of the claimant, the identity of the producer or of the person who supplied him with the product. The same shall apply, in the case of an imported product, if this product does not indicate the identity of the importer referred to in paragraph 2, even if the name of the producer is indicated.

4 In the case of damage caused by a defect in a product incorporated into another product, the producer of the incorporated product and the producer incorporating that product shall be liable.

5 Where several persons are liable under this Convention for the same damage, each shall be liable in full (*in solidum*).

Article 4

1 If the injured person or the person entitled to claim compensation has by his own fault contributed to the damage, the compensation may be reduced or disallowed having regard to all the circumstances.

2 The same shall apply if a person, for whom the injured person or the person entitled to claim compensation is responsible under national law, has contributed to the damage by his fault.

Article 5

1 A producer shall not be liable under this Convention if he proves:
a that the product has not been put into circulation by him; or
b that, having regard to the circumstances, it is probable that the defect which caused the damage did not exist at the time when the product was put into circulation by him or that this defect came into being afterwards; or

c that the product was neither manufactured for sale, hire or any other form of distribution for the economic purposes of the producer nor manufactured or distributed in the course of his business.

2   The liability of a producer shall not be reduced when the damage is caused both by a defect in the product and by the act or omission of a third party.

Article 6

Proceedings for the recovery of the damages shall be subject to a limitation period of three years from the day the claimant became aware or should reasonably have been aware of the damage, the defect and the identity of the producer.

Article 7

The right to compensation under this Convention against a producer shall be extinguished if an action is not brought within ten years from the date on which the producer put into circulation the individual product which caused the damage.

Article 8

The liability of the producer under this Convention cannot be excluded or limited by any exemption or exoneration clause.

Article 9

This Convention shall not apply to:
a the liability of producers *inter se* and their rights of recourse against third parties;
b nuclear damage.

Article 10

Contracting States shall not adopt rules derogating from this Convention, even if these rules are more favourable to the victim.

Article 11

States may replace the liability of the producer, in a principal or subsidiary way, wholly or in part, in a general way, or for certain risks only, by the liability of a guarantee fund or other form of collective guarantee, provided that the victim shall receive protection at least equivalent to the protection he would have had under the liability scheme provided for by this Convention.

Article 12

This Convention shall not affect any rights which a person suffering damage may have according to the ordinary rules of the law of contractual and extra-contractual liability including any rules concerning the duties of a seller who sells goods in the course of his business.

Article 13

1 This Convention shall be open to signature by the member States of the Council of Europe. It shall be subject to ratification, acceptance or approval. Instruments of ratification, acceptance or approval shall be deposited with the Secretary General of the Council of Europe.

2 This Convention shall enter into force on the first day of the month following the expiration of a period of six months after the date of deposit of the third instrument of ratification, acceptance or approval.

3 In respect of a signatory State ratifying, accepting or approving subsequently, the Convention shall come into force

on the first day of the month following the expiration of a period of six months after the date of the deposit of its instrument of ratification, acceptance or approval.

Article 14

1 After the entry into force of this Convention, the Committee of Ministers of the Council of Europe may invite any non-member State to accede thereto.

2 Such accession shall be effected by depositing with the Secretary General of the Council of Europe an instrument of accession which shall take effect on the first day of the month following the expiration of a period of six months after the date of its deposit.

Article 15

1 Any State may, at the time of signature or when depositing its instrument of ratification, acceptance, approval or accession, specify the territory or territories to which this Convention shall apply.

2 Any State may, when depositing its instrument of ratification, acceptance, approval or accession or at any later date, by declaration addressed to the Secretary General of the Council of Europe, extend this Convention to any other territory or territories specified in the declaration and for whose international relations it is responsible or on whose behalf it is authorised to give undertakings.

3 Any declaration made in pursuance of the preceding paragraph may, in respect of any territory mentioned in such declaration, be withdrawn by means of a notification addressed to the Secretary General of the Council of Europe. Such withdrawal shall take effect on the first day of the month following the expiration of a period of six months after the date of receipt by the Secretary General of the Council of Europe of the declaration of withdrawal.

Article 16

1   Any State may, at the time of signature or when depositing its instrument of ratification, acceptance, approval or accession, or at any later date, by notification addressed to the Secretary General of the Council of Europe, declare that, in pursuance of an international agreement to which it is a Party it will not consider imports from one or more specified States also Parties to that agreement as imports for the purpose of paragraphs 2 and 3 of Article 3; in this case the person importing the product into any of these States from another State shall be deemed to be an importer for all the States Parties to this agreement.

2   Any declaration made in pursuance of the preceding paragraph may be withdrawn by means of a notification addressed to the Secretary General of the Council of Europe. Such withdrawal shall take effect the first day of the month following the expiration of a period of one month after the date of receipt by the Secretary General of the Council of Europe of the declaration of withdrawal.

Article 17

1   No reservation shall be made to the provisions of this Convention except those mentioned in the Annex to this Convention.

2   The Contracting State which has made one of the reservations mentioned in the Annex to this Convention may withdraw it by means of a declaration addressed to the Secretary General of the Council of Europe which shall become effective the first day of the month following the expiration of a period of one month after the date of its receipt by the Secretary General.

Article 18

1 Any Contracting State may, in so far as it is concerned, denounce this Convention by means of a notification addressed to the Secretary General of the Council of Europe.

2 Such denunciation shall take effect on the first day of the month following the expiration of a period of six months after the date of receipt by the Secretary General of such notification.

Article 19

The Secretary General of the Council of Europe shall notify the member States of the Council and any State which has acceded to this Convention of:

a any signature;
b any deposit of an instrument of ratification, acceptance, approval or accession;
c any date of entry into force of this Convention in accordance with Article 13 thereof;
d any reservation made in pursuance of the provisions of Article 17, paragraph 1;
e withdrawal of any reservation carried out in pursuance of the provisions of Article 17, paragraph 2;
f any communication or notification received in pursuance of the provisions of Article 1, paragraph 2, Article 15, paragraphs 2 and 3 and Article 16, paragraphs 1 and 2;
g any notification received in pursuance of the provisions of Article 18 and the date on which denunciation takes effect.

In witness whereof, the undersigned, being duly authorised thereto, have signed this Convention.

Done at Strasbourg this 27th day of January 1977, in English and in French, both texts being equally authoritative, in a single copy which shall remain deposited in the archives of the Council of Europe. The Secretary General of the Council of Europe shall transmit certified copies to each of the signatory and acceding States.

Annex (to Convention)

Each State may declare, at the moment of signature or at the moment of the deposit of its instrument of ratification, acceptance, approval or accession, that it reserves the right:

1 to apply its ordinary law, in place of the provisions of Article 4, in so far as such law provides that compensation may be reduced or disallowed only in case of gross negligence or intentional conduct by the injured person or the person entitled to claim compensation;

2 to limit, by provisions of its national law, the amount of compensation to be paid by a producer under this national law in compliance with the present Convention. However, this limit shall not be less than:
   a the sum in national currency corresponding to 70,000 Special Drawing Rights as defined by the International Monetary Fund at the time of the ratification, for each deceased person or person suffering personal injury;
   b the sum in national currency corresponding to 10 million Special Drawing Rights as defined by the International Monetary Fund at the time of ratification, for all damage caused by identical products having the same defect;

3 to exclude the retailer of primary agricultural products from liability under the terms of paragraph 3 of Article 3 providing he discloses to the claimant all information in his possession concerning the identity of the persons mentioned in Article 3.

Appendix 5 E.E.C. Draft Directive on Product Liability

Article 1

The producer of an article shall be liable for damage caused by a defect in the article, whether or not he knew or could have known of the defect. This provision applies also if the article has been incorporated in immovable property. The producer shall be liable even if the article could not have been regarded as defective in the light of the scientific and technological development at the time when he put the article into circulation. The producer is not liable under the provisions of this Directive if the defective article is a primary agricultural product, a craft or an artistic product when it is clear that it is not industrially produced.

Article 2

'Producer' means the producer of the finished article, the producer of any material or component, and any person who, by putting his name, trademark, or other distinguishing feature on the article, represents himself as its producer. Where the producer of the article cannot be identified, each supplier of the article shall be treated as its producer unless he informs the injured person, within a reasonable time, of the identity of the producer or of the person who supplied him with the article. Any person who imports into the European Community an article for resale or similar purpose shall be treated as its producer.

Article 3

Where two or more persons are liable in respect of the same damage, they shall be liable jointly and severally each person retaining the right to compensation from the others.

Article 4

A product is defective when, being used for the purpose for which it is apparently intended, it does not provide for persons or property the safety which a person is entitled to expect, taking into account all the circumstances including its presentation and the time at which it was put into circulation.

Article 5

The producer shall not be liable if he proves:
a that he did not put the article into circulation.
b that, having regard to all the circumstances, it was not defective when he put it into circulation;
c that the article was neither produced for sale, hire or any other kind of distribution for the commercial purposes of the producer nor produced and distributed within the course of his business activities.

If the victim or any person for whom he is liable has by his fault contributed to the damage the compensation payable may be reduced or no compensation may be awarded.

Article 6

For the purpose of Article 1 'damage' means:
a Death or personal injuries;
b damage to or destruction of any item of property other than the defective article itself where the item of property:
  i) is of a type ordinarily acquired for private use or consumption, and
  ii) was not acquired or used by the claimant exclusively for the purpose of his trade, business or profession,
c damages for pain and suffering and other non-material damage.

Article 7

The total liability of the producer provided for in this Directive for all personal injuries caused by identical articles having the same defects may be limited to a maximum amount which is to be determined by a qualified majority of the Council acting on a proposal from the Commission. Prior to any such determination by the Council this amount shall be fixed at 25 million European units of account (EUA). This amount also includes the damages specified in Article 6(c) when they are related to death or personal injury. The liability of the producer provided for by this Directive in respect of damage to property shall be limited *per capita*:

– in the case of movable property to 15,000 EUA, and
– in the case of immovable property to 50,000 EUA.

This amount also includes the damages specified in Article 6(c) when they are related to material damage. The European Unit of Account (EUA) is as defined in Article 10 of the Financial Regulation of 21 December 1977. The equivalent in national currency shall be determined by applying the conversion rate prevailing on the day preceding the date on which the amount of compensation is finally fixed. The Council shall, on a report from the Commission, examine every three years the amounts specified in this Article. Where necessary, the Council shall, acting by a qualified majority on a proposal from the Commission, revise or cancel the amount specified in paragraph 1 of this Article or revise the amounts specified in paragraph three, taking into consideration economic and monetary movement in the Community.

Article 8

A limitation period of three years shall apply to proceedings for the recovery of damages as provided for in this Directive. The limitation period shall begin to run on the day the injured person became aware, or should reasonably have become aware of the damage, the defect and the identity of the producer. The laws of Member States regulating suspension or interruption of the period shall not be affected by this Directive.

Article 9

The liability of the producer shall be extinguished if an action is not brought within 10 years from the date on which the producer put into circulation the individual product which caused the damage.

Article 10

Liability as provided for in this Directive may not be excluded or limited.

Article 11

Claims in respect of injury or damage caused by defective articles based on grounds other than that provided for in this Directive shall not be affected.

Article 12

This Directive does not apply to injury or damage arising from nuclear accidents.

Article 13

Member States shall bring into force the provisions necessary to comply with this Directive within 18 months and shall forthwith inform the Commission thereof.

Article 14

Member States shall communicate to the Commission the text of the main provisions of internal law which they subsequently adopt in the field covered by this Directive.

Article 15

This Directive is addressed to Member States.

Appendix 6 Health and Safety at Work etc. Act 1974

[Sections 1–9 only]

1974 CHAPTER 37

An Act to make further provision for securing the health, safety and welfare of persons at work, for protecting others against risks to health or safety in connection with the activities of persons at work, for controlling the keeping and use and preventing the unlawful acquisition, possession and use of dangerous substances, and for controlling certain emissions into the atmosphere; to make further provision with respect to the employment medical advisory service; to amend the law relating to building regulations, and the Building (Scotland) Act 1959; and for connected purposes.

[31st July 1974]

BE IT ENACTED by the Queen's most Excellent Majesty, by and with the advice and consent of the Lords Spiritual and Temporal, and Commons, in this present Parliament assembled, and by the authority of the same, as follows:—

PART I

HEALTH, SAFETY AND WELFARE IN CONNECTION WITH WORK, AND CONTROL OF DANGEROUS SUBSTANCES AND CERTAIN EMISSIONS INTO THE ATMOSPHERE

Preliminary

1.—(1) The provisions of this Part shall have effect with a view to—

    (a) securing the health, safety and welfare of persons at work;

    (b) protecting persons other than persons at work against risks to health or safety arising out of or in connection with the activities of persons at work;

Preliminary.

(c) controlling the keeping and use of explosive or highly flammable or otherwise dangerous substances, and generally preventing the unlawful acquisition, possession and use of such substances; and

(d) controlling the emission into the atmosphere of noxious or offensive substances from premises of any class prescribed for the purposes of this paragraph.

(2) The provisions of this Part relating to the making of health and safety regulations and agricultural health and safety regulations and the preparation and approval of codes of practice shall in particular have effect with a view to enabling the enactments specified in the third column of Schedule 1 and the regulations, orders and other instruments in force under those enactments to be progressively replaced by a system of regulations and approved codes of practice operating in combination with the other provisions of this Part and designed to maintain or improve the standards of health, safety and welfare established by or under those enactments.

(3) For the purposes of this Part risks arising out of or in connection with the activities of persons at work shall be treated as including risks attributable to the manner of conducting an undertaking, the plant or substances used for the purposes of an undertaking and the condition of premises so used or any part of them.

(4) References in this Part to the general purposes of this Part are references to the purposes mentioned in subsection (1) above.

General duties

General duties of employers to their employees.

2.—(1) It shall be the duty of every employer to ensure, so far as is reasonably practicable, the health, safety and welfare at work of all his employees.

(2) Without prejudice to the generality of an employer's duty under the preceding subsection, the matters to which that duty extends include in particular—

(a) the provision and maintenance of plant and systems of work that are, so far as is reasonably practicable, safe and without risks to health;

(b) arrangements for ensuring, so far as is reasonably practicable, safety and absence of risks to health in connection with the use, handling, storage and transport of articles and sub stances;

(c) the provision of such information, instruction, training and supervision as is necessary to ensure, so far as is reasonably practicable, the health and safety at work of his employees;

(d) so far as is reasonably practicable as regards any place of work under the employer's control, the maintenance of it in a condition that is safe and without risks to health and the provision and maintenance of means of access to and egress from it that are safe and without such risks;

(e) the provision and maintenance of a working environment for his employees that is, so far as is reasonably practicable,

safe, without risks to health, and adequate as regards facilities and arrangements for their welfare at work.

(3) Except in such cases as may be prescribed, it shall be the duty of every employer to prepare and as often as may be appropriate revise a written statement of his general policy with respect to the health and safety at work of his employees and the organisation and arrangements for the time being in force for carrying out that policy, and to bring the statement and any revision of it to the notice of all of his employees.

(4) Regulations made by the Secretary of State may provide for the appointment in prescribed cases by recognised trade unions (within the meaning of the regulations) of safety representatives from amongst the employees, and those representatives shall represent the employees in consultations with the employers under subsection (6) below and shall have such other functions as may be prescribed.

(5) Regulations made by the Secretary of State may provide for the election in prescribed cases by employees of safety representatives from amongst the employees, and those representatives shall represent the employees in consultations with the employers under subsection (6) below and may have such other functions as may be prescribed. [Repealed]

(6) It shall be the duty of every employer to consult any such representatives with a view to the making and maintenance of arrangements which will enable him and his employees to co-operate effectively in promoting and developing measures to ensure the health and safety at work of the employees, and in checking the effectiveness of such measures.

(7) In such cases as may be prescribed it shall be the duty of every employer, if requested to do so by the safety representatives mentioned in subsections (4) and (5) above, to establish, in accordance with regulations made by the Secretary of State, a safety committee having the function of keeping under review the measures taken to ensure the health and safety at work of his employees and such other functions as may be prescribed.

3.—(1) It shall be the duty of every employer to conduct his undertaking in such a way as to ensure, so far as is reasonably practicable, that persons not in his employment who may be affected thereby are not thereby exposed to risks to their health or safety. *General duties of employers and self-employed to persons other than their employees.*

(2) It shall be the duty of every self-employed person to conduct his undertaking in such a way as to ensure, so far as is reasonably practicable, that he and other persons (not being his employees) who may be affected thereby are not thereby exposed to risks to their health or safety.

(3) In such cases as may be prescribed, it shall be the duty of every employer and every self-employed person, in the prescribed circumstances and in the prescribed manner, to give to persons (not being his employees) who may be affected by the way in which he conducts his undertaking the prescribed information about such aspects of the way in which he conducts his undertaking as might affect their health or safety.

APPENDIX 6 HEALTH AND SAFETY AT WORK ETC. ACT 1974

General duties of persons concerned with premises to persons other than their employees.

4.—(1) This section has effect for imposing on persons duties in relation to those who—

(a) are not their employees; but

(b) use non-domestic premises made available to them as a place of work or as a place where they may use plant or substances provided for their use there,

and applies to premises so made available and other non-domestic premises used in connection with them.

(2) It shall be the duty of each person who has, to any extent, control of premises to which this section applies or of the means of access thereto or egress therefrom or of any plant or substance in such premises to take such measures as it is reasonable for a person in his position to take to ensure, so far as is reasonably practicable, that the premises, all means of access thereto or egress therefrom available for use by persons using the premises, and any plant or substance in the premises or, as the case may be, provided for use there, is or are safe and without risks to health.

(3) Where a person has, by virtue of any contract or tenancy, an obligation of any extent in relation to—

(a) the maintenance or repair of any premises to which this section applies or any means of access thereto or egress therefrom; or

(b) the safety of or the absence of risks to health arising from plant or substances in any such premises;

that person shall be treated, for the purposes of subsection (2) above, as being a person who has control of the matters to which his obligation extends.

(4) Any reference in this section to a person having control of any premises or matter is a reference to a person having control of the premises or matter in connection with the carrying on by him of a trade, business or other undertaking (whether for profit or not).

General duty of persons in control of certain premises in relation to harmful emissions into atmosphere.

5.—(1) It shall be the duty of the person having control of any premises of a class prescribed for the purposes of section 1(1)(*d*) to use the best practicable means for preventing the emission into the atmosphere from the premises of noxious or offensive substances and for rendering harmless and inoffensive such substances as may be so emitted.

(2) The reference in subsection (1) above to the means to be used for the purposes there mentioned includes a reference to the manner in which the plant provided for those purposes is used and to the supervision of any operation involving the emission of the substances to which that subsection applies.

(3) Any substance or a substance of any description prescribed for the purposes of subsection (1) above as noxious or offensive shall be a noxious or, as the case may be, an offensive substance for those purposes whether or not it would be so apart from this subsection.

(4) Any reference in this section to a person having control of any premises is a reference to a person having control of the premises in connection with the carrying on by him of a trade, business or other undertaking (whether for profit or not) and any duty imposed on any such person by this section shall extend only to matters within his control.

6.—(1) It shall be the duty of any person who designs, manufactures, imports or supplies any article for use at work— *General duties of manufacturers etc. as regards articles and substances for use at work.*

    (a) to ensure, so far as is reasonably practicable, that the article is so designed and constructed as to be safe and without risk to health when properly used;

    (b) to carry out or arrange for the carrying out of such testing and examination as may be necessary for the performance of the duty imposed on him by the preceding paragraph;

    (c) to take such steps as are necessary to secure that there will be available in connection with the use of the article at work adequate information about the use for which it is designed and has been tested, and about any conditions necessary to ensure that, when put to that use, it will be safe and without risks to health.

(2) It shall be the duty of any person who undertakes the design or manufacture of any article for use at work to carry out or arrange for the carrying out of any necessary research with a view to the discovery and, so far as is reasonably practicable, the elimination or minimisation of any risks to health or safety to which the design or article may give rise.

(3) It shall be the duty of any person who erects or installs any article for use at work in any premises where that article is to be used by persons at work to ensure, so far as is reasonably practicable, that nothing about the way in which it is erected or installed makes it unsafe or a risk to health when properly used.

(4) It shall be the duty of any person who manufactures, imports or supplies any substance for use at work—

    (a) to ensure, so far as is reasonably practicable, that the substance is safe and without risks to health when properly used;

    (b) to carry out or arrange for the carrying out of such testing and examination as may be necessary for the performance of the duty imposed on him by the preceding paragraph;

    (c) to take such steps as are necessary to secure that there will be available in connection with the use of the substance at work adequate information about the results of any relevant tests which have been carried out on or in connection with the substance and about any conditions necessary to ensure that it will be safe and without risks to health when properly used.

(5) It shall be the duty of any person who undertakes the manufacture of any substance for use at work to carry out or arrange for the carrying out of any necessary research with a view to the discovery and, so far as is reasonably practicable, the elimination or minimisation of any risks to health or safety to which the substance may give rise.

(6) Nothing in the preceding provisions of this section shall be taken to require a person to repeat any testing, examination or research which has been carried out otherwise than by him or at his instance, in so far as it is reasonable for him to rely on the results thereof for the purposes of those provisions.

(7) Any duty imposed on any person by any of the preceding provisions of this section shall extend only to things done in the course of a trade, business or other undertaking carried out by him (whether for profit or not) and to matters within his control.

(8) Where a person designs, manufactures, imports or supplies an article for or to another on the basis of a written undertaking by that other to take specified steps sufficient to ensure, so far as is reasonably practicable, that the article will be safe and without risk to health when properly used, the undertaking shall have the effect of relieving the first-mentioned person from the duty imposed by subsection (1)(*a*) above to such extent as is reasonable having regard to the terms of the undertaking.

(9) Where a person ("the ostensible supplier") supplies any article for use at work or substance for use at work to another ("the customer") under a hire-purchase agreement, conditional sale agreement or credit-sale agreement, and the ostensible supplier—

(a) carries on the business of financing the acquisition of goods by others by means of such agreements; and

(b) in the course of that business acquired his interest in the article or substance supplied to the customer as a means of financing its acquisition by the customer from a third person ("the effective supplier"),

the effective supplier and not the ostensible supplier shall be treated for the purposes of this section as supplying the article or substance to the customer, and any duty imposed by the preceding provisions of this section on suppliers shall accordingly fall on the effective supplier and not on the ostensible supplier.

(10) For the purposes of this section an article or substance is not to be regarded as properly used where it is used without regard to any relevant information or advice relating to its use which has been made available by a person by whom it was designed, manufactured, imported or supplied.

General duties of employees at work.

7. It shall be the duty of every employee while at work—

(a) to take reasonable care for the health and safety of himself and of other persons who may be affected by his acts or omissions at work; and

(b) as regards any duty or requirement imposed on his employer or any other person by or under any of the relevant statutory

provisions, to co-operate with him so far as is necessary to enable that duty or requirement to be performed or complied with.

8. No person shall intentionally or recklessly interfere with or misuse anything provided in the interests of health, safety or welfare in pursuance of any of the relevant statutory provisions. *Duty not to intefere with or misuse things provided pursuant to certain provisions.*

9. No employer shall levy or permit to be levied on any employee of his any charge in respect of anything done or provided in pursuance of any specific requirement of the relevant statutory provisions. *Duty not to charge employees for things done or provided pursuant to certain specific requirements.*

Further Reading

America

Products Liability, Noel and Phillips : 1981

Canada

Products Liability, Waddams : 1980

Common Market countries other than the UK

Consumer Legislation in Belgium and Luxembourg, Fontaine and Bourgoignie : 1982
Consumer Legislation in Denmark, Dahl : 1981
Consumer Legislation in France, Calais-Auloy : 1981
Consumer Legislation in Germany, Reich and Micklitz : 1981
Consumer Legislation in Italy, Ghidini : 1980
Consumer Legislation in the Netherlands, Hondius : 1980

General

International Product Liability, Tebbens : 1979

United Kingdom

Product Liability, Miller and Lovell : 1977

Royal Commission on Civil Liability and Compensation for Injury, Cmnd. 7054-I, HMSO : 1978
Consumer Legislation in the UK and Ireland, Whincup : 1980

Index

abnormal susceptibility 59, 124
abnormal use 48, 97, 110, 112, 124, 135
absolute liability 59, 134, 154
acceptance 8, 44, 56–8, 64
advertisements 4, 27, 29–31, 44, 61, 132–4, 140, 176, 178, 180–5
advice and warning 120, 123–5, 169, 179
aerosol dispensers 175
agency 41, 75, 91, 126
agricultural produce 45, 154
aircraft 116, 154, 156
articles for use at work 111, 166–71

babies' dummies 174
balloons 175
'battle of the forms' 8–14
breach of statutory duty 93, 165, 172
British Standards Institute 114, 115, 120, 173–4
business, sale in course of 44, 78, 180

buyer, rights of 39–62
 see also seller
bystanders 110, 139

care, duty of: see negligence
carrycots 173
caveat emptor 44
certifiers 115, 127, 156
children 125, 129
children's clothing 173
collateral contracts 27, 30
Committee on Safety of Medicines 114, 119, 178
compensation 175, 180
 see also damages
conditions 14–17, 40–65
 see also implied terms
consent: see defences
consideration 2
consumer transactions 80–3
contract 1
contributory negligence: see defences
cooking utensils 173
cosmetics 174
cost 46, 48, 96, 110, 118, 121

crashworthiness 109

damages 18–20, 99–101, 155–6, 160
see also compensation
dangerous substances 103–8, 166–71, 175
defect 98, 109, 122, 132–3, 153, 156
defences 98, 125, 135, 154, 156–8, 183–4
delegation of duty 98, 184
dermatitis 59, 105
description, sale by: *see* implied terms
design defects 108–23, 166–76
designers 98, 108–25, 166–76
development risks: *see* defences
directions for use: *see* advice and warning; defences
Directive, draft EEC xxii, xxiii, 127, 153–7
disclaimers: *see* exclusion clauses
distributors 127–30, 136
drugs 40, 93, 98, 113–14, 119, 136, 153, 156–8, 163
durability 55–6, 121–2

economic loss 18, 31, 100–1, 138
electricity and electrical appliances xxiii, 105, 173
employers' liabilities 94–5, 105–7, 111–14, 126
examination of goods by buyer or user 32, 43–5, 48, 60, 64, 99, 111–12, 117, 120
exclusion clauses 5, 13, 20, 36–7, 71–89, 125
express terms 2–18, 24–38

fabrics 179
fireguards 173
fitness 43, 48–56, 59, 60, 62–3, 81
food 176
frustration 21–2
fundamental breach 75–7

furniture, upholstered 174

gas xxiii, 104–5
gifts 40
guarantees 24–38, 80, 86, 141

health and safety at work 105–8, 111–14, 166–71
herbicides 115
hire purchase 60–2, 65, 167, 175

implied terms: *see* description, fitness, merchantability, sample, title
importer 90–1, 127–9, 155, 167
indemnity clauses 80
independent contractors: *see* sub contractors
innominate terms 15
installer 127, 166
insurance 82, 84, 161–3
intervening acts 95, 99, 122, 135

labelling: *see* packaging and labelling
Law Commission xxii, 47, 54–5, 64–5, 155
lawnmowers 120–1
lessors 62, 167, 175
liability: *see* product liability
limitation periods 101

manufacturers xxii, xxiii, 40, 90–101, 103–30, 166–76, 178–9
American and Common Market 131–51
guarantees 27–37
reform of liability 152–63
materials 103–8
merchantability 43, 45–7, 60, 62–3, 81
misrepresentation: *see* representations
misuse of product: *see* abnormal use
modification of product 117, 120, 135
Molony Report 34

INDEX

motor vehicles 5, 20, 24, 27–8, 42–6, 49–55, 57–8, 60, 62–3, 83, 109–11, 118–19, 133–5, 140, 179–81, 184

negligence 90–8, 103–30, 133
nightwear 172, 174
noise 169
novelties 174

Office of Fair Trading 35, 79, 84, 184
oil heaters 173
oil lamps 174
ownership 65–70

packaging and labelling 122–5, 171, 178
Pearson Report 155–7, 161–3
pedal bicycles 175
penalty clauses 17
pencils 173
perambulators 174
private sale 44
producers: *see* manufacturers
product, definition of xxiii
product liability
   America 131–40, 158–9
   Belgium 141–4
   Denmark 149–50
   France 141–4
   Germany 146–9
   Greece 149
   Holland 144–5
   Ireland 140–1
   Italy 145–6
   Luxembourg 141–4
   New Zealand 160–1
   United Kingdom:
     criminal liability 165–85
     express contractual liability 24–38
     implied contractual liability 38–65, 81–2
     non-contractual (negligence) liability 90–130
   see also designers, distributors, installers,

manufacturers, sellers
professional users 124
proof, burden of 91–3, 133, 152–3, 160, 166
puffs: *see* advertisements

reasonable care, meaning of 93–9, 166
recall of products 118–20
repairs 36, 40, 49–51, 56, 58, 63–4
representations 5, 25, 74, 82, 132, 134, 180–5
res ipsa loquitur 92, 133
research 113–17, 168–9
Restatement of Torts (US) 132
risk 22, 65–70, 79

safety check list 94–7
safety records 113, 140, 178
sales literature: *see* advertisements
sample 56
scented erasers 175
second-hand goods: *see* used goods
seeds 180
seller, duties of 1–2, 24, 39–63, 81, 90–1, 101, 127–30, 152, 176, 179–85
services 62–3, 182–3
spare parts 56
state of the art: *see* defences
Strasbourg Convention xxii, xxiii, 127, 153–64
strict liability 58–60, 62, 134, 154
sub contractors 126, 137, 154
substances for use at work 111, 166–71

tests 92, 98, 111, 113–15, 168
title 41, 69, 81
toys 173, 175
tractors 119
trading stamps 37, 40
tyres 179

unfair contract terms: *see* exclusion clauses

used goods 4, 46, 55, 167, 180, 184
vicarious liability 92, 106, 126, 144, 148, 150–1
volenti non fit injuria: *see* defences

warning: *see* advice and warning

warranties 14–17, 40–1
   see also guarantees
wear and tear: *see* durability
wholesalers: *see* distributors
workmanship 125–7
writing 2, 6

Supplement
to
Product Liability Law
by Michael Whincup

EEC PRODUCT LIABILITY DIRECTIVE, 1985

Chapter 8 of *Product Liability Law* explains the need for law reform and discusses the various proposals and counter-proposals which were current at the time of writing. In July 1985 the Council of the European Communities finally reached agreement upon a new Directive and committed the governments of Member States to a specified timetable of action. The details are of immediate importance to all British industries, and are published here to ensure that *Product Liability Law* continues to provide up-to-date guidance for management. We first summarise their effects and then reproduce the provisions themselves in full.

Summary of Directive

(1) The Directive has much in common with the Strasbourg Convention and draft Directive (*see* Appendices 4 and 5 of *Product Liability Law*), but there are certain vital differences which are emphasised below. Like the previous proposals it states the general principle that producers of industrial movables shall be liable without proof of fault for injuries caused by defects in their products.

(2) Products are defective if they are not as safe as one is 'entitled to expect' in the circumstances. Reasonable expectation depends on the presentation of the goods, likely use and time when put into circulation. Safety is judged by standards prevailing at the time of circulation.

(3) A producer is a manufacturer of finished products or component parts, or a producer of raw materials, or anyone representing himself as producer by putting his name or mark on the product, or an importer into the Community. When two or more persons are responsible for the same damage they are each fully liable.

(4) Damages are payable for death and personal injury and also *for substantial damage to personal property. Member States may limit liability for death or injury caused by identical items with the same defect to 70 million European Currency Units (approx. £40 million).* Apart from the problem of deciding whether items are identical and have the same defect, this provision leaves open the question whether, if some widespread and disastrous form of injury occurred, the victims would be compensated on a 'first come, first served' basis or their claims all reduced proportionately – neither of which methods would appear satisfactory solutions from their point of view.

(5) The Directive applies only to products circulated after the effective dates (*see* (9) below). Claims cannot be made more than ten years after circulation, and must be made within three years of the victim's knowing of his injury and the identity of the producer. Liability cannot be excluded by any contract clause or notice.

(6) The burden of proof will be upon the plaintiff to show he was injured by a defective product (*see* (2) above) and to identify the producer (*see* (3) above). The producer may then limit or deny liability by reference to the various defences listed in Article 7, including contributory negligence, all but one of which are in accordance with the Convention and draft Directive. The major new provision enables producers to escape liability on proving that *the state of scientific and technical knowledge at the time their products were put into circulation was such that the existence of the defects could not have been discovered.* This is the 'state of the art' defence rejected by all previous proposals, but required by the British government.

(7) The crucial question therefore is as to the likely effect of this new defence. It appears first to reverse the present burden of proof. Once a product is proved defective (*see* (2) above), the producer will have to show he had no means of knowing of the fault. What precisely this burden of disproof will require depends on the judges' interpretation of the defence. If the producer must show it was *impossible* for him to know of the defect then liability is indeed strict, and in that case the 'state of the art' defence appears meaningless. Even so, one might wonder how many plaintiffs will feel sufficiently sure of this outcome to make their claims in the first place. If on the other hand the defence requires the producer to prove only that he took all the precautions which could reasonably be expected of him at the time (as seems more likely), then in the event of, say, another disaster like the thalidomide tragedy he might well escape liability – and so frustrate the purpose of the reform. It will be noted that adoption of this defence and of the financial limits in (4) above is optional – thus precluding the uniformity of law between Member States which was one of the objects of reform.

(8) Reversing the burden of proof will no doubt enable some accident victims to recover damages who might not at present do so. More victims might thus be encouraged to sue. It is clear nonetheless that the inherent doubt, difficulties and delays in litigation have not by any means been resolved, and correspondingly hard to imagine that any increase in claims will be substantial – or that it could not be covered by marginal increases in insurance costs and purchase price.

(9) The Directive requires Member States to give effect to these provisions by 1988, ie within three years of notification on 30 July

1985. The British government must now prepare a Bill, stating in particular how far industry will be enabled to take advantage of the various possible limitations of liability indicated above.

(10) In 1995 the Commission must report to the Council of Ministers of the European Community on the effect of the Directive. The Council may then decide to abolish the 'state of the art' defence and financial limitations.

© Michael Whincup, 1986.

The Directive

Article 1

The producer shall be liable for damage caused by a defect in his product.

Article 2

For the purpose of this Directive 'product' means all movables, with the exception of primary agricultural products and game, even though incorporated into another movable or into an immovable. 'Primary agricultural products' means the products of the soil, of stock-farming and of fisheries, excluding products which have undergone initial processing. 'Product' includes electricity.

Article 3

1. 'Producer' means the manufacturer of a finished product, the producer of any raw material or the manufacturer of a component part and any person who, by putting his name, trade mark or other distinguishing feature on the product presents himself as its producer.

2. Without prejudice to the liability of the producer, any person who imports into the Community a product for sale, hire, leasing or any form of distribution in the course of his business shall be deemed to be a producer within the meaning of this Directive and shall be responsible as a producer.

3. Where the producer of the product cannot be identified, each supplier of the product shall be treated as its producer unless he informs the injured person, within a reasonable time, of the identity of the producer or of the person who supplied him with the product. The same shall apply, in the case of an imported product, if this product does not indicate the identity of the importer referred to in paragraph 2, even if the name of the producer is indicated.

Article 4

The injured person shall be required to prove the damage, the defect and the causal relationship between defect and damage.

Article 5

Where, as a result of the provisions of this Directive, two or more persons are liable for the same damage, they shall be liable jointly and severally, without prejudice to the provisions of national law concerning the rights of contribution or recourse.

Article 6

1. A product is defective when it does not provide the safety which a person is entitled to expect, taking all circumstances into account, including:

(a) the presentation of the product;
(b) the use to which it could reasonably be expected that the product would be put;
(c) the time when the product was put into circulation.

2. A product shall not be considered defective for the sole reason that a better product is subsequently put into circulation.

Article 7

The producer shall not be liable as a result of this Directive if he proves:

(a) that he did not put the product into circulation; or
(b) that, having regard to the circumstances, it is probable that the defect which caused the damage did not exist at the time when the product was put into circulation by him or that this defect came into being afterwards; or
(c) that the product was neither manufactured by him for sale or any form of distribution for economic purpose nor manufactured or distributed by him in the course of his business; or
(d) that the defect is due to compliance of the product with mandatory regulations issued by the public authorities; or
(e) that the state of scientific and technical knowledge at the time when he put the product into circulation was not such as to enable the existence of the defect to be discovered; or
(f) in the case of a manufacturer of a component, that the defect is attributable to the design of the product in which the component has been fitted or to the instructions given by the manufacturer of the product.

Article 8

1. Without prejudice to the provisions of national law concerning the right of contribution or recourse, the liability of the producer shall not be reduced when the damage is caused both by a defect in product and by the act or omission of a third party.

2. The liability of the producer may be reduced or disallowed when, having regard to all the circumstances, the damage is caused both by a defect in the product and by the fault of the injured person or any person for whom the injured person is responsible.

Article 9

For the purpose of Article 1, 'damage' means:
(a) damage caused by death or by personal injuries;
(b) damage to, or destruction of, any item of property other than the defective product itself, with a lower threshold of 500 ECU, provided that the item of property:
   (i) is of a type ordinarily intended for private use or consumption, and
   (ii) was used by the injured person mainly for his own private use or consumption.

This Article shall be without prejudice to national provisions relating to non-material damage.

Article 10

1. Member States shall provide in their legislation that a limitation period of three years shall apply to proceedings for the recovery of damages as provided for in this Directive. The limitation period shall begin to run from the day on which the plaintiff became aware, or should reasonably have become aware, of the damage, the defect and the identity of the producer.

2. The laws of Member States regulating suspension or interruption of the limitation period shall not be affected by this Directive.

Article 11

Member States shall provide in their legislation that the rights conferred upon the injured person pursuant to this Directive shall be extinguished upon the expiry of a period of 10 years from the date on which the producer put into circulation the actual product which caused the damage, unless the injured person has in the meantime instituted proceedings against the producer.

Article 12

The liability of the producer arising from this Directive may not, in relation to the injured person, be limited or excluded by a provision limiting his liability or exempting him from liability.

Article 13

This Directive shall not affect any rights which an injured person may have according to the rules of the law of contractual or non-contractual liability or a special liability system existing at the moment when this Directive is notified.

Article 14

This Directive shall not apply to injury or damage arising from nuclear accidents and covered by international conventions ratified by the Member States.

Article 15

1. Each Member State may:

(a) by way of derogation from Article 2, provide in its legislation that within the meaning of Article 1 of this Directive 'product' also means primary agricultural products and game;

(b) by way of derogation from Article 7 (e), maintain or, subject to the procedure set out in paragraph 2 of this Article, provide in this legislation that the producer shall be liable even if he proves that the state of scientific and technical knowledge at the time when he put the product into circulation was not such as to enable the existence of a defect to be discovered.

2. A Member State wishing to introduce the measure specified in paragraph 1 (b) shall communicate the text of the proposed measure to the Commission. The Commission shall inform the other Member States thereof.

The Member State concerned shall hold the proposed measure in abeyance for nine months after the Commission is informed and provided that in the meantime the Commission has not submitted to the Council a proposal amending this Directive on the relevant matter. However, if within three months of receiving the said information, the Commission does not advise the Member State concerned that it intends submitting such a proposal to the Council, the Member State may take the proposed measure immediately.

If the Commission does submit to the Council such a proposal amending this Directive within the aforementioned nine months, the Member State concerned shall hold the proposed measure in abeyance for a further period of 18 months from the date on which the proposal is submitted.

3. Ten years after the date of notification of this Directive, the Commission shall submit to the Council a report on the effect that rulings by the courts as to the application of Article 7 (e) and of paragraph 1 (b) of this Article have on consumer protection and the functioning of the common market. In the light of this report the Council, acting on a proposal from the Commission and pursuant to the terms of Article 100 of the Treaty, shall decide whether to repeal Article 7 (e).

Article 16

1. Any Member State may provide that a producer's total liability for damage resulting from a death or personal injury and caused by identical items with the same defect shall be limited to an amount which may not be less than 70 million ECU.

2. Ten years after the date of notification of this Directive, the Commission shall submit to the Council a report on the effect on consumer protection and the functioning of the common market of the implementation of the financial limit on liability by those Member States which have used the option provided for in paragraph 1. In the light of this report the Council, acting on a proposal from the Commission and pursuant to the terms of Article 100 of the Treaty, shall decide whether to repeal paragraph 1.

Article 17

This Directive shall not apply to products put into circulation before the date on which the provisions referred to in Article 19 enter into force.

Article 18

1. For the purposes of this Directive, the ECU shall be that defined by Regulation (EEC) No 3180/78 ([1]), as amended by Regulation (EEC) No 2626/84 ([2]). The equivalent in national currency shall initially be calculated at the rate obtaining on the date of adoption of this Directive.

2. Every five years the Council, acting on a proposal from the Commission, shall examine and, if need be, revise the amounts in this Directive, in the light of economic and monetary trends in the Community.

Article 19

1. Member States shall bring into force, not later than three years from the date of notification of this Directive, the laws, regulations and administrative provisions necessary to comply with this Directive. They shall forthwith inform the Commission thereof([*]).

2. The procedure set out in Article 15 (2) shall apply from the date of notification of this Directive.

Article 20

Member States shall communicate to the Commission the texts of the main provisions of national law which they subsequently adopt in the field governed by this Directive.

Article 21

Every five years the Commission shall present a report to the Council on the application of this Directive and, if necessary, shall submit appropriate proposals to it.

Article 22

This Directive is addressed to the Member States.

Done at Brussels, 25 July 1985.

For the Council
The President
J. POOS

([1]) OJ No L 379, 30. 12. 1978, p. 1.
([2]) OJ No L 247, 16. 9. 1984, p. 1.

([*]) This Directive was notified to the Member States on 30 July 1985.